The Nature of Conversion

The Nature
of Conversion

A STUDY OF
FORTY-FIVE
MEN AND WOMEN
WHO CHANGED
THEIR RELIGION

by Albert I. Gordon

BEACON PRESS : BOSTON

DEDICATED TO
THE MEMORY OF
MY MOTHER
Martha Rosenzweig Gordon

Acknowledgments

ACKNOWLEDGMENT is gratefully made, first to the men and women who, in the interest of this study, made themselves available for the tape-recorded interviews that serve as the basis of this study. I am indebted, too, to the many friends and colleagues—rabbis, priests, and ministers from all parts of this country—who assisted me by opening their files on converts and who at my request helped to secure the cooperation of the men and women whose life histories I have recorded.

I want particularly to note the cooperation of Mr. Leon Paul, former President of the Edith Stein Society, the national organization of Jews who have been formally converted to Roman Catholicism, through whose efforts certain important interviews were obtained.

My dear friends, Professor Gordon Allport, of Harvard University; Professor Nahum Glatzer, of Brandeis University; His Excellency, Eric F. MacKenzie, Auxiliary Bishop of the Archdiocese of Boston; Father James Lloyd of the Paulist Fathers in New York City; Father Robert Quinn of Boston; Rabbis Edward Sandrow, Cedarhurst, Long Island, New York; Max Shapiro of Minneapolis; Zev K. Nelson of South Brookline (Boston), Massachusetts; Sanford Schanblatt of Pittsfield, Massachusetts; Jerrold Goldstein, St. Paul; Alvin Lieberman, Brookline, Massachusetts; the Reverend Harold Ockenga, Park Street Church, Boston; Dean Walter G. Mulder, of Boston University School of Theology; and others, far too numerous to mention, have assisted and advised me as this study progressed.

vii

I am indebted, too, to my colleague, Professor Walter Houston Clark, of Andover-Newton Theological School, where I have taught these past fifteen years, for his valued insights and comments.

Once again, I want to express my sincere thanks to Mrs. Jack (Nellie Rae) Burman, who devoted so many hours to the task of typing this manuscript.

My dear wife, Dorothy Davis Gordon, has, as always, been a tower of strength, support, and inspiration to me. Her insights and her incisive, discerning comments and suggestions throughout the months and years this book has been in preparation have aided me immeasurably in completing the task I set for myself.

ALBERT I. GORDON

Contents

Introduction

THIS book is about converts and their conversion from one of the three major faiths to another. It is primarily an attempt, through autobiographical, tape-recorded interviews, to understand the factors responsible for formal conversion; forty-five men and women, all converts, who reside in various areas of this nation were interviewed.

Of these forty-five life-stories, thirty involve Jews. The reasons for this preponderance should be made clear: First, as a rabbi it was relatively easy for me to check back over the years and find those converts whose life-stories were significant and meaningful. There were, too, many colleagues to whom I could turn for their active cooperation in securing such interviews. Further, I look upon interfaith conversion as a *process* that varies only in minor details, whether the convert be Protestant, Catholic, Jewish, or of any other religion. A study of the histories of these forty-five converts will, I believe, support this view. Finally, conversions to and from Judaism represent perhaps the greatest shift possible within the three great religious traditions in this country and so make them particularly useful examples of the process.

There is no attempt to suggest that the converts whose life-stories are included in this study represent a random sample of *all* ecclesiastical converts. These forty-five speak only for themselves. What we come to know about them as a consequence of these interviews may or may not be representative of all converts. We have no way of knowing. None of the three major religious groups has yet provided exact statistical records of the number of such converts that it receives each year. What little information we have on this score is haphazardly gathered and, at best, represents nothing more than a glorified guess. Without the base of exact statistical evidence it is, at present, hardly possible to establish a random sample of ecclesiastical converts.

It is important, too, to point out that this study was not undertaken to support any hypothesis concerning converts or conversion. Other than my desire to come to know as much as possible about these men and women, I have no desire to prove or disprove anything. The purpose of this study can be summarized quickly—to obtain more detailed knowledge about ecclesiastical converts than has hitherto been available. In seeking the cooperation of clergymen—Protestant, Catholic, Greek Orthodox, Jewish, and Unitarian —I made every effort to make this point clear. I asked only that they recommend to me persons within their own respective communities whom they knew, with whose formal conversion they had been directly concerned, and whose life-stories might be recorded and studied.

The forty-five were not always readily available for interview. Despite the effort expended by my colleagues, suspicions and reservations of one kind or another were often expressed. In many cases, six or more months of persistent effort was required before the assent of certain interviewees could be secured.

In each instance, the same questions were asked of each of the converts, although not always in the same order. The temperaments, suspicions, and attitudes of these men and women often necessitated a change in my approach. With only two exceptions, the interviews took place in the homes of the converts.

The Nature of Conversion

1. Conversion and Converts

THE WORD "conversion" has two distinct and equally valid meanings. It is used, most frequently, to describe "the process by which a person comes to adopt an all-pervading world view or change from one perspective to another. It denotes a major discontinuity in behavior—a drastic shift in orientation of his valuation of reality."[1] William James defined the term as "a process, gradual or sudden, by which a self, hitherto divided and consciously wrong, inferior, or unhappy, becomes unified and consciously right, superior, and happy in consequence of its firmer hold upon religious realities."[2]

Such a conversion may best be described as "inner conversion." As a consequence of a newly acquired sense of unity and integrity of the spirit that results from having "found God" once again, the convert is said to be "twice-born." In addition to his physical birth, he has acquired a rebirth in a spiritual sense. His view of life, his values, attitudes, and behavior have changed. Conversion is a process, continuous and ongoing. It brings about a change from one set of values to another, when old values are discarded and new goals, centered in God, become, for the convert, "the way, the truth, and the life." Such a conversion is generally regarded as a "religious experience," i.e., a response to what is experienced as "ultimate reality."[3]

Inner conversion is common to all faiths, including Judaism and Christianity.[4] The word "conversion," then, means "to turn, or to change." It implies that the convert's movement is in a new direction, away from one course, toward a new direction.

1

Inner conversion has always been of concern to religionists and, later, to psychologists, each seeking to discover the very nature of the process by which it takes place; to understand, as well, the factors that impel men to convert, to become "twice-born."

There is, however, another kind of conversion, equally ancient and recorded on the pages of history. It is the formal act of identifying oneself with a religious faith which has a set of values, attitudes, beliefs, and practices other than those originally adhered to. It is a conscious moving from one organized religion to another. In contradistinction to inner conversion, which generally occurs within the original church setting, this form, "ecclesiastical conversion,"[5] involves a complete shift in allegiance to another and different faith. It may involve an entirely new set of values and a completely new way of life.

In this study we shall be primarily concerned with ecclesiastical conversion because this form of conversion has been increasing markedly as a consequence of the rapidly increasing number of marriages between people of different faiths.[6]

Little attention has been given to this form of conversion, its meaning, and its consequences, and it is hoped that this study will shed some light on a subject that is both intriguing and highly relevant in our contemporary society.

Unlike inner conversion, ecclesiastical conversion is seldom a sudden act. It is rather, most often, the consequence of a gradual, almost imperceptible process. It involves not a "return" to the religion of one's youth and family but a break away from the past and the declaration of a new allegiance. The change from one religion to another need not, as we shall see, necessarily imply the heightened emotional or psychological experiences that are generally associated with "inner" conversion. The convert who moves from one faith to another need not be "twice-born" nor need he now put religious ideas in the central place in his life. His reasons for conversion, as we shall see, may be the consequence of motives that have little, if anything, to do with strengthened or renewed religious feelings.

In addition to reasons associated with marriage, the change from one religion to another may begin as a consequence of dissatisfaction, emotional or rational, with some phase of the religion in which one has been reared. It may result from some unhappiness with parents or with their ways. It may grow out of a coolly calculated plan to break all ties with an unhappy past by formally identifying with the new religion.

Nervous or mental disorder too may play a role in causing a person to change his religion, as may the turbulent psychological changes that are associated with puberty and adolescence. Psychic causes also may help to create the desire (and need) to identify with a different religion. Misfortune in one form or another, ranging from a great cosmic calamity, a war, or social disaster to a purely personal loss or sense of loss, including a loss of faith in God, may be the factor that triggers the determination to shift allegiance from one faith to another. The decision to change religious affiliation may, on occasion, be due to an unpleasant experience, real or fancied, that the proselyte has had with rabbi, priest, or minister. The feeling that his clergyman is a "hypocrite," dishonest intellectually, unethical, or immoral, is recorded in several of our interviews with converts.

It is clear that there is no single factor that ultimately brings about ecclesiastical conversion. The factors vary with the individual and his background, experiences, knowledge, emotional stability and temperament, religiosity, and a host of other causes. It is equally clear that some form of conflict, mental or emotional, is as much involved in ecclesiastical conversion as in inner conversion. There is always a crisis—some moment in which a conflict situation needs to be resolved. This holds true even for those persons who change church or synagogue affiliation to marry. The crisis situation involves a major decision on which one's future happiness is believed to depend.

History too has recorded many instances where, in the interest of attaining full, first-class citizenship with its many opportunities, social, educational, cultural, and political, members of minority religious groups formally accept the religion of the majority. Many Jews in Germany in the nineteenth century are known to have used this means to gain their desired ends. The reasons for changing from one religion to another are varied indeed, as the forty-five converts whose experiences I report in this volume make clear.

These ecclesiastical converts, from all parts of the country, vary in age from sixteen to sixty-five, men and women, most of them married over a period of many years, many with children of their own. None of these converts made the decision to change to a different religion suddenly. In all instances, these converts appear to have arrived at their decision gradually. Some indicated that questions and doubts concerning the validity of their parents' religion began in their early childhood; others report that their questions arose during adolescence. But most of these converts stated that their thoughts turned in the direction of ecclesiastical conversion at the time when they determined to marry a person of another and different faith. Such conversion appears to have little or nothing to do with the inner struggle away from sin, evil, penitence, or even the striving after righteousness.

The exact number of inner and ecclesiastical conversions that take place each year is unknown. Neither Jews nor Catholics nor Protestants keep such records. Insofar as Protestantism is concerned, its greatest emphasis has been placed upon "inner conversion." Here, in most instances, evangelical efforts are expended by the church and its many denominations to reconvert the "fallen away" within Christianity. Such efforts, generally associated with the evangelical work of such men as Billy Graham in our day and a host of "minor league" evangelists, fail to provide thoroughly reliable statistical information. They fail, too, to indicate how many of the most recent "inner conversions" are "repeaters," men and women who have fallen from grace once or many times before, only to return again as "twice-born men." Little reliable information is available about ecclesiastical converts either from the National Council of Churches or from Hebrew Christian organizations whose basic function is their "mission to the Jews."

Although the Roman Catholic Church provides statistics with

respect to the number of converts to Catholicism annually,[7] there is reason to question the accuracy of these figures because the meaning of "conversion" is not sharply defined. The 1964 Directory states that there were 123,986 converts to Catholicism in the entire country, the Directory for 1966 totals were 123,149. The two major sources of these ecclesiastical converts were Protestantism and Judaism.

The Jews too have no official record of ecclesiastical converts to Judaism. Various estimates, each based on surveys and studies made by individuals, suggest that those converts who formally identify with Judaism are accepted by Reform or Conservative Judaism with only a handful entering the Orthodox group. Orthodox Judaism looks with disfavor upon accepting converts, particularly, when the reason for conversion is generally believed to be, in at least ninety percent of the cases, the desire to marry a Jew.

Eichhorn,[8] on the basis of a 1963 study, has estimated that the number of non-Jews who are being converted to Judaism annually is between 2,000 and 3,000. Of these, he believes that 95 percent come to Judaism because of marriage.

Rabbi Daniel L. Davis[9] reported that during the decade 1954–64, 16,000 persons converted to Reform Judaism. He estimates that 90 percent of these converts planned to marry a Jew or Jewess. Data gathered between December 1963 and December 1964 showed that 295 persons had registered for classes in conversion sponsored by the Reform movement—of these, 205 were women and 90 were men. Of these, 170 were Roman Catholics, 21 described themselves only as of Protestant origin; 20 were Methodists, 18 were Lutherans; 12 were Presbyterians, and the remainder were divided among other Protestant denominations. An earlier (1954) study by Eichhorn estimated that 2,500 non-Jews were converted to Judaism annually. About 70 percent of converts to Judaism become Reform Jews, with about 25 percent entering as Conservative Jews and the remaining 5 percent formally affiliating with Orthodox Judaism.

Leaders of the three major religions agree that ninety percent[10] of the ecclesiastical conversions to each religion in these days result from the desire to marry a person of another faith. They agree too, that the number of such conversions is increasing. Christianity in its two major forms is a missionizing religion, and so believes that it has much to gain through interfaith marriages where conversion is involved. It is, however, not always certain that such conversions always lead to the establishment of "good" Christian families and homes because to many such converts the conversion is only a means toward a particular end, marriage.

Judaism has not actively sought proselytes throughout its long history and is, in the main, ambivalent in its attitude toward conversion. Sincere converts, regardless of racial, national, or religious origin are, according to its most Orthodox interpreters, to be welcomed. Such persons are regarded as "Righteous Converts." Yet, the question of the utter sincerity of the convert is not always readily ascertainable, for so much depends upon the judgment of the rabbi whom the candidate approaches. Traditionally too, there is the feeling that conversion should take place "for its own sake," out of a love of Judaism and a desire to identify with the Jewish people and not for extrinsic reasons, among which is the desired marriage of a non-Jew to a Jew or Jewess.

Although the matter of "sincerity" still plays a major role in the ultimate decision that must be made concerning the applicant, most Reform and Conservative rabbis and a few Orthodox rabbis today accept such candidates, hoping that their judgments in this respect are correct.

Ecclesiastical conversions are most often the consequence of a gradual, often tantalizingly slow change in the point of view of the convert. Emotions play their role, not only in the case of those persons whose reasons for conversion are solely intrinsic but also in those whose conversion is largely motivated by love and the desire for marriage.

This study of forty-five converts leads me to believe that the vast majority of all ecclesiastical converts have not had a religious experience. There is seldom a "struggling away from sin," as Starbuck[11] puts it. Nor is there a "striving after righteousness." If these responses are evident in any degree they are only incidental to other objectives. If, as a consequence of conversion, the convert moves from a state of emotional conflict to a condition of inner peace, the reason for the change may more often than not be the result of a happy marriage.

Ecclesiastical conversion is, I think, a further indication that the individual in our day is often faced with stresses and strains, anxieties and insecurities that bespeak his loneliness in our contemporary world. The indifference and dissatisfaction with the religion of one's youth, the belief that the church or synagogue in which one has been reared has failed to speak out clearly on the issues of our day or that the God in whom one has believed has somehow failed, appear to have prompted many of the converts to whom I have spoken, to lose whatever faith they ever had. Some turn hopefully to another form of organized religion, to church or synagogue, with the hope of finding what they regard as a solution to their problems and a better understanding of the society of which they are a part.

Others, disillusioned with all religion, accept the regimen of the church or synagogue because, in a world they view as morally relativistic, they seek discipline and absolutism. The dictates of the church or synagogue will, they believe, provide them with this basic need.

There are still others who are totally indifferent to religion. If, as a consequence of their desire for marriage to a person of another faith, conversion is expected or required of them, the desired partner can be easily accommodated through conversion. "After all, what difference does it make? One religion is as good (or bad) as another."

If restlessness, anxiety, and indifference increase within our society, I venture to suggest that ecclesiastical conversions will increase in the years ahead. For those to whom religion means much as well as for those to whom it means little, conversion will prove to be a way out.

As Gordon W. Allport[12] has pointed out,

the universe is simply incomprehensible. Each of us wonders. We do not understand the interrelationships of the fragments we know and because we are so anxious to understand the nature of the universe and the meaning of life, it seems to me that more and more persons will turn to religions other than their own for more satisfying and relevant answers.

Conversion must, in some way or other, affect the individual who is converted. The experience of conversion means, for him, not only the weakening or breaking of certain ties to family and friends. It means also the establishment of new ties and new relationships. The convert cannot escape the consequences of these new involvements. He pays a price for conversion. The members of his family, too, are affected by the conversion. They may, as a consequence, be deeply hurt and resentful, or, on the other hand, they may derive great satisfactions and happiness.

Conversion also affects the unity and solidarity of two religious groups: the one the convert leaves and the one he enters, as Rubenstein[13] has observed. It weakens or strengthens either one or both groups, depending upon the qualities of heart and mind that characterize the proselyte. In this sense, the church or synagogue as religious institutions have much at stake in their acceptance or rejection of candidates for conversion.

Like a pebble dropped into a quiet pool of water, the act of the individual radiates out in an ever-widening circle, influencing and affecting families, groups, religious bodies, and society in varying degrees. But there is always some effect, some reaction, however insignificant and imperceptible it may appear to be at the moment.

The forty-five converts whose stories are examined in this volume provide us with a fascinating commentary on the nature of conversion, the factors that brought about their conversion, and the degree of success or failure that has resulted therefrom.

2. Requirements for Conversion

ALL THREE major religions provide for the conversion to their faith of those persons whom they regard as "sincere." Both Judaism and Christianity declare that the truths inherent in their faith are such that they wish to share them with all who will listen. Judaism hopes for the day when all men will worship the one God. Christianity seeks to bring the "good news" to all the world. Although Judaism has only sporadically "missionized," Christianity has, from its very beginnings, actively engaged in the missionizing effort. Christianity believes that the convert must be ready to base his life on the affirmation that Jesus Christ is Lord. Conversion, in its barest essential, is arriving at the point where this affirmation can be made with conviction.

The requirements for ecclesiastical conversion differ widely, not only among the three major faiths but among the various divisions, denominations, and sects within each.

All are agreed, however, that there is need to ascertain the sincerity of the candidate for conversion, for it is this above all else that ultimately spells enrichment or decay and disintegration of church and synagogue and the spiritual view of life to which each adheres.

Protestantism

Protestants believe in Jesus Christ as Lord and Savior, and for them the Bible is the basic source of knowledge concerning what is good and right. They think of God as the ultimate source of man's happiness and seek constant fellowship with Him. Further, they

9

believe in the Church as the institution through which the followers of Christ express their communion with Him. The desire to do God's will is paramount. The obligation to seek to advance His kingdom must never be forgotten.

Although the requirements for conversion among various Protestant denominations differ widely, in almost all of the Protestant denominations the belief in Jesus Christ as the Messiah, Son of God, and Savior of Mankind is required. If a person moves from one Protestant church or denomination to another he is said to "transfer." This, however, is not to be mistaken for conversion in any sense. It is, simply stated, the movement of a person from one Protestant church or denomination to another without any basic change, major or otherwise, in belief or practice.

In the case of those who seek entrance from outside, Protestant denominations set certain definite creedal requirements.

Generally candidates for conversion to Protestantism must indicate (1) a recognition of sin, (2) the utter hopelessness of man without the strength and support that comes from the Savior and man's hope for Redemption. A candidate for conversion must, of course, believe in Jesus as the Messiah, the Son of God, and the Savior of Mankind. Unless these basic beliefs are fully and sincerely accepted, a candidate for conversion is not to be accepted. The Protestant procedures with respect to conversion are usually quite informal and certainly not fixed. They depend in large measure upon the convert and the views of the Protestant minister who is directly involved. If the convert has not been baptized, he must be baptized in accordance with the particular practice of his denomination. If the baptismal ceremony is performed, the legality of the conversion ceremony is seldom, if ever, questioned.

There are three forms of baptism, each of which is acceptable to some denomination and all of which are now acceptable to most church bodies. They are (1) sprinkling, (2) immersion, and (3) pouring. These are, of course, symbolic means of indicating that a cleansing of sin and purification of heart and identification with Christ has taken place. Baptism is regarded as the means by which entrance is made into the Christian fellowship of the Church. It is required of all who would regard themselves as Christians. Roman Catholics and Protestants today recognize the validity of baptism performed by each other. A Protestant who enters the Roman Catholic Church must support his contention that he has been baptized with documentary proof, as must a Roman Catholic if he converts to Protestantism.

Converts to Protestantism must undergo a training period, guided by the pastor. Its nature and length varies, depending upon the instructor, and the period of instruction may range from six weeks to a year, depending on the circumstances, knowledge, and background of the candidate.

Although conversion procedures within Protestantism vary, as we have indicated, certain elements common to all denominations are apparent:

> The applicant for conversion must take a course on Christian doctrine which would include a knowledge of the Ten Commandments, the Apostles' Creed, the Lord's Prayer, an understanding of the Sacraments of the Church, and, of course, he must accept Jesus as the Messiah and personal Savior. The profession of Christian faith is the foundation upon which all else is based.[1]

The text of the Apostles' Creed, which is also used in the Roman Catholic Church, reads:

> I believe in God the Father Almighty, Maker of heaven and earth:
> And in Jesus Christ his only Son our Lord: Who was conceived by the Holy Ghost, Born of the Virgin Mary: Suffered under Pontius Pilate, Was crucified, dead, and buried: He descended into hell; The third day he rose again from the dead: He ascended into heaven, And sitteth on the right hand of God the Father Almighty: From thence he shall come to judge the quick and the dead.
> I believe in the Holy Ghost: The holy Catholic Church: The Communion of Saints: The Forgiveness of sins: The Resurrection of the body: And the Life everlasting. Amen.

Variations of procedure within Protestantism are understandable in view of the numerous church bodies that comprise it. For a detailed account of the official requirements of all religions and denominations within the Christian and non-Christian world, see Solomon's *A Handbook on Conversions*.[2]

Roman Catholicism

The Roman Catholic Church is and always has been actively concerned with the winning of converts to the Church and to the way of life that it represents.

Conversion to Roman Catholicism represents not only the acceptance of membership in the Church but full acceptance of its doctrines as well as submission to the laws of the Church.[3] The Church as the guardian and teacher of revealed Truth openly invites all men to discover the true religion as it is represented by the Church.

While any priest of the Church may influence a candidate to seek identification with the church, the most active missionaries on its behalf are the Paulist Fathers, who, by the dissemination of information about Roman Catholicism, through information centers, public lectures, pamphlets, and other material, expound upon the truths of Roman Catholicism for the benefit of all who seek to know more about the faith.

The Knights of Columbus, the largest of the Catholic laymen's organizations, is also actively engaged in seeking converts. However, the very nature of the organization precludes it from doing more than bringing the prospective proselyte to the attention of the priest.

According to Father James Lloyd,

The person who seeks admittance must be morally certain within his own mind and heart that God wants him to be a Roman Catholic.

He must take every means to become well-informed in the teachings of the church and his commitment as a Catholic. This is to be achieved through the "instructions" and lessons given him by the priests who serve as instructors. The number of such lessons varies, depending in large measure upon the Priest-instructor. Although private instruction is provided if circumstances so require, most candidates are invited to enter formal classes that have been established for this purpose. Such classes vary in size, usually, in the large urban areas, classes number about twenty-five pupils. These classes offer about twenty-four lessons. They meet once or twice a week with each session one hour in length.[4]

The subject matter varies depending upon the priest instructor and the special interests and needs of the candidates.

In the classes conducted by the Paulist Fathers at the Catholic Information Center in Boston, Massachusetts, *Outline of Catholic Teaching,* by Father Keating, is the textbook around which the course of study is built. Lessons in Bible and liturgy, catechism, etc., are also included in the course of study.

Father Robert F. Quinn, C.S.P., of the Paulist Fathers in Boston, who has been responsible for these classes, has indicated that two-thirds of those in attendance (the average attendance is 25) are non-Roman Catholics ranging in age from 25 to 35. About one-half of the non-Roman Catholics have already been baptized in another Christian church but are inactive in that church, while about forty-five percent of the remainder are unbaptized persons who are nominally Christians. About one percent of those attending these classes are Jews. Classes meet from three to six months.

In similar classes conducted by the Paulist Information Center in New York City, twenty-four class sessions are conducted twice a week, for three months. The subjects dealt with in these lectures are:

1. God and Man
2. Divinity of Christ
3. Church of Christ
4. History of the Popes
5. Revelation and Faith
6. Trinity and Creation
7. Creation (Continued)
8. The Incarnation
9. Redemption & Mystical Body

10. Means of Grace
11. Sin & Penance
12. Baptism & Confirmation
13. Penance (Continued)
14. Holy Eucharist & Communion
15. Sacrifice of the Mass
16. Step by Step through the Mass
17. A Dry Mass
18. Extreme Unction & Holy Orders
19. Contract of Matrimony
20. Sacrament of Matrimony
21. The Lost Things
22. The Ten Commandments
23. Saints, Prayers & Doctrines
24. General Review

The opportunity for questions and discussion of these and kindred subjects is provided in class instruction or in private consultation.

The formal Profession of Faith and the baptism then take place (if the validity of the baptism of a Protestant is questionable) at a special mass.[5] While not uniform throughout the Roman Catholic Church, the following text of the Profession of Faith is widely used. Note that the Apostles' Creed is a part of the Profession:

I, ————, touching with my hand God's holy Gospels, enlightened by divine grace, profess the faith which the Catholic, Apostolic, Roman Church teaches. I believe that Church to be the one true Church, which Jesus Christ founded on earth: to which I submit with all my heart.

I believe in God, the Father Almighty, Creator of heaven and earth; and in Jesus Christ, His only Son, Our Lord: Who was conceived by the Holy Spirit, born of the Virgin Mary, suffered under Pontius Pilate, was crucified, died, and was buried. He descended into hell; the third day He arose again from the dead; He ascended into Heaven, sits at the right hand of God, the Father Almighty; from thence He shall come to judge the living and the dead. I believe in the Holy Spirit, the Holy Catholic Church, the communion of saints, the forgiveness of sins, the resurrection of the body, and life everlasting. Amen.

I believe that seven sacraments were instituted by Jesus Christ for the salvation of mankind: namely, Baptism, Confirmation, Holy Eucharist, Penance, Extreme Unction, Holy Orders, and Matrimony.

I believe that the Pope, the Bishop of Rome, is the Vicar of Jesus Christ on earth, that he is the supreme visible head of the whole Church, and that he teaches infallibly what we must believe and do to be saved.

I also believe everything which the Holy, Catholic, Apostolic and Roman Church defines and declares we must believe. I adhere to her with all my heart, and I reject every error and schism which she condemns. So help me God and these His holy Gospels which I touch with my hand.

Baptism is, of course, associated with the idea of the cleansing from sin, the new birth, and identification with Christ.[6]

Here, as in the case of those seeking conversion to Protestantism and Judaism, the priest must believe in the candidate's sincerity of purpose. He, in the final analysis, must make the decision concerning the candidate's acceptability to the Church.

Judaism

The traditional attitude that should be taken toward a candidate for conversion to Judaism is best expressed by the words of the Sage, Rabbi Yochanan, recorded in the Talmud:[7] "Always, the left hand should repel and the right hand, attract." The intention is clear— although every precaution should be taken to be certain that the candidate is both worthy and sincere, he should not be treated harshly. Let the candidate know that he is being judged but once the judgment in his favor has been made, help him to appreciate the meaningfulness and relevance of Judaism so that he may ultimately become an authentic convert to Judaism.

The Talmud[8] specifically prescribes the traditional procedures of inquiry that should be used of one seeking conversion to Judaism, an excerpt of which is included here:

Our Rabbis taught, when a man desires to be converted to Judaism, he is asked: "What induces you to be converted to Judaism? Do you not know that in these days the Israelites are persecuted and oppressed, despised, harassed and overcome by afflictions?" If he replies, "I know and yet am unworthy (of the privilege of membership in Israel)" he is forthwith accepted and is given instruction in some of the minor and major commandments. . . . As he is informed of the punishment for the transgression of the Commandments, so is he informed of the reward granted for their fulfillment. . . . He is not, however, to be persuaded or dissuaded too much.

If he accepts (all the restrictions and disabilities) he is circumcized, . . . immersed in the ritual waters while two learned men stand at his side and acquaint him with some of the minor and some of the major Commandments. Following the immersion he is deemed to be an Israelite in all respects.

Although conversion procedures are clearly defined, Orthodox Judaism discourages those candidates who desire to convert as a consequence of a desire to marry a Jew, and the number of conversions under Orthodox Jewish Rabbinical auspices is very small. Conservative and Reform Jews are considerably more lenient, believing that the sincerity of the candidate is not automatically disproved because marriage to a Jew is contemplated.

Candidates for conversion are expected to know the beliefs and practices of Judaism. They are expected, too, to know Jewish history and the customs and ceremonies of the Jewish people. Some rabbis require that candidates learn to read and understand the meaning of the Hebrew prayers, as well.

Orthodox Judaism

Orthodox Judaism requires that the duties and obligations incumbent upon Jews, as prescribed by Jewish law, shall not only be known by the convert but that the assurance be given that he intends to follow them. In all instances, it must be clear that the candidate has definitely rejected the tenets of his former faith, that he will lead a Jewish life, and will rear his children as Jews. Nor is the acceptance of Jewish religious principles alone regarded as a sound basis for conversion, because Judaism, the religion, is regarded as inseparable from the Jewish people. Hence, the convert must commit himself to (1) the Jewish religion and (2) identification with the Jewish people.

The Orthodox Jewish legal requirements for conversion are also recorded in the "Schulchan Aruch" (the Prepared Table) or code of traditional practice.[9] Accepted by the majority of Orthodox Jews, its provisions, compiled by Rabbi Joseph Caro (1488–1575), are generally regarded as binding even today. These requirements include the following:

1. Instruction in the basic doctrines of Judaism, i.e., the unity of God and the prohibition of idol-worship, must be given.

2. If the candidate for conversion has accepted these root-ideas, he is further instructed in the "MITZVOT" (Command-ments) including the ritual of Jewish life.

3. The ceremony of circumcision, in the case of a male, may then be performed as a sign that the proselyte has entered into the Covenant made between God and the children of Israel.

4. The proselyte, male or female, is then required to undergo ritual immersion in a "MIKVAH," a pool of water especially designated for ritual purification as a symbolic act of purification.

5. A Tribunal or court consisting of three learned Jews must attest to the fact that each of these acts has been properly per-formed. They must further testify to the sincerity of the proselyte, as well as to his knowledge of the basic doctrines and ritual of Judaism.

6. The convert is then given a Hebrew name ("——— son or daughter, of Abraham,") indicating that he is now considered to be a descendent of the first Hebrew, the Patriarch Abraham.

Conservative Judaism

The *Rabbi's Manual* (1965 edition) published by the Rabbinical Assembly, the national organization of Conservative rabbis, devotes fourteen pages of its official handbook to the subject of conversion. In the main, Conservative rabbis prescribe the traditional practices and procedures of their Orthodox colleagues. In one major respect, however, they differ. While acknowledging that many candidates for conversion plan to marry a Jew, the Conservative rabbis do not necessarily regard this as sufficient reason for their refusal to prepare such a candidate for conversion.

The principal motivation of an overwhelming number of candidates for conversion is the desire to marry a specific Jewish individual, a motive which, per se, is not viewed enthusiastically by Jewish law and tradition. *However, through judicious guidance by the rabbi, such a prospective convert may gain a deep and sincere appreciation of the Jewish religion, leading to his or her becoming a "Ger Tzedeck" in the fullest sense of the term.* [Italics mine][10]

Other significant excerpts from the Manual are:

The convert to Judaism often becomes much more devoted to the tradition as interpreted by a conscientious teacher than the native Jew whose Jewish education may have been neglected or inadequate.[11]

A minimum of six to eight months of intensive study of assigned material should be required for the average applicant for conversion. A period of one calendar year is strongly urged.[12]

It is highly desirable that (the applicant) be introduced to Jewish families in order to effect as pleasant and easy a transition period as possible into the Jewish faith and the Jewish community.[13]

The rabbi and two colleagues or two qualified laymen constitute the Beth Din, or religious tribunal, who shall examine the knowledge and attitude of the prospective convert and preside over his or her admission into the Jewish faith.

If and when the tribunal is convinced of the sincerity of the applicant and that his decision is based upon his love of God, he is then instructed in the observances and religious duties, the fundamentals of Judaism, with special attention to the meaning and implications of the God-Idea. In addition to the personal instruction and discussion led by the rabbi, appropriate textbooks are offered for study in order to augment the knowledge and information already obtained. No time limit is set for these lessons inasmuch as all instruction depends in large measure upon the character and quality of the applicant.

If the candidate is a male, the conversion procedure requires

(1) the rite of circumcision, in accordance with the Covenant of Abraham and (2) ritual immersion in a Mikvah (a pool of water used exclusively for ritual purification). If the candidate is a female the ritual immersion ceremony alone is required.

Two blessings are recited by the proselyte at the time of the immersion:

1. Blessed art Thou, O Lord our God, King of the Universe, who hast sanctified us by Thy Commandments and hast commanded us to perform the rite of Immersion.

2. Blessed art Thou, O Lord our God, King of the Universe, who hast kept us in life, sustained us and enabled us to reach this significant season.

The immersion ceremony, not unlike the Christian baptism, is intended symbolically to signify the "washing away" of sins and the beginning of a new life.

The convert, having performed these rites, is henceforth recognized as a full member of the Jewish religious community. According to Judaism he is now no different from all other Jews, legally, religiously, and socially.

Reform-Liberal Judaism

This branch of Judaism, although from its beginnings concerned with proselytizing, has until 1966 never undertaken a positive, militant program in that direction. Many of its pamphlets and other publications provide information concerning the nature of Judaism and offer every assistance to persons seeking to acquaint themselves with the theology and ritual life of the Jew.

Its philosophy is clearly stated in its *Rabbi's Manual*.[14]

ADMISSION OF PROSELYTES

Judaism welcomes all sincere converts without regard to racial or national origin or to their former religious faith. The Biblical laws excluding certain peoples from admission to the community of Israel were declared obsolete early in the Talmudic period (*Yadayim* 4.4). Tradition prescribed that a prospective convert must be warned in advance of the many religious responsibilities which a Jew must assume and of the disabilities he may suffer; but it was further ordained that the candidate should not be unduly discouraged (*Yevamoth* 47a). Jewish literature has much to say in praise of converts and records the names of many illustrious and pious proselytes.

The traditional halacha requires male converts to submit to circumcision and afterwards to receive a ritual bath; women are converted by the ritual immersion. But in 1893, the Central Conference of American Rabbis declared that no initiatory rite was necessary; the prospective convert should simply declare, orally and in writing, in the presence of a rabbi and no less than two associates, his acceptance of the Jewish faith and his intention to live by it. At times this formal admission of the proselyte took place during a Sabbath service, but the procedure outlined in this Manual is the more usual one.

It is understood that the formal conversion is to be preceded by a suitable period of instruction by the rabbi or some other qualified person. This will enable the rabbi to satisfy himself not only that the candidate has sufficient knowledge, but is a person of responsible character who is sincerely desirous of living as a Jew.

Not all Reform rabbis are in complete agreement with this formulation or with its requirement. Petuchowski[15] has estimated that twenty-eight percent of all Reform rabbis will officiate at a marriage involving a Jew and a non-Jew without expecting that any or all of these requirements be fulfilled. The traditional ritual of immersion and the requirement of circumcision, in the case of a male, is eliminated. Formal study and class sessions are generally required. The rabbi or someone designated by him serves as class instructor. The period of instruction may vary from community to community. In all instances, Jewish history, beliefs, and practices are included in the course of study. As we have already noted (see Chapter 1), the majority of converts to Judaism enter through Reform Judaism.

Individual rabbis, Reform and Conservative, often add requirements of their own to those already listed. Among these are the following:

1. A pledge to affiliate with the Temple.
2. A pledge to attend worship services regularly.
3. A pledge to give children a Jewish education.
4. A pledge to observe the ritual and ceremonies of Jewish life, with particular emphasis upon observance of the Sabbath, the Holy Days, and, in some instances, the Dietary Laws.

Reconstructionism

The Jewish Reconstructionist Movement, which is generally regarded as "left" of Conservative Judaism, includes both Conservative and Reform-Liberal rabbis. It recommends conversion procedures that, in general, follow those observed by Conservative Judaism. In the case of some of its adherents the immersion ceremony is optional on the part of the proselyte.

The philosophy of Jewish Reconstructionism, as stated by Ira Eisenstein,[16] one of its noted leaders, is not in agreement with the practices suggested above.

The mistake generally made is in thinking that a religion should be "universal" in the sense that it should be accepted by all men, that every people on earth should adopt the civilization, traditions, associations, *sancta* of that religion. The truth is that the universalism of a religion should consist in the universal applicability of its values. Missionary activity, therefore, should consist in getting others to accept one's values, not in making proselytes, in getting others to adopt one's cultural patterns, or ancestors and history.

The usual objection to this conception of religion and of the relation of religions to one another, is that no cognizance is taken of the fact that some religions are better than others, not only superior for their own adherents but *objectively* superior. However, upon reflection it will appear that no religion can be regarded as superior to any other. The mere fact that, at any given time in history, it may possess a superior set of values does not make the religion itself superior since those same values can be appropriated by other religions, and expressed in terms of the *sancta* of those religions. To say that the *sancta* of one religion are better than the *sancta* of another is, however, meaningless. The fact is that the *sancta* of one religion are invaluable and precious to the members of that religion; and are generally of no value at all to members of another. They may have certain purely esthetic values; but they cannot possibly have the appeal to outsiders which they have to those born and brought up within the group . . .

As soon as we recognize, therefore, that different religious groups really represent different culture patterns, we see how futile and wrong it is to attempt to impose them upon those who prefer their own. If there is truth in a particular religion, and that truth is lacking elsewhere, it can be easily adopted and adapted, and everyone will benefit."

Eastern Orthodox Church

The Eastern Orthodox Church regards itself as the "source of Christianity." It looks upon Roman Catholicism, Protestantism, and other Christian churches as splinter churches.

Governed by an Ecumenical Council, this church does not regard any of its teachers as infallible. Rather, it is the "Holy Spirit" alone that "shall lead us into all truth."

In America, the Eastern Orthodox Church is not large and it is exceedingly wary about conversion and converts. It does not encourage either but is ready to accept converts if those who wish to join the Church do so in good faith. The majority of converts to the Eastern Orthodox faith are converted because of their desire for marriage to a member of a Greek Orthodox church.

If a person expresses his (or her) interest in joining this church, and if, further, his interest in the Church is judged to be sincere, he is admitted to membership in the Church.

It is the priest who must be responsible for the instruction and training of the applicant.

The candidate for conversion must acquaint himself with the

history of the Greek Orthodox Church in a period of instruction that depends entirely upon the response of the priest to the candidate for conversion, his belief in the integrity of the applicant, and his intuitive feelings with regard to the ability of the applicant to "absorb" and comprehend the teachings.

The priest must be convinced as to the candidate's sincerity. "We are wary of people who want to convert to our church." "We ask, Why? What do you wish to gain? to acquire? What can this Church do for you? What do you need?" If the priest is convinced as to the candidate's sincerity he may agree to provide a series of instructions. Such lessons are offered by the local priest, with the proviso that children born of the convert will be reared in the Greek Orthodox Church. A series of five to seven lessons is undertaken. These lessons include a study of the religious ideas of the Church and an introduction to the ethnicity of the Church's membership. The "ways" of the Greek people are also studied and discussed.[17] Greek language skills are taught, as is Greek history. Orthodox religion in terms of doctrine, divine liturgy, the symbolism of the Church, as well as its sacramental aspects, are all carefully considered and discussed.

Among the positive doctrines a convert is expected to affirm are acceptance of the Nicene Creed, which forms a part of the Roman Catholic mass and is also used by some Protestant denominations. The text of the Nicene Creed follows:

> I believe in one God the Father Almighty, Maker of heaven and earth, And of all things visible and invisible:
> And in one Lord Jesus Christ, the only-begotten Son of God; Begotten of his Father before all worlds, God of God, Light of Light, Very God of very God; Begotten, not made; Being of one substance with the Father; By whom all things were made: Who for us men and for our salvation came down from heaven, And was incarnate by the Holy Ghost of the Virgin Mary, And was made man: And was crucified also for us under Pontius Pilate; He suffered and was buried: And the third day he rose again according to the Scriptures: And ascended into heaven, And

sitteth on the right hand of the Father: And he shall come again, with glory, to judge both the quick and the dead; Whose kingdom shall have no end.

And I believe in the Holy Ghost, The Lord, and Giver of Life, Who proceedeth from the Father and the Son; Who with the Father and the Son together is worshipped and glorified; Who spake by the Prophets: And I believe one Catholic and Apostolic Church: I acknowledge one Baptism for the remission of sins: And I look for the Resurrection of the dead: And the Life of the world to come. Amen.

Following upon the period of instruction the candidate is expected to accept the obligations of membership in the Eastern Orthodox Church. He is then prepared to receive (1) baptism, (2) confirmation, and (3) the Holy Eucharist. If he has accepted these three sacraments, he is then permitted to sign an official document of conversion.

The validity of the Roman Catholic sacraments such as baptism and confirmation are recognized by the Church. If, however, the applicant for conversion is not a Roman Catholic these requirements are still enforced.

Unitarian Universalist

Unitarian Universalist views are generally far removed from and to the left of orthodox Christianity, and this denomination is included primarily because its philosophy with respect to conversion differs radically from all other forms of Christianity.

Unitarian Universalist societies or churches have no formal requirements for conversion. The word "conversion" is, in fact, seldom if ever used to describe the experience that ultimately brings members into the Unitarian Universalist denomination. The gradual process by which a person arrives at the conclusion that the views of this group represent, for him, meaningful and relevant truth, is described as "a process of growth."

When the conclusion is reached that affiliation with the Unitarian Universalist philosophy through its societies or churches is desirable, the membership book is signed. Such a person may be formally received, either at a service or in the privacy of the minister's study. Inasmuch as each of the societies is autonomous, the procedures vary. In most instances, nothing more than attendance and active participation in the thought-life and activities of the church is expected.

* * *

Requirements and procedures for ecclesiastical conversion are, as we have noted, diverse. They vary among denominations and individual churches. Within Judaism, they differ also. In all instances, however, the function and purpose of religion as each group understands it is made clear by its particular requirements. In each case, conversion implies not only a rejection of formerly held religious views, but a change and acceptance of another markedly different faith and practice.

3. *Something About These Converts*

MANY QUESTIONS need be asked about the forty-five converts who have been interviewed. What kind of people are they? What kind of homes did they come from? What were their parents like? How "religious" were their parents? These and a vast number of other questions require specific answers if the nature of conversion with respect to these forty-five is, in any degree, to be understood.

Of the forty-five converts interviewed, twenty-nine were women and sixteen were men. All but six were married. Thirty-five had children and of these children, one-half were grown. In some cases, the children of the convert were already married and rearing families of their own.

Of the thirty who converted to Judaism, eleven persons (eight women and three men) were formerly Roman Catholics. There are also nineteen former Protestants (thirteen women and six men) who accepted Judaism as their new religion. All three of the converts to the Greek Orthodox Church are women. Of these, two were formerly Protestants and one was a Roman Catholic. Of the nine converts to Roman Catholicism, five had been Protestants (three men and two women), while four were formerly identified as Jews (three men and one woman). The two converts to Protestantism are women, and both were former Jewesses. There is also one man, a former Roman Catholic, who is now a Unitarian Universalist.

Of the thirty converts to Judaism, twenty-one (sixteen women and five men) declared that their formal conversion to another faith was prompted and motivated by a desire to marry a Jew.

26

Further, it was their belief that as a consequence of conversion religious unity within the home would help to assure the success of the marriage. Of these sixteen women who converted to Judaism, ten were formerly Protestants and six were Roman Catholics. Four of the five men in this category were formerly Protestants, while one had been a Roman Catholic.

Only three of the nine persons in our sample who converted to Roman Catholicism (two women and one man) did so for reason of marriage to a Roman Catholic.

The three converts to the Greek Orthodox Church (all women) formally accepted their new religious affiliation as a consequence of their wish to marry a member of that church.

Of the two converts to Protestantism (both women) one indicated that her conversion was related to her desire to express her loyalty to her deceased husband, a Protestant.

The lone Unitarian Universalist in our sample turned to his present religious philosophy for purely intrinsic reasons.

Twenty-eight converts (twenty-two women and six men) of the total number of forty-five converts on whom we are reporting indicated that the primary motive for their conversion was clearly extrinsic. Conversion served as a means toward an end that was not *directly* related to the quality or nature of their adopted religion.

Eleven persons in our sample said that their conversion had nothing whatsoever to do with marriage. These individuals stated that logic and reason alone brought about their ultimate conversion. Another six had been married for many years at the time of their conversion.

Thirty-two (ten men and twenty-two women) were reared in metropolitan areas along the eastern seaboard, ten (four men and six women) came from the Midwest, while two (one man and one woman) had their origin in the West. One man was born in the South. Fourteen (six men and eight women) were born and reared in cities having a population of five hundred thousand or more. Seventeen (seven men and ten women) lived in cities with a population ranging from fifty thousand to just under a half million, and fourteen (seven men and seven women) lived in towns of from twenty-five hundred to just under fifty thousand. None of our sample came from communities of less than twenty-five hundred people.

Because it is often suggested that the natural division between the generations and lack of communication between them may be even more significant if the parents are foreign-born, the origin of the parents of these converts was ascertained. Of these forty-five, the parents of eight of the men were foreign-born while the parents of another eight men were born in the United States. The parents of seventeen of the women converts were foreign-born while, in the case of twelve women, their parents were native-born.

In all but two instances (one man and one woman), each of these converts was born in the United States.

Forty-two of these converts are white while three (two men and one woman) are Negroes.

In seven cases (all women), the converts were the children of mixed marriages, where mother and father were of different religious background and maintained their separate religious affiliation following their marriage.

The interdating practices of our sample indicate that, of the total number, seven men and twenty-two women dated with persons of other faiths, beginning at the high school level and thereafter. In the case of the men, they stated that no objection to this practice was voiced by their parents. Of the twenty-two women who interdated, only six indicated that they did so despite the objection of parents, particularly their mothers. The other twenty-three parents, according to these converts, raised no objection whatsoever to the interdating practice at any time.

As of the level of education, among the sixteen male converts, two completed only elementary school and the remainder completed high school. Of the fourteen high school graduates, eight graduated from college, and of these, five have advanced degrees. The educational level of the twenty-nine female converts is significantly lower. Eleven of them completed only elementary school; eighteen completed high school, and of these eighteen, five graduated from college, two of them having graduate degrees.

Of these forty-five converts, thirty-six (fifteen men out of sixteen and twenty-one women out of twenty-nine) lived away from home as young adults; six, as early as their high school years, and thirty beginning with their college years. Independence for these people expressed itself by actual physical separation from parents and family. Often this separation provided the impetus that led to the formulation of religious values and standards totally different from those of the parents. Uncertainties and doubts concerning familial religious values and beliefs perhaps born of contacts and relationships with diverse people of varied backgrounds often developed into resentments and an open break with formerly accepted standards.

In most cases these converts appear to be strong-willed, generally highly opinionated persons. They speak with very positive convictions, not only with respect to their religious beliefs but on other matters as well. Whether this is in some measure due to a personal insecurity which obliges them to speak with such certainty, it is difficult to say. Of the forty-five converts, this trait was noticeable in all but three cases.

Conversations with these converts about their reactions to persons of other colors lead me to believe that they are generally free from bias on the basis of color. At least I found no overt indication of deep-rooted prejudice or bias.

A marked emotion-laden response became readily apparent when these converts spoke of religions other than their adopted one. I found, in all but five instances, a tendency to look down upon other religions. This was true even in the cases of those whose reason for conversion was directly associated with marriage. Now that they had converted, they seemed to frown upon other religions, including the religion of their parents. This, however, did not directly affect their attitude toward parents or siblings. In all cases except those that involved broken homes and marital unhappiness, the desire to retain close ties with parents and family was apparent.

Despite the obvious feeling of superiority now that they had adopted a new religion, there was no indication in any instance of a desire to propagandize on its behalf or to seek other converts. They did not attempt to do so even with their own children, believing that each person must make his own decision in the matter of religion.

Generally I found no strong indication of liberalism, either in politics or in social attitudes in these converts. None belongs to any organization that is directly devoted to the advancement of civil liberties or toward a greater degree of social justice for humankind.

The initial move toward conversion began, for most of these persons, in their late twenties and thirties. Thoughts concerning conversion commenced at about the time when the possibility of marriage to a person of another faith also presented itself.

Of these forty-five, nine persons began to think about conversion between the ages of thirteen and twenty; sixteen of the converts first began to consider conversion during their twenties; sixteen indicated that they began to think seriously about conversion between the ages of thirty and forty; while two persons actively entertained the idea of conversion after the age of sixty. Only two persons indicated that the idea of adopting another faith occurred to them prior to their thirteenth birthday.

What role had religion played in the early life of these converts? Of the eleven former Roman Catholics who had converted to Judaism, we have already noted that eight were women and three were men. Of these eight women, only one stated that she came from a "strictly religious" home. Two persons described their parental home as "moderately religious," while five converts indicated that their homelife had "no religion." In the case of the three male converts to Judaism, two described their early homelife as "not religious," and the third indicated that he came from a "strictly religious" home.

Of the nineteen former Protestants who had been converted to Judaism (thirteen women and six men), the religious life of their early homes was not much different. Seven of the women described their families as "not religious," four others declared their early family life to have been "moderately religious," while only two spoke of their early homelife as "strictly religious." In the case of the six male converts from Protestantism to Judaism, three indicated that their early homelife had been "nonreligious," two came from "moderately religious" homes, while only one declared his homelife to have been "strictly religious."

All five of the former Roman Catholic women who had been converted to Judaism, whose homelife had no religious influence, declared themselves to have been "indifferent to" or had "lost faith" in Catholicism prior to their conversion to their new faith. One woman whose family had been "moderately religious" also stated that she had become indifferent to Catholicism in her late teens. Only two persons, one from a strictly religious home and the other from a moderately religious home, stated that they had maintained religious interest in and concern for Roman Catholicism. In the case of the three male converts from Roman Catholicism to Judaism, all declared themselves to have been indifferent to Roman Catholicism long before their conversion.

Of the nine converts to Roman Catholicism, four (three men and one woman) were Jews. Only one of the Jewish men described his early homelife as "moderately religious," while the three others declared that their homelife had been "nonreligious." In each of these four cases, the convert declared that for many years there had been a quest for some meaningful religious identification which had not been satisfied in early homelife.

Of the five former Protestants (three men and two women) who became converts to Roman Catholicism, four (three men and one of the women) described their early family homelife as "moderately religious," while only one, a woman, stated that her homelife had been "nonreligious." In the case of only two of these persons (both men), there had always been a yearning for some strong meaningful religious tie.

Two Jewesses were converted from Judaism to Protestantism. In one instance, the early homelife had been nonreligious, while in the other case there had been a "moderately religious" background. In both cases, there appears to have been an earnest quest for stronger religious ties that were finally satisfied by conversion to Protestantism.

All three of the women who converted to the Greek Orthodox religion came from homes that were "moderately religious." Of these, one had been a Roman Catholic and the other two had been Protestants. There is no indication that any of these three had even moderate religious ties or anything more than a nominal religious identification prior to conversion.

The one former Roman Catholic who later identified himself with Unitarianism described the home and family life of his youth as "strictly religious." Until his adolescence he and all his family had assumed that he would ultimately become a Roman Catholic priest. His loss of faith in the Church and its tenets began early and was climaxed by his ultimate break with his religious past, in his early twenties.

A summary of the early religious homelife of all these converts indicates that fifteen came from what they termed "religious" homes; nineteen were reared in homes and families that were "moderately religious," while eleven were reared in "nonreligious" homes. There is, however, no indication that the degree of religiosity of the homes from which these converts came seriously affected their attitudes or responses to such a degree that we can unequivocally point to this factor alone as the deciding factor that ultimately led to their conversion.

Many of these forty-five converts have come from homes which they describe as "broken," i.e., where alcoholism, desertion, open quarreling, or noncommunication between the parents has led to separation or divorce. Nine of the thirty converts to Judaism (five former Roman Catholics and four Protestants) indicated that the family life of their parents had not been happy. Of these, four indicated that alcoholism was the decisive factor that had made for an unhappy homelife and eventually resulted in divorce. Three of the converts spoke of an early separation and ultimate divorce that made their homelife unhappy. In the other case, the convert spoke of a lack of communication between the parents that made a happy homelife difficult of attainment. In still another case, the death of the father while the interviewee was still in elementary school seriously affected the happiness of the home. In all cases, there is reason to believe that the lives of our subjects were seriously affected by these unhappy experiences.

Of the nine persons (five Protestants and four Jews) who were converted to Roman Catholicism, three of the former Protestants and two of the former Jews stated that their lives had been seriously affected by some form of stress and strain between parents that resulted in separation (one case), a domineering parent (three cases), or death of a parent (one case).

No instance of unhappiness was reported in the case of the three converts to the Greek Orthodox religion (two Protestants and one Roman Catholic).

Of the two converts to Protestantism (both former Jews), one was seriously affected by the death of her husband, which appears to have led her to convert to his faith, while the other appears to have been affected by the prolonged serious illness of her mother.

The lone former Roman Catholic who later affiliated with Unitarianism declared that alcoholism on the part of his father seriously affected his homelife.

A total of seventeen out of the forty-five cases have given some indication that their early homelife was affected, directly or indirectly, by the homelife in their childhood.

A sense of loneliness and insecurity characterized thirty-eight of these converts. Their conversations made it clear that there had been but little communication, not only between their parents and themselves but with siblings as well.

I never really had anyone to talk to. My grandmother who raised me was a fine person, but I never felt that I could really talk to her. My mother really never gave us kids any attention.

*　　*　　*

I really couldn't talk very much about my ideas about God and Jesus when Mother was sick. My father would have thought I was crazy to entertain the ideas I had. So I just had to carry these ideas inside me and not talk about them.

*   *   *

My parents would have looked upon me as a kind of dangerous character if I had suggested that I no longer found pleasure in attending the Roman Catholic Church. The Church was their life. My ideas would have upset them, so I just kept my thoughts to myself.

*   *   *

My father was always working at his tailoring shop and my mother, wonderful woman that she was, was quite illiterate. I had one brother who was eight years older than I, and we never had anything in common. So how could I talk to any of them?

It is however not clear that parents or other members of the family were always at fault in this respect. In four cases, the difference in age between the interviewee and the next older or younger sibling was sufficiently great to cause this lack of communication. In twenty-nine instances, a natural resistance and sensitivity on the part of the convert appeared to be the answer. Their anxieties and questions concerning themselves and their values were revealed throughout these interviews.

A more minute and detailed examination of these converts and what their conversion has meant to them and to the church or synagogue with which they have identified is provided through the interviews in the suceeding chapter and in the appendix.

4. Eighteen Interviews

Peter Kaufman

Peter is my baptismal name, the name I took when I entered the Roman Catholic Church. I've always loved that name. Little did I realize that the day would come when I could bear it with a sense of pleasure and satisfaction. Of course, the name my parents gave me at my "Briss" (circumcision rites) when I was initiated into the Covenant of Abraham and became a Jew is still my legal name. They called me "Abraham." But the name I really love is "Peter."

My mother was born in Russia but came to America as a little child. My father's family also came from Russia, from the very same town where my mother's family came from. My mother received what little education she got, in the public schools of Ohio. She really couldn't go very far in school because of the dire economic necessity that required that she help earn enough to support the family. In those days it was absolutely essential that the children work if the family was going to eat regularly. Her father had been a carpenter, and often he was without work. Those were difficult days for her family.

My father got even less formal schooling. I'm sure that he never finished grade school. He was a simple, honest man, a good tailor. But that's about all. I always thought of him kindly. He was never a very happy man. I remember that he didn't enjoy his work too much. He was always a kind of sad-looking man. He had been a good Hebrew student in the Old Country. Here he learned the tailoring trade. My mother and he were married after a very brief

35

courtship. They had been introduced by mutual friends whose families had also come from that same Russian hometown.

After my father died, my mother tried to keep the tailoring shop but branched out in dry goods, and, even though it was a great struggle, she saw my brother and me through high school and college. My brother is a physicist, and a good one. I always did well in academic subjects. People who knew us boys used to call me "the scholar." I guess they really meant that I had a rather philosophical bent, and this often amused or intrigued them. I did well enough to win a scholarship to go on to college. I went to Oberlin because it had the kind of courses—in literature, art, and music—that appealed to me. I loved to read. The great books, the outstanding literature of the world—all this was of great importance to me. A high school teacher of mine had made a great impression on me. He was a fine scholar, and it was he who really directed my reading and my thinking. It was he who suggested the possibility of my getting a scholarship, and, to this day, I am deeply grateful to him for all that he did for me.

My mother was and is an exceedingly bright person. I understand that my father always had felt that he should have continued the life of a student. But the intellectual curiosity and concern of both my parents was, as I understand it, quite marked.

From all that I remember of my early childhood and from what my mother has told me, my parents lived a good life together. It was a good home, a happy home. My relationship with my brother, who was eight years older than I, was, generally speaking, also good. Of course, the difference in our ages meant that in my early years we had nothing in common. We "discovered" each other about the time of World War II, when I was eighteen and he was twenty-six. Suddenly, we found ourselves going out together. This was like receiving a brother out of the blue.

I remember that I had a few uncles and aunts, with whom my mother maintained close, affectionate ties. They and their children, my cousins, lived not too far away, and we saw them fairly often. Either they came to our home or we visited with them. They were all quite Orthodox Jews, as were my parents. But my mother was the more religious of the two. My father, although he loved to study the Bible, the Commentaries, and the Talmud, was less seriously religious. He loved to study. It meant so much to him. I can't think of many Jews of his generation who did not take the life of the synagogue seriously. It was the very center of their life, religiously and socially. Everything centered around it. My mother kept a kosher house, as did all the other members of the family. I do remember that she would eat out of her home but never any non-kosher meats or things like that. We observed the Sabbath, the Holy Days, and Festivals, but we seldom attended the synagogue service on the Sabbath. I guess that was because she had to keep her store open. She needed whatever she could earn. I went to Hebrew school and I was Bar Mitzvah. I think I stopped going to Hebrew school shortly after I was Bar Mitzvah. Altogether I think I went to that Hebrew school for about two years. It wasn't much of a school, and I didn't spend enough time there to really learn very much, formally, about Judaism. But it was all I got. Certainly, there was nothing profound about my Hebrew education. I think it would be right to say that I got a "smattering" of Hebrew education. It was all quite superficial.

Just the other day, I met a cousin of my mother's whom I had not seen for twenty years and she reminded me that I was always the most religious youngster in the entire family. She recalled that once, when we were all out together, my mother had ordered a frankfurter for me but I would not eat it until I was sure that it had a kosher label imprinted on the casing.

My mother was proud of her sons. My brother had gone on to New York University. He worked his way through school. And he had done well, but it was I, her youngest, from whom she and the others in the family expected great things. You see, I was what they called a "scholar." I went on to Oberlin and had a wonderfully exciting college career. I was stimulated by the professors, the courses—everything about it pleased me. I graduated "cum laude" and, of course, my mother was so pleased.

There was always a ferment on the campus. Ideas of all kinds were floating about. The discussions and arguments we used to have were really good. As for religion, if you came with a religious faith you stood a fair chance of losing it, because religion like everything else was the subject of much argument and debate. What college campus isn't full of that same exhilarating spirit? In my case, I became more interested in religion, on the campus, than I believe I had ever been before. I found myself reading and studying many religions, but I found that Judaism intrigued me the most.

We had a saintly refugee who came to the college from Germany. Being Jewish, I was asked to help this man, whose English was very imperfect, and I did. He was a most unusual man, learned and attractive in every way. He was very well up on literature and certainly very well up on Judaism. He was a practicing Jew, and we became friendly. Because he had no family, I suppose I became something like a son to him. For almost four years we were good friends. It was he who taught me Hebrew again. Then we studied the Bible and carried on discussions about Jewish theology. This was all exciting to me because, really, I knew very little about Judaism in my youth. I thought that it did not have any intellectual respectability. At times I felt I was an atheist; at other times I thought of myself as an agnostic. But, as a consequence of this friend and teacher, I began praying the traditional prayers every day. I went to the synagogue on Sabbath whenever possible. I even remember writing to my mother and asking her to send on the Tefillin (phylacteries) so that I might pray daily in accordance with Orthodox Jewish ritual practice. I did it for a while, but it was so time-consuming that I gave it up.

But along with all that, I was also reading and discussing the New Testament, Karl Marx, Freud, and the Epistles of St. Paul. And I found too that I became interested in the problem of Christ and his relationship to Israel.

I think it only fair to say that I had, by this time, acquired some Catholic college friends. Some of them were very impressive; others were unimpressive. But I was surprised about one thing. I had hitherto considered it kind of absurd to believe the things that the Christians believed in. I was impressed upon meeting people who, on other subjects so sane and reasonable, could believe in the idea of the incarnation. This struck me as very strange and worth my looking into. As a consequence of my study of Judaism, I began to feel the need to understand the relationship between Judaism and Christianity. With all this, the problem of Christ and Christianity intrigued me also. So you see, I was really quite involved in the study of religion, with special emphasis on Judaism and Christianity and the fascinating relation between these two religions.

All this while, I was a practicing Jew, but a Jew with problems. Not only was I trying desperately to find and understand the relationship between Judaism and Christianity, but I was concerned, too, about what might happen to my relationship with my wonderful friend, the professor, if I told him about my concern with Christianity. Well, I summoned up the courage to talk to him about it. I did not want to offend him or disturb him, and I was sure it would. I did not say too much because it would be hard for him as well as for me. In the meanwhile, I decided to join the Navy (all this happened during the war years). I left school during my junior year, and I was in the service for three years. I was in on the invasion of France and, later, out in the Pacific. I saw some action. About that time the bomb was dropped over Japan, and then the war was over. When I came out of the service, I went back to school for my senior year. My friend, the professor whom I liked so much, was still there.

Now all this while I had been thinking about Catholicism, about joining the Church. This seemed to me to be the right thing to do. But it was still not completely clear to me that I must do this. When I came back to my senior year, I was leaning heavily in that direction. I did not commit myself to anything, but I decided to take instruction to find out more about Catholicism. You see, all this while I was trying to understand the real relationship between Judaism and Catholicism. I could not get over the fact that, at about the time Judaism seemed to be so weak, Christianity was, so to speak, picking up the old tradition and building on it. And, of course, the oldest form of Christianity was Catholicism, so I just had to know more about it.

I have a very skeptical view of purely mystical experiences. The whole theme of Catholicism is Incarnation. Now, I think that anyone without my faith, looking at my actions, would have plenty of opportunities to find ways to explain what I did in another fashion than I do. All this while I found myself increasing the number of Catholic friends I had. I had a few Catholic girl friends. One girl in particular interested me very much. I began to feel that maybe I was turning more and more to Catholicism because of my interest in her, so I actually broke off with this particular girl so that I might think about Catholicism completely independent of her. This particular girl lived in my hometown. My parents knew that I had been seeing not only Jewish but Catholic girls as well. I remember that they objected very much to my interdating. But I told them I never intended to marry outside of the Jewish faith. But I must say that I liked this girl very much. Yet, I suspected my own motives, and I never did anything about the Catholic Church until I had broken off with her.

You see, during these years I was coming to believe that I was following the will of God by turning to the Church. I do not mean that I had any visual or auditory unusual experiences. It was something else. Let me try to explain. I think the fundamental factor was this. No purely sociological explanation of the historical phenomenon of the Jewish people was satisfying to me. The Jewish people and its unusual place in history just couldn't be explained by any of the usual type of reasoning. There was a mystery about the Jewish people. The only thing that could explain this people was that it had a God experience. I believe that the Jewish people is unlike any other people in the world. Now, having that opinion, having the conviction that there was a mystery attached to the Jewish people, and being fascinated as I was by the person of Jesus, it satisfied my mind as I read the Prophets, that the birth of

Jesus was indeed the great culminating experience of Judaism. That the Jewish mission could only be understood in terms of Jesus' coming. This Man was going to spread the idea of human decency, the love of God and of one's neighbor throughout the pagan world. In other words, all that happened in Judaism was climaxed and culminated by the coming of Jesus.

I think of Jesus as God, but this was not easy for me to come by. It was easier to think of Him as a great Prophet or Teacher, perhaps even the greatest. But I realized that the thoughts of God are not the thoughts of man. It would be like God to do this fantastic thing in a fantastic universe. God could become man if He so chose. Why then could He not appear as Jesus?

These were my thoughts. It took a long while for me to formulate them, but I came to feel the divinity of Jesus. It was a kind of revelation to me, not in any mystical sense or experience, but by the reasoning process I arrived at this conclusion. The Church, based on Jesus then, was God's choice, and I wanted to follow His will.

I had two problems to cope with. The first had to do with my teacher, the professor to whom I felt so close. The other had to do with my parents and family. How could I tell them?

Now it so happens that the professor had heard, through a mutual friend, that I was thinking seriously about Catholicism. He called me into his study to discuss it. Previously, I had raised a few questions about Catholicism, but he had not really known the depth of my interest. At this final confrontation, during my senior year at college, he listened to me and to my arguments. I could see that I pained him, and I know that I didn't want that to happen. But, very quietly, he spoke with me and said that he considered it my duty to tell my parents what I was feeling about Catholicism or he would be obliged to do it himself. This was such a trying experience for me. But I knew that he was right. I *had* to do something. After I thought about it for a while, I decided to tell one of my uncles whom I liked very much, hoping that he would talk to my parents. Some of my college friends had somehow heard about what was going on. One, a Protestant, had a long talk with me about it. He told me bluntly what he thought of me for considering Catholicism. The whole thing was just about as trying an experience as I can imagine. But always I came back to the feeling that what I was thinking was, in fact, the will of God.

Even after I had spoken to my uncle and told him that I was contemplating conversion to Roman Catholicism, I thought that the right thing for me to do was to be baptized at once and then confront my parents afterwards. But after more thought I decided that this was not the ethical thing to do. So for a few days I did nothing. Then I got the phone call from my parents to come home at once. Well, of course I did exactly that, and this led to a painful, hysterical session with them. The first confrontation with them extended over a period of about three or four days. This uncle is a particularly successful businessman. He is a very kindly, humane person. I had chosen to talk to him because, years earlier, not knowing what would happen later, he had told me that once he had been attracted to some aspects of Catholicism. I thought he would be sympathetic. It turned out that he was very unsympathetic.

You can hardly imagine the time I had with my parents and all the rest of the family. There are no violent people in my family, but there were verbal threats. They kept the money that I had saved during the war when I sent my salary home. It was in their name as well as mine. They followed their sincere conviction. But I became very angry and hurt. Today, in retrospect, I understand better why they acted as they did. As I look back, I am sure they still loved me all through the years, but they broke off with me completely. I did not hear from them or see them more than once or twice in the next five years.

I converted to Catholicism about a month or two after that confrontation with my parents. Actually, I had arranged for the baptism about the time when my parents called me back home. So I postponed it at that time, but almost immediately thereafter I went ahead with my plans.

Was I going with any girl while all this was happening? Yes,

I was and she was a Catholic. But it didn't last very long because I was so anxious to become a Catholic that nothing else seemed to matter. As a matter of fact, almost immediately after the conversion I got interested in the idea of becoming a priest. Perhaps that was impulsive on my part but that's the way I am.

When the break with my parents occurred, I decided to get away and go to a graduate school and get an M.A. I went out to the Midwest once again and spent a year working intensively in philosophy. It was a wonderfully happy year for me.

Once again I decided to become a priest and join a religious order. I was accepted and I entered a monastery and spent two years during the novitiate preparing myself for that important day when I would be a priest. I spent three years in additional study and received fine training in Catholic theology. But I began to have serious doubts of my suitability to that kind of life about a year before I had to make a final decision. Well, I finally decided against the priesthood. During this time, my parents came to see me once or twice, particularly when they heard that I had become ill. They wrote about once or twice a year.

I left with full agreement by the order. I came back into the world and my first thoughts were to go into teaching. But before I could connect I took all kinds of odd jobs. It was during that period in my life that I met my future wife. She was then writing for a Catholic magazine. We were married about a year after we met. It was then that I decided that in order to teach I should have a Ph.D. degree. So, once again, I went back to a university, and finally, after getting the degree, I got a good teaching post in a leading Midwestern university. We are living happily in a college environment. My wife and I have four fine children. It has been a good marriage in every way.

As for my parents, I'm sorry to say that my father died while I was still preparing for the priesthood. My mother is now friendly with us. She is happy to know that I married a fine girl. We just don't talk about religion. But the whole situation is still painful to her, especially on the occasion of Jewish Feasts like Passover.

Have I changed much since I converted to Catholicism? I believe

the answer is "yes." I think I had a sense of commitment to God
when I was a Jew. I also had a sense of social justice as a Jew.
But I have both of these as a Catholic. Perhaps I have it more, but
I should have it more than I do. I try to love God and my neighbor.
That, I think, is the purpose of religion.

If my children were to marry outside of the Catholic faith it
would be upsetting to me because I consider one's religious convictions to be terribly important and I think the chances of happy
marriages are heightened by an identity between two people with
respect to serious convictions. But I would rather that my children
would marry a fine specimen of a Jew than a poor specimen of
humanity who happened to be born a Catholic.

We really have few contacts with my family. It's almost as if they
played no role whatsoever in my life. We *do* see my wife's family.
We have good social contacts. We belong to one society of Catholics
who, like me, were born Jews. We find it stimulating because it consists of people who love Israel. We are at home with one another.
It is a help when you have such a relationship, particularly when I
know that some Jews, when they find out that I am a Jew who
converted to Catholicism, look upon me as a traitor. Then too,
some Catholics who find out that I am a Jew who converted, look
upon me with suspicion. So it is good to be in the company of other
Jews.

It's a difficult thing to say whether, if I had it to do all over again,
I would do it. The circumstances were actually not of my choosing.
My college professor and my uncle forced my hand. I'm not
questioning for one moment my becoming a Catholic. It's only a
question of when I should have done it. For me, it was the correct
decision.

Serene Daniels

I am a native of Massachusetts. I was born in one of the many fish-
ing villages on the coast, a member of a large family of ten children.
My mother was born in the same town, and my father is a native of
Italy. My mother was a Lutheran. Whatever religion my father

may have been in Italy (I suspect that it was Catholic), I knew him only as a Lutheran. He never talked much about his family or religious background other than that he was a Lutheran. My parents were quite religious people. They attended church regularly as we children did. We went to Sunday school and were of course baptized.

All of us children are married. Three—two brothers and one sister—married Roman Catholics, but none converted to Catholicism. They all have remained Protestants. And they are getting along beautifully. We all have a good relationship visiting with each other when it is possible. My father died about seven years ago. My mother now lives with my husband and me. The fact that I converted to the Greek Orthodox religion doesn't seem to bother her at all. It just seems to make no difference to her. She figures we have our own lives to live and our children to bring up. "This is *your* affair" is the way she has put it more than once. She still attends the Lutheran church even though she lives with us. I do not recall that we have ever fought over religion.

All of us children went to grade school and high school in our old hometown. It was a good, pleasant life. We all got along very well and we had a lot of friends, boys and girls of Protestant and Catholic families. We all lived close together. We were happy in each other's homes. It was all like one happy family.

My father worked in a quarry for many years. He was a good man and we all loved him very much. He and Mother went to church every Sunday morning and I would say that he took religion very seriously. But it never bothered him that some of us children had married outside the church. He was much more concerned that when we married we should marry good people. That was the kind of man he was.

I met Stu, the boy I married, when he was working in my hometown on a summer job. He's a Greek. His parents were born in Greece. But they had come to the United States about twenty-five years earlier, and they lived in Stoneham all those years, living with other Greek families in that town. All the children went to public

school. Some of my friends in my hometown had met Stu that summer and they introduced us. We got along well right from the start.
Stu is a leatherworker. He learned the trade when he finished
grammar school, and, through all these years, he has been working
at the same trade. Although both of his parents died some years
ago, there is a fine relationship between his brother and sister and
us.

When I met Stu I knew that he was Greek and that he was of a
different religion, but it really made no difference to me. I knew
very quickly that I loved him so all the rest really didn't matter.
And Stu has told me that our differences in religion never made any
difference to him either. We saw each other quite often during that
summer, and we became quite serious. He had a good job waiting
for him in Stoneham so he had to go back, but we still saw each
other often. He would come up to my hometown and we would go
out together. I was only about seventeen years old when I first met
Stu.

My parents had met Stu and liked him, but they didn't know his
nationality so they asked me. When I told them that he was Greek
I half expected that they might object but they didn't. I guess they
thought we were just kids and it didn't mean anything. As a matter
of fact they never really discussed his nationality or religion with
me. If they had known how serious we were I suppose they might
have said something. But we didn't give them or anyone else a
chance to do any talking because we eloped.

It was the elopement that bothered them more than anything
else. Not religion and not his being Greek—just that we were kids!!
Well, maybe we were, but we've been married happily for twenty-
eight years now and we have four wonderful children, all grown up
and fine in every way. So I think we have done very well.

It was only three years ago that I converted to the Greek
Orthodox religion. All these years I remained a Lutheran even
though my children were all reared as Greek Orthodox. My four
children were all baptized in the church, and there never was any
question about how they would be raised. The two older children

are now married. My boy married a French girl. She converted to Greek Orthodoxy. My daughter married a Catholic, but she has not converted. But she has had her marriage blessed in the Greek Orthodox Church. Even though they married outside of their religion, they are pretty close to our church.

Why did I not convert to my husband's religion for all these years? Well, the truth is, I wanted to make up my own mind. I wanted no one to push me. I guess it would have remained that way if I hadn't become very ill. About three years ago, I became desperately ill, and I thought I was going to die—and every one else in the family did also. I was so very sick and it was then that I really felt the need for religion. You see I had stopped going to the Lutheran church because there was no such church in the town in which we lived. So I just didn't go to any. It was enough for me to know that Stu and the children were going to the Greek Orthodox church. I had never felt that I really needed a church for myself until I was so desperately ill. Only then did I feel that I should go to communion. But I didn't really have a church of my own to go to.

A strange thing had happened to me many years before, when my children were small. I had taken my children to the Greek Orthodox church to be baptized, and the priest there said that I had to be baptized. I told him that I had been baptized many years before but he said, "You have to be baptized the Greek Orthodox way." Well, I allowed it for the sake of my children, but I was very angry about it and I remained upset about that all those years. If I had been baptized once, why should I have to be baptized again? But here I was ill, and I felt that I needed a church. I felt as if I should go to communion, but I didn't have a church. There was just no place to go. My husband tried to explain to me about the rules of the church, but I couldn't take his explanation because I couldn't figure it out. After all, communion is communion. It was important to me. I mean you can't be a heathen. I was pretty much upset about it.

I kept bringing the children to the church Sunday school. I had many friends in the Greek Orthodox community. They were friendly to me, but they knew that I hadn't been married in this church. Yet, I guessed, on the basis of their friendship, that it didn't make any real difference to them. After all, it happens very frequently; this marrying into another religion is very frequent in the Greek community. Well, whether it was frequent or not, I was very much upset. I thought to myself, "My kids are going to church. They take communion. They are baptized in this church. Why, then, shouldn't I be part of this same church?" So I came to Father S and told him that I felt that the time had come when I should formally convert to the Greek Orthodox religion. Father S knew me very well. He had never pressured me to join the church and he had always been most kind. He was a younger priest who had replaced the older priest with whom I had had such an unhappy experience. I told him that, in the interest of family unity, we might as well all go to one church. Father S was pleased. So were Stu and the children. So, after a few formal lessons with the priest, I was converted. I really didn't need much instruction. I had lived so many years close to this church that I really knew all about the church and the Greek community. I had been coming to the church all these years without belonging. I had absorbed a lot from all the Greek people I knew and, of course, from Stu and the children. Well, it was all a formality for me, and yet it was very important to me. It meant that, officially, there were no differences in any way in my family; we were all one. After my illness, when I was so worried about what would happen to me in case I died, I now felt safe. I could now receive communion. It meant that if anything happened to me I could be buried properly and receive the rites of the church. What I am trying to say is that being a part of the Greek Orthodox church I now feel secure. I needed something and I know now that I needed the security of the church.

I feel ever so close to the Greek Orthodox faith. I really feel that I belong, that I am a part of something very important. I feel really happy about it.

My mother is still alive. She is pleased because I have done this thing. Even though she never has changed from her Lutheran faith she understands why I changed and she feels that if it meant that I was bringing my family together and gaining security for myself that's all that really matters.

After all, it wasn't as if I had to change any real part of my faith. I believe in Jesus Christ now the same way I did when I was a Lutheran. I see more ceremonial and ritual in the Greek Orthodox church, but I don't think that there have really been any great changes in any of my Christian beliefs. I come to church regularly with my husband. Both he and I are happy about the conversion. I think I can say in all honesty that we are happier now than we have ever been in our lives.

Conversion to Greek Orthodoxy was the best thing that ever happened to me. It took that illness to remind me of what I was missing in my life. But thank God, I did the right thing and I feel good about it all.

Agatha and Richard Johnson

AGATHA: My grandmother is closer to me than any other member of my family. I was raised by her and I owe her just about everything. She has done more for me than anyone else, including my parents.

My father and mother were divorced when I was just a child. My father was born a Catholic and my mother a Protestant. I'm sure that my mother never converted to Catholicism. From all that I have heard about it they just didn't get along, and so they were divorced. There was no problem about getting a divorce because they hadn't been married in the Church. Later, my mother remarried. This time, too, she married a Catholic, but what was different was that she actually converted to the Catholic faith. And, from what I hear, she became a very strong Catholic. It was after the divorce that I went to live with my grandmother, my father's mother. She was a wonderful person. She treated me so well, I shall never forget her love and kindness to me. I was baptized as a child, but that was primarily my grandmother's doing. She was a good Catholic, and she looked out after me in every way.

My father had been in the Navy. I really saw very little of him when I was a child. I heard about him through Grandmother, and my mother. Mostly it was my grandmother who spoke to me about him. I was reared as a Catholic, of course. The Church meant a great deal to my grandmother.

Now, there was divorce too in my grandparents' lives. Shortly before I went to live with my grandmother, my grandparents were divorced. Later, my grandfather was remarried and he lived in a little town in eastern Pennsylvania.

With all the divorces, there was still a strong feeling for Catholicism. I was baptized and confirmed and I made my first communion. But I have come, over the years, to dislike Catholicism. There were many reasons for it. Certainly, one of them was the idea of confession. I always felt that confession made me out to be a pretty inadequate human being. I still remember that I used to get punished for asking questions about things I should have simply memorized in catechism. I was supposed to accept what they taught you—just accept it—but I really never could. I attended a parochial school until the sixth grade. My grandmother saw to it that I went. But always there were questions in my mind, and when I asked questions I couldn't understand why I never got answers that seemed to me to be adequate. Rather, more often than not, I was told that I was wrong. The Sisters had a very fixed, dogmatic way of teaching. I disliked that school thoroughly, and I prevailed on my grandmother to take me out of that school and enroll me in a public school. She certainly wasn't too happy about doing it, but she did it because I asked her. I still remember that my grandmother's friends were shocked because they thought it was unforgivable that I left the Catholic school in order to attend a public school, but it didn't bother me one bit, and my grandmother, even though disappointed, defended me before her friends.

But those were good years for me. I can't think of anyone being better to me than my grandmother.

RICHARD: Well, my parents were Congregationalists, at first, both of them. I was born in a small town in upper New York State. Both were American-born. When we moved to another town when I was about seven years old, my parents joined the Episcopal church because that was the nicest church and had some of the nicest people in town. I would say that my folks were religious people. There was nothing fanatic about them. I have two brothers and two sisters, all of whom are younger than I. We all went to Sunday school regularly and, of course, to the public school. It was a happy family. We kids got along fine together. My parents got along very well, and there never was any feeling of anything other than pleasure in our all being together. We moved to the new town because my father got a good job in a large construction company. It was during the Depression years that things really got very tough for us. There was no work for my father. He went on WPA and I remember working at odd jobs and during the summer. We moved a few times during those years, but in the same town, in order to get as low a rent as possible. But we always kept our church affiliation, and we joined Christian Endeavor Youth Fellowship in the church. I went on to high school and played on several of the school's athletic teams. I played right end on the varsity football team up until I graduated from high school. But immediately after graduation, I got a job driving a truck, and later I went into the Navy, right after the war broke out. I was in the Navy until the end of 1945. I served overseas all of the time. When I was discharged I came back to my hometown and got the old job back again. In fact, I was with that company for twenty years, until they went out of business. It was a good job. I enjoyed it very much. I was advanced with that company, serving as manager for close to ten years.

During those years I dated a lot. There were girls of different religions whom I took out, but I never gave such things a thought. I don't recall ever taking out a Jewish girl because, really, there were very few Jewish girls in town.

AGATHA: My life was much more restricted than Richard's. It became that way, I guess, because my grandmother was really not pleased because I was no longer in the parochial school. And she used to talk about it. So, feeling that I was hurting her, I decided to go to the Catholic high school, but it was really much against my wishes. I got into the same turmoil as I was in before because, instead of accepting religious classes as I should have, I began once again to ask questions, and the Sisters really got exasperated with me. I didn't have too many friends in that school, but not only because of the questions I asked. It was also, I think, because I was living with my grandmother and my parents were divorced. That didn't set well with these Catholic families. Well, all this bothered me so when I found that I could get a job, I quit high school in the eleventh grade and went to work.

Oh yes, I forgot to mention that Protestant boy I was going with when I was a junior in high school. That, too, caused a lot of trouble. It wasn't considered right for me to do that. My grandmother didn't seem to mind my dating this boy, but she was disturbed when there was talk about getting married. Of course, as I look back at it, my primary interest in this boy and all this talk about getting married was really just to get out, to get away, to be on my own. Actually I had become engaged to him. I remember that the principal of the high school, who was a priest, called me into his office when he heard that I was going with this Protestant boy; and he accused me of things I was not guilty of, primarily of sleeping with this boy. Without listening to what I had to say, he expelled me from the school. Just two days later he sent for me and said that he had acted very hastily and improperly and wanted to reinstate me in the school. But, by then, I was so angry, so hurt, that I remember saying some things to the priest about how could he have acted that way. He was supposed to represent the one true religion and he was not listening to what I had to say about my relationship with this boy and I was disgusted. That was when I refused to go back to school and got a job, instead. But the priest had really been right about me, because I became pregnant by that boy. He had no job and the going was very tough, so I decided that I would not marry him but I would have the baby. That boy's folks knew all about things between us. They tried to be helpful to me, but I couldn't feel very close to them. They were religious fanatics. They were Seventh Day Adventists. Well, his parents kept on talking to me about how it would not be right if the baby didn't have his father to help take care of him and love him, so even though it didn't mean very much to me, I married this boy. We lived together for two years. Those weren't happy years for either one of us. We just didn't get along. So, we got a divorce. It was all a nightmare.

Now all this while I was maintaining contact with my grandmother. At first she was terribly upset with me because of my quitting high school and then about Jim and, later, about the baby. But she became more sympathetic as time went on. When I got the divorce I went to work. I had been taught typing at high school, so I got a job as a typist. I was taking care of the baby. When I went to work I had my son in a day care center. I supported him all the time. I got no help from Jim. He just didn't have any money.

RICHARD: Aggie hasn't told you anything about her music. I think that was what really helped her.

AGATHA: Oh, yes, the music! When I was nine years old, my grandmother started me at piano lessons. The lessons were only fifty cents. Shortly after I got started at that, I decided I wanted to take voice lessons too. Well, we couldn't afford that, so, for the first time I contacted my mother, who had remarried and lived far away from where we lived. That was about my only contact with my mother in those days. I certainly wouldn't have done that if I hadn't been so very anxious to take voice lessons. My mother really had no interest in me or my grandmother. She never communicated with me, but we did know where she lived. So she paid a dollar a week for my singing lessons. And you may believe me, I really enjoyed it. So all those years, I was studying piano and voice.

After the divorce and the typing job I found that I simply wasn't earning enough. One day a friend suggested that I get a job in a store selling records. It was a most pleasant job, but what made it especially nice was that I met a lot of jazz musicians. One day some of the fellows who played especially well came around and one of them started playing the piano. I just started to sing. These boys were working at small nightclubs in the area. When they heard me sing, they thought I was very good. And, the next thing I knew, they offered me a job as a vocalist with them to sing at a New Year's Eve date, and that was followed by their going to the local nightclub owner and saying, "There's a chick in town that sings." So he offered me a job—fifty dollars a week. Well, I was pleased, of course. I had moved back in with my grandmother and she was taking care of the baby. And all was going well. I enjoyed my job very much. I began singing in other clubs and cafes. It was on one of these dates that I met Richard.

RICHARD: I met Aggie at the bar. It was the only place in town that had entertainment. It was in the neighborhood I lived in. I could see that Aggie was not a happy person even though she enjoyed her singing and all that. When I asked her about herself, she told me all that had happened to her—and it was plenty. I must say, I felt awfully sorry for her. And she was such a nice kid too. So I guess this is what really got us started going together.

AGATHA: I really didn't like Richard when I first met him. I tried to avoid him but couldn't do it. He would see me at the nightclub and the first thing in the morning he would call and say, "Good morning, how are you?" and I would say, "What do you want?" (real nasty-like) and he would say, "I just wanted to ask you out for breakfast." Well, this kept up for about six months. One of the things that troubled me was that Dick was a Protestant, and I really wasn't anything. When I got my divorce, I gave up Catholicism. Or maybe I should say, I gave up being a Catholic because the Church didn't recognize my right to get a civil divorce. I can't quite say what I was sore about, but I certainly didn't want to remain a

Catholic. When I got my divorce, I started going to the Unitarian church in town, not regularly, but every once in a while. I found out that I was closer to Unitarianism than anything else. All those ideas I had had for so many years, they all seemed to be Unitarian ideas! Well, Richard asked to marry me, and, even though I had had an unhappy experience with marriage, I became fond of Richard and about a year after we met, we agreed to marry. So I asked Richard to get married by the Unitarian minister, and he agreed. We got a small apartment. Richard had this good job and was doing very well. Within three years we had two children. I would say that things were going well for us. We were very happy with each other. But I think we came to a point in our life where we needed something. I found, as time went on, that the Unitarian ideas were too far out for me. Maybe it wasn't the church's ideas but the minister's. He seemed to be way out in left field. And his ideas disturbed me.

RICHARD: As I would mention to my wife, when we would come home Sunday morning from the Unitarian church, I didn't feel as though I had been to church. I didn't know exactly what it was that was missing, but I felt just as though I had been to a neighbor's house for a visit instead of having been to church. I gained nothing from it. We both realized that we needed some church. It was strange that we should have felt that way, but that's the way it was. We began reading about various religions. One day, I came home from work and found my wife reading some literature on Judaism and we started discussing that.

AGATHA: I happened to get hold of the book on Judaism when, at one of the meetings at the Unitarian church, the rabbi spoke. He had some interesting ideas so, after the meeting, I went up to him and asked him if he could recommend some book on Judaism for me to read. He invited me to come over to his temple, and, about a week later, I saw him in his study and he gave me this book.

It was about this time that I began to feel quite sick. After seeing a couple of doctors, I was told I needed an operation. Well, between the operation and my uncertainties about religion, I was really feeling at low ebb. I needed some faith and I didn't seem to have any. All this made me feel that I ought to have a religion in which I could really believe. Up to this point I felt that what I didn't believe in far exceeded what I did believe in. All this while, in my discussions with Richard I found that he too really wanted to believe in something, and he had nothing either!

RICHARD: I guess you can say that I was as insecure and unhappy as Aggie. Our children were already going to the Unitarian Sunday school, but, to me, it was really no religion.

AGATHA: So I went back to the rabbi and told him that the book he had given me had proved so interesting that I would like to read more. I told him, quite frankly, all about my background and all about Richard. And I explained that we were not happy with Unitarianism. Perhaps if I read more and Richard agreed, we could convert to Judaism. Well, the rabbi was very reluctant to talk about conversion for us. He said that we would have to know a lot more about Judaism before we could be in a position to make up our minds about what to do. He gave me a lot of material to read, books and pamphlets. I took it all back home and read it carefully, and Richard read it too. We spent hours discussing it. The more we read and the more we talked, the more convinced we became that we ought to become Jews.

The Rabbi invited us to come to the synagogue on Sabbath and on Rosh Hashonoh (New Year) and Yom Kippur (Day of Atonement). We were really impressed and very much moved. We felt that Judaism really should be our religion. We wanted to become Jews. Still the rabbi kept on urging us to think very carefully about taking this final, great step. He pointed out that it wasn't easy being a member of a minority people like the Jews. But the more he talked negatively about our becoming Jews, the more we seemed to feel that this was the right thing to do. We felt that Judaism was really a very liberal religion, that it had a long tradition to fall back on, and that whatever was good in Unitarianism was already to be found in Judaism. We found ourselves believing in one God and not in Jesus as the Son of God. All the while we kept saying to each other, "This is where we belong!"

RICHARD: Aggie's grandmother was now quite old, and we had asked her to live with us because we felt that we could take good care of her. Everything had been fine between us until she sensed that we were thinking about becoming converted to Judaism. Well, anything you don't understand becomes a real problem. She didn't understand anything about Judaism. So she really got terribly upset. But, of course, we had already decided that we wanted to go through with it so, politely but firmly, we told her that our lives were at stake and we had studied and thought a great deal about it and we could not leave off doing what we knew we had to do, even for her. When she realized that we were very serious, she said no more about it, although she obviously wasn't very happy.

AGATHA: It was at this point when we went to the rabbi—both of us—and told him that we wanted to convert. He couldn't argue with us any longer because, by then, he knew that we were both very serious, very sincere. We didn't have to study very much more because we had already done so much. The rabbi explained that Richard and Billy would have to be circumcised, and that we would all, including the children, have to receive the ritual immersion, take Hebrew names, and pledge ourselves to live as Jews and live in accordance with the ritual and customs of the Jews. You see, the rabbi is a Conservative Jew, and all this had to be done according to the ancient tradition. We agreed to all that he mentioned. So, about three years ago, the four of us—Richard, I, and our children—were formally converted to Judaism.

We keep a kosher home (observe the dietary laws). We changed all our dishes. We keep the Sabbath. I bless the candles on the Sabbath Eve. Richard blesses the wine. We recite the blessing over the bread. The children now go to Hebrew school regularly, and Richard and I are learning Hebrew also. We attend Sabbath Eve services regularly. Richard works on the Sabbath so he can't attend the Sabbath morning services, but I come very regularly with the children. We observe Passover and eat matzoh instead of bread. I think that generally speaking, we are more observant than a lot of the other Jews in this town. I belong to the temple sister-hood and to Hadassah and a few other Jewish organizations. We are both interested in the temple, and Richard is a member of the temple's social action committee.

RICHARD: The Jews in town seem to have accepted us very well. There doesn't seem to be any problem in our relationship with them. We get invited to their homes, and we invite them to our home.

AGATHA: You will understand how serious we all are about Judaism when I tell you what happened to my little boy not so long ago. Billy ·is eight years old. Recently he had a slight operation and had to be in the hospital. Well, the hospital is by no means Jewish or run Jewish. Well, the day after the operation they brought in his lunch and served him meat, and on the tray there was a glass of milk. So Billy started to explain to everyone who would listen what the laws of kosher were and why he couldn't eat milk and meat things to-gether. Of course, all those people were completely baffled. So he refused to eat unless it was all kosher. He simply refused to eat. Luckily there was a Jewish doctor around so he came in and listened to Billy. Of course, he understood. He told us about how he had to go back into the hospital kitchen and explain the laws of kosher to all these people. What was so important to us was that Billy was really trying to explain that he was a Jewish boy and that he observed kosher just as he did at home; he wanted it in the hospital, too.

What could I do if my children, when they grow up, decided to marry non-Jews? Well, I would object very strongly. Yes, I would. But I wouldn't disown them under any circumstance.

RICHARD: That's exactly the way I feel about it. I would prefer that they didn't marry outside of their own religion. But, assuming them to be of age, I would feel that they would have to make up their own minds. But I would certainly feel bad if they didn't marry Jews. I would be ever so much happier if they married Jewish people.

AGATHA: We are happy that we converted to Judaism. We feel that this is the religion we have been looking for all our lives. It has made our marriage better and happier and has really made a great change in our lives.

Lorna Cohen McCormick

Although I was born a Jewess, I have converted to Christianity, the Congregationalist denomination, to be exact. This took place after the death of my husband, who was a Congregationalist. I'm especially pleased to be able, in this way, to indicate my loyalty to him and to the way of life he represented.

I am a native American. My parents, both of my brothers, and my sister have lived in Woburn, Massachusetts, all of our lives. This small town just outside of Boston is really the only area of the country I know. I have never traveled. My husband, Don, also lived his short life here. My two sons were also born here. This is home to me.

My grandparents, on both sides, were born in Russia. They emigrated to the United States. My father's parents established a small retail business in Woburn. My mother's folks were also in a retail business in the same town. I gather that they were fairly well observant at home, but both sets of my grandparents kept their places of business open on the Sabbath. This was not unusual because most of the Jewish families in the town, and there were really very few, did the same thing.

My parents were quite liberal in their views, but they not only acknowledged their Judaism but, in their own way, observed the Sabbath by always having a special Sabbath meal. My mother

regularly kindled the Sabbath candles, and, I remember too, my
father used to chant the Kiddush at the Sabbath Table. My parents
did not observe the dietary laws strictly, but they did not use pork
products in their home.

I have two brothers and one sister. They all live in and around
the Boston area. All are married, and they, with one exception, all
are affiliated in one way or another with the Jewish community.
One of my brothers married a Presbyterian, but they never had
any children so there was never any problem of affiliation with
respect to children. This brother was never converted to Christianity. He is, in fact, very much of a Jew. My other brother teaches
in a Hebrew school in his town, in his spare time. My sister is
married to a Jew, and they have three children. They are all being
raised as Jews. I would say that they most closely approximate the
Conservative-Jewish point of view. There is a very fine relationship
between all of us and my parents as well. We get along fine in every
way. We are very close to each other. My husband, Don, when he
was alive, was very well accepted as a very dear member of the
family. Don was very well liked by all the family. He was an unusual individual, he had a nice personality, and it just was natural
for him to be liked.

Don had been born and raised in Woburn. I got to know him
when I was in high school. We both attended the same school. It
was really a high school romance. Don's father was a member of
the school board. He was a successful merchant in town and was
highly respected.

Woburn's Jewish community is fairly large today, but it really
was very small when I was going to school. When I was growing up
it was fairly small. There were just a handful of Jewish people. I
remember going to a Sunday school here, but I don't really remember
very much about it. My brothers attended Hebrew school in that
congregation. They were Bar Mitzvah. I never did go to Hebrew
school. I remember wanting to go, but my mother thought that
Hebrew school should be for boys. About all the Hebrew education
I got except for the Sunday school, which really wasn't very good,

was in my home. That was about all of the Jewish education I received. It was, as I view it now, completely inadequate. The schools were part of the small synagogue in the town, but it really didn't give us children very much.

Our home was quite Jewish. We observed the Sabbath after a fashion. We certainly observed Passover and the High Holy Days. I mean, we attended services but really didn't know very much about what it all meant. But there was never any question about any of us being Jews.

I had practically no Jewish friends simply because there were not many Jews around. The number of Jewish children in school was extremely limited. But there were other members of the family around, cousins and uncles and aunts. It really wasn't a lonely life. I had many friends, as did my brothers and sister. The neighborhood we lived in was mainly Italian. There were also a few Irish. In the main the area was Catholic. I was accepted very well. There just never was any problem for me, as I recall. I went on to high school and enjoyed that too. I met Don in my sophomore year at high school.

Don was a Protestant, of Scotch-Irish descent. He was a Congregationalist. His family had lived in Woburn for many years. They were one of the town's leading families, highly respected and admired.

I had seen Don around school but during the war years they had a teen-age canteen in the town recreation center. We used to go down there weekends, and we would play Ping-Pong and had dances. Well, apparently, he found me attractive. At first I wasn't interested in him at all but gradually he became my beau. There were few Jewish boys and girls around. If I wanted to go out it was most likely to be a non-Jewish boy. I used to see Don around. We dated but really not too frequently. After he graduated high school he joined the Navy and we would write to each other. When he got out of the Navy, he enrolled at Amherst and I didn't hear from him until his second year at that school. He was a couple of years older than I. When I graduated from high school, he was already out of the Navy and registered at Amherst. We corresponded fairly regularly, but it really didn't get serious until I was at Boston State Teachers College, following my graduation from high school. Don used to come home for his vacations and we saw each other, but I dated other boys too, mostly non-Jewish. It never seemed to disturb my parents, and it certainly was the normal thing for me to do.

Don wasn't an especially good student because he had never really learned how to study, but he certainly was a bright boy and awfully good company. During the latter part of his college years we became closer, and we began to get really serious about each other. But we didn't decide to marry until Don had graduated from Amherst.

I had a guilty conscience about wanting to marry Don because, although I really wasn't very much of a Jewess, I did know that it was expected that I would marry a Jew. Somehow, I didn't mind all the dating with non-Jews, but I really did not want to marry outside of my faith. Somehow there was a feeling in me for Judaism. I felt a part of the Jewish community, although most of my life my contacts were with the Christian society really.

When Don wrote his folks, while he was still at college, and told them he would like to get married, his parents wrote and just mentioned the difference in religion but that really was about all. They knew my folks and they said they liked me. And my folks liked Don very much. They had known him for years. Maybe if Don's folks had disliked me we would never have gotten together. But we were accepted by both families as good, decent individuals. Our respective families seemed always to emphasize the individual rather than the groups, religious or ethnic, from which they came. My mother actually never said very much about the situation until she discovered that we were really serious. Then she became very upset because I was planning to marry out of the faith. She seemed to think that she had, somehow, failed in my upbringing. She was disturbed, too, about what her friends would say. She told me that she wanted me to marry within the Jewish faith and my whole family did too.

Don and I talked this all over, but we decided we were made for each other and, insofar as we were concerned, that was it. We decided that we would be married by the Congregationalist minister in town. It was the church which Don's family attended. But this decision was not easy for me. I really wanted to have the Unitarian minister officiate. I felt that this would be a compromise, but he was away on vacation. Inasmuch as we both wanted to get married right away and Don had found a good job in an insurance office, I agreed to have the Congregationalist minister officiate. We went over to see him and he knew of our situation—that I was Jewish. But I would not convert to Christianity. I made that point quite clear. Well, at first my folks didn't like the idea, but they finally went along with it. I can't say that they or my brothers and sister were happy about it, but they went along too. My father didn't express an awful lot of concern. I think he liked Don very much. My parents and all the family attended the service. The marriage took place out in the yard. It was a beautiful garden wedding. It all got started beautifully, and Don and I were very happy. We had two children, both boys. Don was coming along very well in his business. Everything seemed quite perfect. Then, one day Don had a sudden heart attack. He was only thirty years old. It was just unexplainable. He was in Boston one night with some of his business friends and they took him to Mass. General Hospital. He phoned me from there. I spoke to Don and to the doctor as well, and I was assured that everything would be all right, but within an hour he was gone. It was a real tragedy.

Both his parents and mine were as kind and helpful as they could be. They certainly tried to help me over the shock as much as they could, but, of course, I had to live with it all. We had had a very happy marriage in every possible way. Neither of us was given to running around a lot. Don was so very much interested in his business and I was at home, caring for the children and trying to be a good wife.

I had attended Don's church ever since our marriage. I joined the women's circle of the church but I wasn't ready to join the church. I found myself being drawn into the women's circle of the church, and, I must say, I enjoyed it. Even though I was not a member of the church, the women were all wonderful to me in every way.

Of course there were people in town who raised eyebrows because Don had married me, a Jewess, but the prominence of Don's family really overcame all those petty people.

I remember that when my first son was born I had expected that he would be circumcized according to the Jewish practice, but Don seemed to be bothered by this because he was not circumcized, so we ended up by not having our son circumcized. But for a long time, this really bothered me. My parents had asked me, when the baby was born, if he would be circumcized. I remember finally telling them that we had decided against it. I rather expected them to be disturbed about it but, to my surprise, they weren't. They accepted my decision.

All this while since Don's passing I have had excellent relations with my own family; my father has since died. My sister and I are really very close to one another. I see my brothers very often and my mother is still a dear close friend in every way. I am accepted by them, and they visit me and my children very frequently.

I really had known nothing about the Jewish faith, just a few basic things, but not very much. All this while I was thinking about my children and how they ought to be reared. Some time before Don's passing a friend of mine in the neighborhood told me that she was going to take a special course over at the Congregational seminary that isn't very far from here. The course sounded interesting so I asked if I could register as well, and, of course, there was no reason why I couldn't, so I just went along. I think I learned more there about both Christianity and Judaism than I had ever known before in my whole life.

Of course it was hard for me to accept Jesus Christ, but the change came about gradually. Before I realized it, I began to feel very much at home in the Christian faith.

Before Don died, we really had no strong religious faith. Don attended church and I, on occasion, went with him. But actually, it had been years of having nothing. When my oldest boy was born, we agreed that he should have some religious affiliation but exactly what it would be, neither of us could say. We both, Don and I, had religious instincts; there was religion within ourselves. But still I couldn't make the move to formally convert to Christianity.

There had never been any thought of Don's converting to Judaism. I had never even thought to ask him about that. It had to be me who would make the move. I began to read the Bible and tried to make some sense out of it. I really tried to find out just where I really belonged. I had always had a very strong sense that God is around me. I have my own theology, really.

I began to see Congregationalism as a very liberal religious philosophy. I began to feel that Jesus had a certain all-important message to bring to the world. I felt that Jesus was, in fact, God's messenger. He had such a tremendous impact in that time of history. I began to feel that He really spoke for God. God was really speaking through Him. But I do not think of Him as having been immaculately conceived. To me, He is the real son of Mary, and Joseph is His father. I do not pray to Him or through Him. He is not the intercessor of my prayers. It took me several years prior to Don's death to arrive at these conclusions. I never joined any of the church classes, but out of regard for Don I continued to attend the church services, and there, I began to arrive at the conclusions that ultimately led me to formal conversion to Christianity. People have called me a mystic. I really don't know whether I am or not. I began to feel that this was all a part of God's plan for me. Whether my conversion had anything to do with my desire to maintain a loyalty to Don and the church to which he had belonged, I really do not know. I simply cannot say.

Whenever I spoke to the minister, I felt that I was talking to a really good man who wanted the best for me and my children.

I actually joined the church, by which I mean I was converted, about two weeks after Don's death. It made me feel better almost immediately. After Don's death I arranged to have the children baptized too. Don's death was a tremendous religious experience for me. I felt the very strong presence of God and I also felt very, very close to the church. Even though I had my own parents to turn to, I never got from them what I received from the church.

My parents-in-law, the minister, and his wife attended the private conversion service, but my mother did not attend. I wouldn't really have expected her to be there. It would have been too difficult for her. With the conversion I felt that I had sealed a contract between me and God and the church. Was this also the sealing of a contract with Don? I really am not sure.

Because my theology is quite liberal, I do not find that I have to compromise with what I understand to be the views of the Congregational church. For example, I do not feel that the celebration of Easter requires me to believe that Christ has actually risen, that is, that His body rose and went to heaven. I do not believe in the resurrection of the body; rather I hold to the view that the spirit of man lives on beyond the grave. It is more a matter of hope. It means believing that although things may be dark for the moment there is always hope for the future. That is what I am teaching to my sons.

It has been quite a struggle for me to decide what to do with my life since Don's death. Generally speaking, I think I am a very well-organized person. At first I was thinking about going back to teaching. I was trained as a teacher and a few courses would be sufficient to get me back in that field. But somehow, I decided against it. My father-in-law invited us to occupy his old house, the one Don had grown up in, so I decided to sell the other house we had lived in and move here with the children. It has been just perfect for us. While all this was happening I was, of course, still thinking about what career to follow. I had been thinking about going into some kind of religious work. At that point, I felt that the only meaningful part of my life was in religion. In no other way did I feel that I could find a meaning in life. That was when I remembered the course I had taken at the seminary. The more I thought about it the more convinced I became that this was the right thing for me to do. So, one day, I simply went to the school and registered for the course leading to a minister in religious education degree. I spent four years taking courses there while, of course, running my home and taking care of the children. I had to learn much about Christianity. There really was so little I had known.

After I graduated, I accepted a position at a nearby church which is nondenominational. I am in charge of the Sunday school. Between that and my home, I find myself very busy and very happy.

As I look back upon the eight years that have passed, I feel that I have done the right thing. I am very happy in my church work. I feel that I am a good Christian; at least I try to be. I have had four opportunities to marry since Don's passing. In all cases the men have been Christians; one of them was a Catholic. I want to remain a Christian, and if I do marry again it will be to a Christian.

I cannot say that I would favor mixed marriages, generally speaking. It would depend on who the individuals are and if they believe they can really work out their problems, personal and familial. If it would cause a big controversy I would not favor it.

If my sons should someday fall in love and want to marry either a Jewish or Catholic girl, it wouldn't really bother me. I would make sure that I gave them all my feelings. I would try to let them know the problems they might come up against and the compromises they might have to make. I would try to have them see the whole picture.

I have acquired a great sense of security through the church. The emphasis on love in Christianity is truly great. It means ever so much to me. It was an important decision to make, but, for me, conversion to Christianity was the right course. About that, I am very certain.

Edward Van Dermer

I am what some anthropologists would call an "Old Line American." My mother's family came to this country in the very early eighteen hundreds. My grandparents on my mother's side and their parents before them were Kentuckians. My father's family came to this country, via Canada, somewhere in the late sixteen hundreds. My mother's people were "Royalists" during the American Revolution. They were deported to Nova Scotia by the Loyalists during those trying days. My father's family came to Pennsylvania and settled just outside of Philadelphia. They were farmers and landowners, not wealthy, but rather a middle-class family. My father's family was of Dutch origin. But he was not a member of the Dutch Reformed Church. I had been told that his family were Baptists. At least that's what they were in this country. I have no idea about the religion of my mother's ancestors. I know, however, that my grandmother, on my mother's side, was a Christian Scientist. I am told that my grandmother (my mother's mother) was in Mary Baker Eddy's original Guardian Group. The family had moved from Quebec but a short time after the Revolutionary War, into Connecticut. My grandmother was, of course, born in this country. What I am trying to say is that my family's history is really part of early American history.

My parents met in Columbus, Ohio. You see, my father had attended Ohio State University and was studying bacteriology. My mother had come to visit an aunt who lived in Columbus. A party given in honor of my mother brought about their meeting. Mother was a music student. She loved to play the piano and was generally regarded as a good musician. I'm told that there was a real streak of eccentricity in her family. If, however, you had money to support an eccentricity, these—according to what I've been told—English families didn't frown upon such things. For instance, I've been told that my grandfather, who had inherited a great amount of money, took a large part of his inheritance and decided to raise ostriches in Canada. Well, between the climate and his utter lack of knowledge of that very special kind of business, you can just about imagine what happened to his wealth and to the ostrich-raising business. But to people generally, he was just an eccentric.

Although the English people generally belong to the Church of England, my grandmother took up with Mary Baker Eddy. This was unusual because it was a brand-new movement and far different from the conservative religions of most people. So she, too, was regarded as an eccentric.

Most members of both my parents' families really had no church loyalties. They "belonged" but they really didn't "identify." None was really close to any religion or felt strongly about it.

I would think that you could probably say that our family was more mixed up than a lot of families would be. There was a definite pattern of churchgoing, but, however much it may have meant to others, I'm of the opinion that churchgoing was taken for granted like brushing one's teeth. It was the proper thing to do. But there were other things that were emphasized, such as reading. In my family it was regarded as highly important. There was a reason behind it, an important reason. Reading led to knowledge, and knowledge meant ability to cope with the world. Churchgoing was generally something to satisfy the direct or indirect demands of one's society. Knowledge was something to meet one's own needs. There was a difference. The more my sister and I read, the more meritorious we were in the eyes of my parents.

Getting back to my folks, they met at a house party, fell in love, and, within six months, were married. My father and mother were really very much different in disposition and character from each other. Father was much more staid and steady. Mother was much more imaginative! They were both really good people. And other people liked them too. My father became a bacteriologist and was a highly respected citizen of his community. People liked them both. They were both fun and what you would call "solid citizens."

My sister and I both went to Sunday school in the Christian Science Church, but I'm afraid we were not doing more than meeting our familial obligations. It didn't really "take."

I attended the grade and high school in our town and did very well. There never really was a time when *not* going to college or university was ever considered. It was simply assumed that, at the proper time, we would go on to some school of higher education. It was just another step upward and forward for us. I had, for years, dreamed of attending Pennsylvania State College, where I wanted to major in physics, so it was quite natural for me, with the approval of my parents, to apply to that school. When I was accepted, it was a happy day for me and all the family, you may be sure. Fate is a strange thing indeed. I had, among other reasons, decided on Penn State because I was pretty much of a social being. I liked people. My folks had always had many friends. There was much visiting back and forth. My sister and I also had our own friends and we got along well with them. So it was natural that I should choose a coeducational school where I could meet girls as well as boys. Little did I guess or even think that this decision would affect my whole life. For it was at Penn State that I met my future wife.

Vera had lived in Pittsburgh. She had gone to an excellent girls' high school and was especially gifted in mathematics. She hoped, some day, to become a math teacher. She was a year ahead of me in school. We happened to meet on the tennis courts at school. I loved tennis and would, every moment I could get away from my studies, try to get over to the courts. Well, it was there that Vera and I met. But we didn't marry until about eight years after our first meeting. And that is where the story of my conversion really begins.

You should know by now that I never was a really religious person. To me it has always seemed impossible that anyone with any degree of scientific information could be a religious person because there is too much of a conflict between what you see and what you should believe. Before I even went to high school, gosh, I was reading Herbert Spencer. Of course, it was in a very superficial way and I was not understanding more than two or three words out of ten, but it was nevertheless sufficient for me to develop an attitude. No, I am not a religious person today. I don't see how I can be. To me it's quite significant that people like Oppenheimer and Einstein and practically all the first-rate scientists are not religious people. They may be ethical minded, but they are not religious in the formal sense of the word. Yet, as I have indicated, my family always felt the need to affiliate with a church.

Now Vera is Jewish. All of her family is Jewish. And Judaism meant much to them. They would have been extremely upset if there had been other than a religious service for Vera and me, more specifically, a *Jewish* service.

I am fortunate in the woman I married. I mean that we are extremely happy. Ours is a good marriage. It was one of those lucky chances that, sometimes, you run into. You are likely to be married only once, and if you are married in such a way that you alienate or hurt the people that are going to be close to you, I don't see any point to that. On the other hand, I think that parents too can make the same kind of mistake when they object to a marriage and thereby alienate their children because of their choice of a husband or wife for their daughter or son. Children alienate parents and parents alienate children. Every effort ought to be made to prevent this whenever and wherever possible.

Actually I'm talking about my "in-laws." They are good people and good Jews. Both were American-born and both had a real love of Judaism. They have strong, positive feelings for Judaism. So, naturally, they would have wanted Vera to marry a Jew. And, of course, I wasn't a Jew or, as I have explained, very much of a religious person.

Now it is important, I think, that you should know that neither I nor my parents had any prejudice against Jews, or anyone else that I can think of, in our systems. We were just raised free from that sort of thing. I had several Jewish friends among my acquaintances but I never really thought about that. It just didn't matter what their religion was as long as they were nice people.

My wife's parents never really objected to Vera's going with me, a non-Jew. But, as I think of it now, I do remember that they objected very strongly when Vera's brother married a Jewish girl who came of Russian, East European background. Vera's family is of German-Jewish origin. They rather looked down upon the Russian Jews. And, what's more, they never really got over it so that, even today, there is an undercurrent of feeling between my "in-laws" and that girl.

Vera's folks really were not the sort of people to ever tell you or ever really let you know directly what they wanted. It was Vera's feeling from knowing them as she did that they would be hurt if we were not married by a rabbi, and I could believe that they would be hurt.

But there is still part of the story I haven't really told you. And that concerns Vera more directly. Apparently, at about the time I met her, Vera was engaged to a Jewish boy, and, not much later, she married him. This marriage proved to be a very unhappy one. Eventually—I think it was about five years later—it ended in divorce. I had kept track of Vera. I confess I liked her but I had no contact of any kind with her or her family during all those years. I had not married but it wasn't out of love for Vera because, actually, our whole relationship had really been quite casual. There just was no reason to think that we would someday meet once again and decide to get married. Some marriages fail. Why they do, it is often difficult to know. Here were two Jews, both of good families, who simply couldn't make a "go" of their marriage. When, by sheer accident, Vera and I happened to meet about a year after her divorce, once again on the campus where I had gone to attend a scientific meeting and where Vera was now teaching math, it was nothing more or less than sheer accident that brought us together. That's all I can say about that. But I think that I can understand why Vera's parents would be less likely to object to me, a non-Jew, as a possible partner for Vera, since she had suffered a disappointment in her first marriage to a Jew. If it could happen under these circumstances when the religions were the same, it certainly couldn't be worse if there were marriage between people whose religions or indifference to religion were unlike. They were especially understanding and appreciative when they heard that I had told Vera that I was seriously thinking about converting to Judaism.

I felt all along that this would be a good marriage. I felt quite strongly too that it would be better to start the marriage with two people feeling very much the same. Since I did not have a strong religious feeling and my wife did, it was really better that I convert to her religion. There was so much to be gained for us both, by such a move. Certainly, I thought, formal conversion on my part would even please Vera's parents. I can only say that later I discovered that there had still been some feeling against this marriage because it involved a non-Jew. But in no instance was I to discover that an unkind word or act had been said or performed because of such objection.

Vera agreed with me that the formal conversion and proper preparation for it would be the prelude to our marriage. So, I began to visit various rabbis, both Conservative and Reform, not only to get their interpretation of the requirements for the conversion but to discuss with them as well the implications of conversion per se. I must say that I met some fascinatingly interesting men, different in so many ways; yet each had a quality that interested me greatly. There was one, however, who annoyed and distressed me thoroughly. Finally, after these many meetings, I decided that I would want the Conservative rabbi to instruct me and see me through the conversion. He required that I be circumcised according to traditional Jewish law and I, wanting to do things right, agreed. I studied over a period of six months. There were many books and much discussion, but it was a valuable and constructive period because I came to know Judaism through the mind and eyes of a highly intelligent rabbi. This helped assure my appreciation for Judaism, I'm sure. I received the Hebrew name, "Abraham," and went to the Mikvah (Ritual Immersion). Frankly, I think a number of things could have been better stage-managed, but everything turned out well despite the fact that at the Mikvah I almost gave up the whole idea. There were a couple of men around there who looked as if they could have been characters in the Stillman Gym down in New York—watching the fighters prepare for their next fight. Somehow it was out of keeping with the solemnity of the occasion or its religious significance.

Well, all's well that ends well. In just about two months after all the formalities had been concluded and I was pronounced a Jew, Vera and I were married by a rabbi. It was a religious ceremony just as Vera had wanted. My mother attended the wedding and Vera's folks were there, of course. They all gave their blessings, so to speak. My mother accepted it perfectly well. My father had died a short while before. As for Vera's folks, they gave true acceptance to it all from the beginning. After all, I was Vera's choice and whatever else could be said, I certainly was a man of some standing in the community. I was no kid and neither was Vera!

After our marriage, Vera continued to teach at a nearby college, and I was busy with my work, which had grown over the years. All in all, things were looking up for us. Vera and I were happy and there was a friendly, even warm, feeling between her folks and me. Vera's family was an old-time family. It was highly respected. Her family, and her grandparents before, had been members of one of the leading traditional Jewish congregations for close to a hundred years. Vera and I joined a synagogue. Of course I know that some people affiliate without really feeling any religious ties. With them, it is just a matter of belonging. But with us it was different. Vera had always had a strong religious feeling. I was just beginning to understand what religious feeling really was. Perhaps I had better say that Judaism had more intellectual significance for me rather than emotional importance. I found in Judaism a satisfying intellectual experience. The result of study with the rabbi and much reading on Judaism really helped me to experience Judaism on a high intellectual plane. I found significant answers for questions that had disturbed me for years. What puzzles me is that so many Jews who claim to be intellectuals are so uninterested in Judaism. It is distressing also to find so many Jews who do not know Jewish history. It seems to be a point of pride *not* to know what happened to the Jewish people—or is it indifference?

Vera and I have been married for thirty-five years. We have three children, two sons and a daughter. The daughter is the youngest. The older of the boys is thirty-two. My boys were Bar Mitzvah and my daughter was confirmed. We gave the children a fair Hebrew education. The older boy, John, is married. He works for the Federal Government. Just about six months ago John married but not to a Jewish girl. Because the marriage is so recent, I'm not yet certain whether or not the girl will convert to Judaism. This may happen provided people don't press her. Vera and I are both a little unhappy about it, but what else can you do? Yes, we are bound to be somewhat upset about it.

John had discussed his love affair with us and he wanted to get our reaction to his marriage to this girl, of Episcopalian origin. There was really little that we would say other than to express the hope that she would, someday, convert to Judaism. Vera and I realized that we could not play God. John's girl is really a very nice person, an intellectual type, just the same as my son is. She had grown up among Jews and has a great feeling for Jewish people. My younger son is not married, but my daughter is married to a very nice Jewish boy for whom we have a great fondness.

My son's intermarriage has opened up a whole series of discussions within our family. My own feeling is that the children have to live the life they choose for themselves. You can only help them up to a certain point. I think, very frankly, that particularly Jewish mothers try to hold on far, far too long to their children. This is like playing God and I don't think it is justified. Children have to form judgments of their own. They have to live with judgments they have made or at least change them. So you see, even a convert can have his problems.

Has conversion changed me? Really, I don't think the actual conversion changes you. It may change your approach to something but it doesn't really change you as a person. At least, it hasn't changed me. I have some close friends in this Jewish community. With others there is a very warm, pleasant feeling. I think that conversion has generally been effective in my case, but, if I had to do it all over again, my answer would probably be "no." The answer assumes that everything else would probably have been the same. But everything else would *not* have been the same.

The reason I say "no" is that I am not at all convinced that anybody can be what he was not brought up to be. That is all I am trying to say. I can't have the childhood experiences that Jews have. I didn't live in a Jewish family. Of course, conversion may have a positive effect, but it is, I think, not to be compared with the feeling one gets when raised in a fixed environment. I think I would say—have to say, "no."

Warren Bagley

I am the son of a West Indies Negro. I have no idea what my mother's origin was. Although my father was a Catholic, my mother was a Protestant and I was reared in the Protestant religion. I had two sisters. We were all reared as Protestants. My father was about fifteen years older than my mother. He died when I was a very young child. All I really know about him is what my mother told us and that really wasn't very much. My parents met in Kansas City. Father was a manual laborer. He had no formal education, but, according to my mother, he was a smart man and a good man. My mother came from a large family of colored folk who had moved up to K.C. from the South. They were very poor people. I really know very little about how they met except that my mother said that they "just hit it off" and were married. But I remember very clearly that Mother always referred to him as a Catholic. She was an Episcopalian. Somehow, from my very earliest years I was interested in meeting Catholics. I guess I was curious about what my father was really like and this difference in religion between them aroused my curiosity.

As I say, I just knew that some day I was going to become a Catholic. I never spoke about it but it was in my mind.

My grandmother (my mother's mother) was really more my mother than anyone else. You see, my mother wasn't a very stable person. She was so young and loved the bright lights and really couldn't be bothered taking care of us children. She spent very little time with us. It was my grandmother who cared for us and watched over us all the time we were growing up. She was quite a gal. She tried to do whatever she could for us. She had certain theories about raising children. We weren't to be hampered in any respect. Whatever she could do for us she would do it. This kind of thing. There was always this kindness. She was always trying to understand us even when we knew that she disagreed with us. As a matter of fact she was more of a mother to us than a grandmother.

At one time when my mother had found a good paying job in another city she wrote and asked us children to come to live with her. My sisters, both younger than I, decided to do just that. But I didn't want to leave my grandmother. So they moved and, as I discovered later, had a wonderful relationship with her. But I stayed on with my grandmother.

Of course Mother had remarried too. Even the prospect of having a father didn't move me. I just felt that I would be an outsider if I went to live with them. Whatever it was, I felt that I belonged more to my grandmother than to my mother. I had all the love for her I could have had for a mother. To me, she was it. When she died it was like losing a mother. I was about fifteen when that happened.

We lived in a Negro neighborhood, but there were some white people living rather close by. I got to know white people and had some good close friends among the white boys. Many of these white families were of foreign origin, Poles, I guess. They were all Catholics. So, I got to know them and their religion pretty well. I went to a mixed school and never had any trouble. In those days there was very little of the kind of thing we see now—no fighting, no hating each other. It may have been different elsewhere but where I lived everything was fine. I went through high school and got along well. The kids, the teachers, the principal—everybody was friendly and I really felt no special pressures because I was a Negro.

I even had two years of college. I worked in all the spare time I had at odd jobs of one kind or another and managed to make enough to keep me going. I was a pretty happy fellow. I was a pretty good athlete at high school so I decided that I would try to get some training as a recreational director when I went on to college. I hoped that eventually I would become a social service worker or do something in the recreational field. I always found work in that field. I got myself a job at the YMCA, where I worked in the boys' department. I set up a recreational program for young kids between the ages of six and eighteen and worked especially with junior high and high school kids.

I always got along well with people—whites or Negroes. I met all kinds of people—the higher income bracket and the poor Negroes and whites—and never really felt pressured by anybody. All that work in the "Y" was, of course, in a Protestant environment; yet I was meeting Catholics too and, somehow, I always singled them out as "special." Why this was, I cannot say but that's the way it was.

When the war broke out, I was drafted into the Army. I was with whites and Negroes. This hadn't made much difference before and I don't feel now, as I look back upon it, that I had too much trouble with the whites—more, of course, than I would have had in my own hometown. After all, so many of the Army boys were not used to looking upon the Negro as an equal.

It's a strange thing, but while I was in the Army I not only found myself associated mostly with Catholics but attending the Catholic religious services as well, going to masses and generally acting as if I were a Catholic when, of course, I was still an Episcopalian. I just began going. All my friends were going and I went. This continued even when I was transferred from one outfit to another. I do not recall that there were ever Episcopal services that I could have gone to. Perhaps I really didn't look carefully. I just began to think of myself as really being a Catholic. I took up collections in the church and took part in the social activities. The only thing I wasn't doing was taking communion, which really is the main thing about being a Roman Catholic. It's just hard to explain why. . . .

I found myself reading a lot of history, particularly Church history. I read a lot about Roman Catholicism, but I also read about Judaism and Protestantism as well.

As the result of all this I came to two conclusions: one, that I was going to become a Roman Catholic and two, if anything happened to prevent me from doing that, I would join the Jewish faith.

All my reading made it clear to me that if one wanted to really know the history of Christianity, it was necessary to study the beginning of the Roman Catholic Church and the Church's teachings. After all, Protestantism came out of Roman Catholicism. The Christian religion goes back to the time of Christ, while Protestantism is only about five hundred years old. If this was true, then I ought to start with the one religion that came into being that had Christ as its central figure. I always felt that Jesus was the Messiah, that He was Divine. I believed then and I believe now that the Messiah had come. That is my absolute belief. Christ is the Redeemer. I looked upon all the other forms of Christianity as they are represented by Protestantism as having been taken or borrowed from the Roman Catholic Church.

Being a military man who has always believed in the importance of discipline (after all, my grandmother taught me that discipline was the most important thing in life), I could see the value of the discipline of the Church. That was, for me, the right way.

You see, from the earliest years I got into physical and athletic work I came to appreciate discipline. Good athletes become better athletes when they discipline themselves. I could see the difference between the undisciplined athlete and the one who, in order to train his body, really worked at the matter of discipline. So, instead of its being a bother, the discipline of the Roman Catholic Church, its insistence upon doing things in a particular way and at a particular time, only served to impress me more and more.

I have a great respect for authority, good and bad authority. For instance, I don't believe in crossing the street if there is a sign there that says "don't cross." I think people should respect these things. I think that sign was put there for a purpose. I believe in obeying the rules. There may come times when you have to question the authority, when it doesn't seem practical to obey the authority, but that doesn't happen very often. In the main, discipline and authority are there for good purpose and I try to obey it.

Some people who have talked to me about why I became a Roman Catholic seem to think that there is more to it than I have

suggested. They say, "Now look, you're a Negro and you are used
to authority. So that wouldn't be a problem for you. That is like
doing what comes naturally with you. But maybe you joined because you really didn't have any good home life except with your
grandmother and you needed security. Maybe, too, as a Negro, you
feel insecure because you are a member of a people that has been
having a hard time these days. Maybe the Church, with its authority
and its decision making, gives you that added security. Maybe *that's*
why you became a Roman Catholic." Well, maybe there is something to what they say, from *their* point of view. But I never gained
any economic security by joining the Church. Even in the Army
when I found myself turning to the Church, I was almost always
with Negroes and, at that time, Negroes were segregated. So I
couldn't have gained much security by joining the Church and then
going back to a segregated Army outfit. I think that, with me, it
really was a matter of appreciating authority and discipline. I spent
all the years since I was drafted, in the Army. I only retired three
years ago. Segregation or not, I feel like an Army man and from the
very beginning of my service, I felt just exactly that way.

The last ten years in the service were spent in integrated units.
Actually I found that often I forgot or had the tendency to forget
that I am a Negro, one of a minority group. I spent those years
out of an all-Negro environment, and I think I really didn't think
very much about whether I was a member of a minority or majority.
I was treated fairly. I was advanced in rank. No, the more I think
about it, the less do I feel that I joined the Church in order to gain
a greater security for myself.

After all, when I was a kid and when I went into Catholic
churches so regularly, the Church was pretty well segregated. The
Church's schools, hospitals, and just about everything were either
all-Negro or all-white. And the pastor of the Negro Catholic church
was a white priest. This should have angered me but it didn't. It
was only about the time I went into the service that I recall there
was a Negro Roman Catholic priest.

There is one part of my life I haven't spoken about. That is about my marriage. Yes, I had a wife and I have three children, two girls and a boy. My wife died about ten years ago. When I married, I was still living in Kansas City. My wife was a Negro. She had been born and reared in K.C. She came of nice people. She had gone through high school and had been working at a job in a laundry. I met her through some mutual friends. She was a good person in every way. Between the two of us, we made a fair living. Of course, we were living in a neighborhood that was all Negro. We got along very well. This was all before I got into the Army.

My wife was an Episcopalian. She was a good church member. I recall that we went to the same church, but I went to that church not so much because I really was happy with it, but rather because that was my grandmother's church. Even though we went to the Episcopal church, I wanted our children to go to a Catholic school. My wife offered no objections. Today they are good Catholics. That is what I had really wanted and my wife did not argue about it at all.

I did not formally convert to Catholicism until after my wife's death. I just couldn't do it while she was alive. I think that would have upset her. All through her years she regarded herself as an Episcopalian, and I certainly wasn't going to upset her. So, even though she knew how close I felt to the Catholic Church, I just never took the step.

You see, my wife didn't follow me as most military men's wives do. Only once did we live on a military base. She felt that it would be easier to raise the kids in the city and not move them around as military people do. So it was to her credit that she followed my wishes and let the children go to a Catholic school. I explained to her my ideas about the importance of discipline. I felt that there was too much wildness among kids, and the sooner we taught our children the meaning of discipline the better. And the best place to get that was from Catholic schools. That is why, I think, she accepted what I had said and did what I wanted. When the kids said they wanted to be Catholics she never said one word against it. And, insofar as this idea of discipline is concerned, I was proved right.

My children have a great respect for law and order, for authority, and a respect for God, who is the greatest Authority. You can't go through life, live in an organized society without this sense of discipline and authority. Parents alone can't bring this view about with their children. They need religion, which emphasizes these things.

I can't say that all the years of my married life were happy. Actually, we sort of drifted apart. I was in the Army; she was at home. I would come home two or three times a year. I supported her and the kids. I never failed. And she did a good job of rearing the kids. Since her death the kids have been living with an aunt, my wife's sister. They are quite grown-up now. They are really their own bosses. But she keeps an eye on them. Two are now in college and doing well. I can't say how good Catholics they are. They are free to do anything they want to do. I write to them often and when I write I say, "Don't forget that there is a God and that you have a responsibility to Him." You see, just as I feel that God has a responsibility to man, so do I feel that man has a responsibility to God. I believe that there is Order in the Universe, that there is Justice in the Universe, that there is a God who directs things.

For me, the Catholic Church is just right. But I don't feel that you have to be a Catholic to go to Heaven, if there is a Heaven. I feel that there are a lot of Catholics that will miss it and I feel that many from outside religions will be there. I'm not the kind who believes that being a Catholic is the only way. There are lots of good people, all heading in the same direction. To me, I have the teachings of the Catholic Church as my guide for fulfillment. I feel that I can get from this church a better concept of life than I could from being just the average Protestant.

I am working in recreation work once again. I got back to this kind of work since I retired from the Army. I live alone but I do not feel alone. I have many friends, both white and Negro, and I have the church and the friendship of some wonderful priests.

I was converted here, in New York City, after taking a long series of lessons from a priest who conducted a class for converts. I remember discussing and even arguing with him, but I was never told that I could not use my mind or that I had to believe and accept everything. I come to the church not only on Sundays but for other church activities. I help the young boys in the church to become better athletes. We get along fine.

Would I do it again? Yes, I certainly would. I knew years ago that someday I would become a Roman Catholic. *This* is fulfillment for me.

Thomas Sanders

I was born in a little town in Nebraska in the early 30's. My parents, both born in the United States, were strict religious fundamentalist Methodists. There was no smoking, no dancing, no drinking, no movies, *no anything,* in our home or the people with whom my parents were friends. It was the strictest kind of life you can imagine!

My father was a farmer. My mother was the daughter of a farmer. My mother's father was poor as a church mouse. He wasn't a very religious man although he *did* go to church. But, according to my mother, he was a disappointed man. He had expected to do better than he did and, upset with himself, he drank a lot. My mother always said that because of his drinking, she was determined that we should be raised very strictly. That would account for her determination to see to it that none of these things she remembered so vividly and disliked so heartily would ever happen to me and my sister.

My father gave up farming because he too had a lot of bad luck. So he went into mechanics and became a maintenance machinist. He was quite a man. He would come home from work literally covered with dust and dirt. About all I could see of him was his white teeth.

Those were Depression years. My dad barely made a living. These were hard years for my parents as well as for us kids. But everyone around us was having a rough time as well. So it all seemed quite normal.

I can't say that I was a particularly happy kid. I think that I began to have fun when I went on to high school and went out for the wrestling team. I enjoyed that very much and, I must say, I was pretty good at it. My sister and I both graduated from high school (she's a few years younger than I).

After I got out of high school I went into the Air Force. I couldn't find a decent job. No one wanted to hire someone who didn't have his service out of the way and, besides, I didn't feel that I wanted to go on to school. While I was in the Air Force, I changed my mind about going to school so, after I came out, I enrolled at a small Methodist college in Iowa. I went there because my parents insisted that I go to a church-directed college. Even at that I had to borrow four hundred dollars, which, naturally, didn't last long.

You see, my parents were good church people. They went to church every single Sunday. They never missed. And, of course, my sister and I went along as well. We were all baptized and confirmed.

As for college, I was there less than a semester. The only job I could find in town was "fry cooking." I made next to nothing, so I ran out of money very quickly. Besides, I really was disappointed with the school. It was poor academically. They weren't telling me anything. I didn't mind the Bible classes, but I felt that I was wasting my time. Unless I went into the ministry—which I certainly had no mind to—even the Bible courses, I felt, couldn't do me much good.

There really was a lack of communication between me and my parents. My father was very taciturn, always has been and still is. Frankly, I think that he is afraid of exposing himself to any sort of criticism. He doesn't mind listening to ideas, but he's afraid to express *his* ideas for fear they will be criticized. He always seemed to be happy with the family but there just wasn't any real communication between him and me. He and my mother got along well.

When I got out of the Air Force, I only had seven cents, so I had to try to find a job at once. I went to work in a packing plant in Sioux City for a very short time and got enough money to get a bus home. When I got home, I found that the folks had gone away for a brief vacation. When they returned I told them that I was planning to go to some college. That was when they insisted that I go to some Methodist church-directed school. But they had no money to help me so I borrowed the four hundred dollars. But, as I say, I lasted less than one semester. I simply had no money to continue and besides, I just didn't like the school.

When I got home, the folks were upset, especially my mother. But they really weren't rough on me. They just hoped I would "find myself"—whatever that means. I stayed home until I got a part-time job (jobs were still hard to find); then I would live away from home because I felt that I was being a financial burden to my parents. I couldn't talk very much about what I wanted to do with my life to either my mother or my father. But it was always especially hard to talk to my father. He would listen but never say anything. Oh, he was good to me and he helped me with things, but there was no real conversation. Besides I always resented the way he did things. For example, you remember, my father was a machinist. His talents lay in that direction. When I was a kid I remember that whenever something went wrong with my bike I would tell him about it. Rather than advise me as to how to fix it and explain to me what to do, he would simply repair it himself. So I learned nothing from the experience. And, you know, that always hurt me. I wanted to learn and he never taught me what he could have done so easily.

Another thing that always "bugged" me was something that happened while I was in the service. Prior to that time I had only run into implied prejudice against various races and groups. It seems that everyone in the town I lived in was against what they called foreigners and against Negroes too. They were, I think, against any group other than their own. They would imitate accents and cast slanderous remarks or make fun of names of Jews or Italians or Irish. That was definitely a part of their makeup. When I came into the Air Force I found that I was extremely prejudiced myself. I developed even stronger prejudices while in the service against everyone other than white, Anglo-Saxon Protestants. I certainly limited my friends to that one group. Some Negroes served under me. I don't think I was too kind to them. As I say I was really a prejudiced person. But I think these people, Negroes and the others, had a very strong influence on my later life. Maybe I was just immature. I think I had become that way because not only my parents but all the townspeople I knew had been that way. Later, I came to resent the people who had helped to make me that way.

When I got a few dollars after working around for a while at a variety of jobs, I decided to go to the state university. Somehow, I felt that I would do better there. The folks were pleased that I wanted to go back to school. This time there was no insistence about my going to a church school. I can't really say why I thought I would be interested in studying archeology, but, after one quarter, I quit that and just took general subjects.

While at school I met my wife, Ruth. It was in a French class. She is the daughter of a Lutheran minister. You see, I thought I ought to broaden my interests so I enrolled for this French course. Ruth's father had died in the mission field in British Guiana. She had formerly lived in Minneapolis. So she and her mother came back there. But Ruth wanted to go on to school. Ruth's mother had also been a very strong Lutheran. We got acquainted in the class and we sort of took to each other. She too had the feeling that religion was important, but she had not been very happy with Lutheranism. Maybe it was her folks' way with that religion that disturbed her, but, at any rate, it was clear that she wasn't going to be very close to that religion. You see, her relationship with her mother had not been very good. She always felt that her mother had the idea that children should be caged in until they are twenty-one years old, and then that they should be sent out into the world. She believed that, somehow, children at that age would suddenly blossom out overnight and become marvelous human beings. When I got to know Ruth's mother and her younger brother, I found that neither were marvelous human beings. I really am sorry for both of them. Her brother, who later married, was divorced. And I feel that it all starts with the attitude of Ruth's mother. She is not an easy one to understand. Neither Ruth nor her brother were the least bit interested in the Lutheran religion. They do not have pleasant memories about their father either. He was so strict with them.

Shortly after I met Ruth I found out that she had been attending the services in a Jewish synagogue rather regularly. When I asked her why, she said, very simply, "Because I like it." I seemed to gather from her that it had a calming influence on her. She had been so hurt and even resentful about so many things associated with her parents that this Jewish religion, so far from what she had known in her early years, had a wonderful influence on her.

Now I know you will be surprised when I tell you that I had known her for only a couple of weeks when we decided to get married. I was going to school. I had no other source of income. Ruth had no money either but we didn't let *that* stop us for very long. Before she and I got married though, she went on a brief trip to California and I got a job driving a truck, just to make a little money. When she came back, we got married. So I hurried up and got another job working nights in a hotel. We got a tiny apartment near the university—one that was hardly fit for human habitation. But that night job at the hotel gave us just enough money to get by on. I was still going to school and Ruth was taking some courses—until the baby came. Then we both had to quit school.

My parents were rather pleased that I got married. At first, I thought that my mother resented it just a little but she has never really let it show. She holds onto herself pretty carefully. She's a real character—my mother. She is a regular churchgoer. Yet, I don't really think that she is religious. I would say that she is emotional rather than religious. All the friends my parents have are based on church friendships with the possible exception of a neighbor or two.

After the baby came, my wife managed to go back to the university and, actually, she graduated with honors. I don't really know how she did it but she was determined. We were very much in love. Even though I didn't have a good job it was just enough to let us get by. During the days while she was at school, I would care for the baby. So it all worked out rather well.

Oh, I forgot to tell you about Ruth's mother's reaction to our getting married. You see she had wanted Ruth to be a professional person or something. I don't know what she had in mind exactly, but I certainly didn't figure in her plans for Ruth. She felt that I was beneath her daughter. She didn't like the relaxed way I always tried to live. I try not to be too straightlaced about things, and she is just the opposite. She objected to me in every way. Ruth's mother is a hard worker. I'll say that about her. But she certainly doesn't know what to do about her children—how to raise them or how to deal with them. Yet, she has very high standards, personally. She just doesn't know how to relate to her children. She treated her son in pretty much the same way she did Ruth. Always giving him ultimatums. Everything with her was "either . . . or," either do this or do that or either do it *my* way or not at all. So you can see why she didn't get along with either Ruth or myself.

While I was working nights at the hotel I kept on watching for a better job. I liked hotel work. I worked behind the desk and kept the night audit and so forth. I got the experience on the job. When Lee was born, my parents, seeing how hard we were struggling just to make ends meet, bought us an old car so that we could have some kind of satisfactory transportation. I guess that they hoped that it would be easier for us to bring the baby over to their house more often so they could see her. They really were nice to us. They saw to it that we had the money to get Ruth into the hospital when it came time for her to have the baby.

Little Lee really made us both very happy. That baby took the place of a lot of university courses. But, of course, I was worried about getting a better job and making more money because we needed it so desperately. Well, as luck would have it, I *did* manage to find a better paying job in another hotel and that eased the financial burden a bit. I was earning more money, but things were going on in that hotel that created an unhealthy atmosphere. I just knew there was something wrong. So I began to look around for another job and I found one. This was a larger hotel and the pay was better, but because the man who had hired me was let out, I too was fired. So I went back to work at the first hotel, where I had gotten started in this business. Well, I stayed there for five years, learning all I could about auditing and other financial phases of the hotel business. All at once there came a bunch of offers from various businesses. I took a turn at several of these jobs but didn't really like them very much. I had decided to take the civil service examination for an important job in governmental service and, to my great pleasure, I passed and got a really good job. Ever since, I have been advanced and have been on the job for many years now. I seem to have settled down now.

As soon as I got into the government service, Ruth and I looked around for a house and we got a nice place with a small yard for Lee to play in.

It's really because of Lee that Ruth and I came over to Judaism. You see, having a daughter, you begin to realize that there are a million responsibilities with raising children. You worry about the possibility of her getting into the wrong company and getting into trouble. We, Ruth and I, were thinking all the time of how we could insure Lee's future as much as possible. We felt that we could do much for her by just being ourselves and trying, on as warm a basis as possible, to get her to see that we were concerned with her happiness. But we both realized that actually the rules a person must live by must come from society. It is the society in which one lives that must give the family the rules by which to live. It all comes from outside the home. We realized that the whole world really has to live by general rules that society sets up. The more we thought about it, the more we felt that society gets its rules from religion. So, on that account, we agreed that our daughter had to be brought up in a religion. Then she would have some primary groundwork in morals and ethics. We can give her love, but we can't teach her the way she can be taught by religious teachers. At least, that's the way we thought. I happened to be the prime mover in this. But the basic question still had to be decided—*which* religion was it going to be? Neither one of us had any warm feeling for Methodism or Lutheranism. Actually we felt that we had *both* rejected Christianity. How could Jesus be divine? We didn't believe that. To us, he was never more than just another man. He was not God incarnate. We never observed Christmas because, after all, it was a religious Christian holiday. In fact, one year, we did have a Christmas tree in our home but it was a *black* Christmas tree— only because it amused me. I guess that showed what I thought about the whole idea of Christmas. Despite that we gave gifts to each other and to Lee at that season because gift giving is something else again. My parents gave Lee gifts then, as did Ruth's mother. At Easter time I still go to church with my parents out of respect for them—but for no other reason. And it still bothers me that I go to church at that time of the year because I really don't feel at all associated with the Easter festival. It's just an accommodation to my parents and nothing else.

Ruth and I actually began to shop around a little bit for a good religious school for Lee where we could feel that we were doing something constructive for her. So, after looking around, we decided to come over to see the Sunday school at this synagogue where Ruth had gone years before. We asked the rabbi if we could enroll her in the school and he said "sure."

She was doing so well over there that we decided to come to services, join the Parent-Teacher Association of the Sunday school. We did that for about a year when we realized what we were really doing. Actually we were drifting toward Judaism ourselves. And we were very much pleased with ourselves about the whole thing. This made us realize that you couldn't be partly *in* and partly *out* of something like religion. So, one day, we both came to see the rabbi, and told him that we both wanted to convert to Judaism. Maybe I wanted *affiliation* more than I really wanted conversion. There is a difference in my mind between these two ideas. The rabbi asked us all kinds of questions and gave us negative arguments that we already knew. He was doing his job, I guess. Within a few months, after three or four meetings with the rabbi, he said, "Well, if you are still determined to go through with this, I'll help you but you will have to attend classes and really learn something about Judaism." We agreed to do this. It was a large class. I don't know if all the people there were candidates for conversion, but I had the feeling that many of the people there were converting because of marriage. We read quite a few good books about Judaism, and, I will say, we really learned a lot and were happy about the whole thing. Here was a religion we really could accept. It didn't make intellectual demands upon us that were contrary to our own way of thinking.

I never thought about converting to Roman Catholicism because I think it's wild. Of course, that's a personal opinion. I do not want my daughter to think that the Pope in Rome is anything other than a man.

We never turned to Unitarianism because, to us, it's an "in-between" group. I feel that they really don't know what they are. I don't think they can define any rules for anyone because all they do best is to ask questions without really knowing the answers. They question other religions and other points of view rather than develop one of their own.

We were favorably impressed with the rabbi, who really tried to teach us, not by forcing his ideas on us but by drawing our ideas out and then explaining where we differed from the norms of Judaism. Much to our great pleasure, we found that we could really accept Jewish beliefs. We had no trouble at all.

I was given the Hebrew name, "Tobias," and Ruth retained her own name because Ruth was that famous convert after whom the book of the Bible is named. Lee was not converted because she is simply being *raised* in it. She knows that she is a Jewess.

We are so pleased with the way Lee is coming to learn about morals and ethics and the Jewish attitude toward things. We think that she is learning the rules of life better through the synagogue than by any other way. We feel that we really have done the right thing both for Lee and for ourselves as well.

We try to observe Jewish practices in our home. We observe the

Sabbath by having a Sabbath meal. We kindle the Sabbath candles. We have the Sabbath bread, the "Challah." We have the Sabbath wine, and I say the "Kiddush" (Prayer for Sanctification) over the wine, but I say it in English because I haven't studied Hebrew, although I certainly will do so one of these days. We come to services quite regularly on Friday evening. And what we both like is that we are not obliged to accept everything the rabbi says 100 percent. I guess that's the secret of why Judaism is still so strong after these many centuries.

The conversion ceremony wasn't Orthodox. There was no immersion ceremony nor was I circumcized, but I feel that I am a Jew and Ruth does too. We don't belong to any Jewish organizations outside the Synagogue. Maybe in time, we will.

Do you remember my telling you about how prejudiced I was as a youngster and how strongly prejudiced I was when I was in the Air Force? Well, let me tell you that all that has changed now too. Let me tell you what happened.

Ruth and I had wanted another child for a long time but having another child was, according to the doctor, too hard for my wife, so we decided that we would adopt a child if we could. One evening while watching TV we saw an announcement about the possibility of adopting a child from an Asiatic country. We got excited about that. We made inquiries and finally we managed to adopt a little girl—a little Negro girl! She is part Negro. We know about her background. She is a lovely child and we really love her. What seems so strange is that, for me, this is a complete reversal of my former attitude toward Negroes. I think that the attitude of one of my college instructors and the attitude of our rabbi on this subject is what helped me to change. What surprises me even more is that my parents have accepted it too. And, you will recall, they were the ones who were my original teachers in prejudice. I thought that they would react unfavorably when we converted to Judaism but, strangely, they also accepted that gracefully.

I expect that there will be some problems to solve when the two girls begin to grow up, but we'll just have to let time take its toll.

We're so pleased about our conversion to Judaism. If we had it to do all over again, you may be sure we would. If at sometime in the future Lee decided to marry a non-Jew, a Roman Catholic or a Lutheran or anyone other than a Jew, I would feel slightly hurt. I think that the reason would be because she hadn't followed *me* rather than because she didn't follow Judaism. But whatever her decision, it is for *her* to make and not for me. After all, we did the same thing, didn't we?

Benjamin Chasin

I converted to Roman Catholicism from Judaism after much serious thought. And, I'm certain that it was the right thing to do. I don't think that I made this move out of a rebellious spirit or for any other reason that is really negative. I converted because I am convinced that Roman Catholicism is the true religion. It is right for me! It is logical and reasonable! It has answered my questions and fulfilled my needs.

I am forty-five years old. I was born in New Jersey and attended the elementary and high schools of Newark. I went on to college and majored in math and physics. So, you see, I am sufficiently intelligent to make choices without too much trouble. I have a great respect for intelligence and an appreciation for learning. What I have done with respect to religion is not the result of a whim but the consequences of study and debate and genuine concern. Religion means a great deal to me. I do not regard it lightly. My decision to convert to Catholicism is the result of careful thought and honest conviction. I am a Jew, but I am a Roman Catholic by religious conviction!

I have one brother. As far back as I can remember he has been an atheist. He has no identification with Judaism. He is married and has a little boy, aged twelve years, but there has never been any religious feeling in him. Even as a child I do not recall that he ever gave any indication of religious feeling. Of course he is about ten years older than I. I never really got to know him well. Our difference in age seems to have been a barrier between us. He has been

married now about fifteen years. He lives very well. He has a
business of his own and seems to get along very well. But religion
is of absolutely no concern to him or to his family. What will happen to him I don't know. We just have little rapport. I remember
that we never really got along. Perhaps it was the difference in age,
or maybe of temperament. But from the very earliest years that I
can remember it was that way. I feel that my brother is an arrogant
and intolerant person in every way. He is a nightclub owner. As I
say, in every way that I can think of, we are different from each
other.

My father, too, is an atheist. He came from Russia many years
ago, in the 1880's. Yet I remember that he did have a Hebrew background. When I was a little boy, I recall that my father used to
recite his prayers every day. He put on Tefillin (phylacteries) each
morning when he prayed, in the manner of an Orthodox Jew. But I
remember that, all of a sudden, he stopped. I associate this with a
friendship that he took up with an atheist, a Gentile atheist. What
happened to cause him to change I will never know but *something*
must have happened that was important to him.

My mother didn't maintain a strictly Orthodox home but she
wasn't an atheist. She was just an illiterate woman with a good
heart and good intentions.

She had no education of any kind. But neither my mother nor my
father ever went to the synagogue even on the High Holy Days. I
know that my mother was really not antireligious. I think that the
change in my father's attitude toward religion came about when
I was about ten years old.

My folks never kept a kosher home. They never really did anything that could be called religious. They never practiced or observed any of the Jewish ritual except, as I have already pointed
out, that my father, in my early years, used to pray the traditional
Hebrew prayers daily. He belonged to a couple of societies of Jews
(I don't recall their names), but they were just friendly groups of
people with no religious affiliations whatsoever.

My father used to own a restaurant years ago. But before his retirement about ten years ago, he went into the bar business. I don't know whether this disturbed me or not. Maybe it did. I guess it *did* bother me a bit.

Insofar as my mother is concerned, she really knew very little English. I remember that when I was in the Army she was all alone (my father had left her). She had nothing to do and to make some productive use of her time she attended an adult education class in order to learn English. I have some of her notebooks at home and she seems to have done remarkably well.

My parents separated when I was about thirteen years old. I was never Bar Mitzvahed. I never received one little bit of religious education. I don't think my brother was ever Bar Mitzvahed either.

My father was an uneducated man. He never had any formal education that I can remember. When he came to this country at about eighteen he went right to work in a liquor store. He has been in a variety of businesses. He was always a very enterprising, independent person. He had a lot of get-up-and-go, a lot of self-reliance, and he always came up with new ideas which he always tried in whatever business. He is in his late seventies now. I hear from him occasionally, but my ties have always been closer to my mother. Why he and my mother never got along, I really do not know. When he left home he just never came back. My father has two brothers who live in Delaware. I am told that they are observant Jews. They are affiliated with synagogues and, from what I have heard, are respected members of their Jewish communities. My father was a Socialist. He had strong left-wing leanings at one time, but now he is rabidly anti-Communist. I know that he was never a Zionist. After his break with Judaism when I was a youngster he never really had any association with the Jewish people. Well, perhaps that is putting it too strongly because now, where he lives in Florida, he is living in a Jewish hotel. I mean that he is living among Jews. But he is still a nonreligious Jew. His interest has always been in business. He has had no intellectual stimulation of any kind that I am aware of. He just made up his mind this way and that has been the way it has been through all these years.

He really is a very nice person. I have been able to talk with him all through these years. He is a nice, gentle kind of man. He is approachable in conversation and has gotten more so, through the years. My mother died a few years ago. She lived a rather lonesome kind of life. She had a sister with whom she had maintained some relationship through the years. They lived rather close to our home. They were within walking distance from us. In the main, I would say that there was a rather distant relationship between my aunt's children and us. The coldest, most distant member of the family was always my brother. When it came to anything—religion or anything else—there was always a kind of sneering attitude toward it all. I cannot really understand why he was this way. But that was the way it was. I always had the feeling that when it came to religion he was trying to say that he wouldn't believe in anything as old-fashioned as that. I guess he thought that this view of his meant that he was being modern.

But all of my friends and all of his friends were Jewish. I cannot remember having non-Jewish friends during all those early years. Oh, yes, there *were* some Gentiles in my life when we lived in a non-Jewish neighborhood when I was a kid. That was the time when my father had a business in a Gentile neighborhood. We lived upstairs over the business at that time. But when my parents separated, my mother moved back into a Jewish neighborhood. I knew then that these other kids were Jewish, that they went to Hebrew school and to the synagogue, but I never remember raising questions about why they did and I didn't. I guess I, too, was pretty much of an atheist as a kid. I did stay out of school on Rosh Hashonoh and Yom Kippur, but I never went into a synagogue. I just didn't want to offend, but I really had no religious feeling. Even after my parents separated, my mother, who, I felt, had some religious feeling, never went into a synagogue. I think it was because she felt that, because of the separation, she was rather out of everything. She was a person who had few friends and few associations, and she was, in a large sense, rather out of it all. Even though they were separated, my father contributed to her support.

My brother was always a source of irritation to me. He was so haughty, so arrogant. He always made me feel inferior. I don't really know why I should have felt that way because I always did well in school. Even when I majored in math and physics and was doing rather well, I didn't feel that I was doing well enough. I wasn't too happy about my school or my schoolwork. Maybe it was because there really was a connection between my schoolwork and the feeling I had about coming from a broken home. I'm pretty sure now that the separation had an effect upon my equilibrium. Maybe too, the fact that my brother had been the one who urged me to study math and physics because he said "they were the coming thing" made me unhappy. I never took kindly to anything he said. He had no appreciation of the fact that it might be the coming thing for some other guy but not for me. And I was too uncertain of myself to make whatever decision I had to make by and for myself.

I was able to go to college because it was tuition-free. I worked nights to make a few extra dollars, at various trivial jobs, clerical or office jobs. At one time I went to school at nights and worked during the day. But it all took money to go to school, so I had to work hard to make the extra money to stay in school. All in all, it took me ten years to get the college credits to graduate. And of course, there was the Army that took a chunk out of my years. My Army years were rather lonesome ones. I had a few friends—not many— but they were not really what you would call close friendships.

I used to date girls but not very often. As I recall they were Jewish girls, but it wasn't done deliberately. It was rather that I knew them and not Gentiles. While at college I never attended Hillel Foundation or any other Jewish group. I just lived my own kind of life, met people, had some friends, and that was all. After the Army (I served in the India-Burma theater) I went back to school and completed my schooling under the G.I. Bill. I always got along with people, both in and out of the Army.

When I got back home I communicated with my mother and only on rare occasions with my brother. I seldom heard from them while I was in the Army. I don't think I ever heard from my father, and on rare occasions from my brother. Most of my mail came from my mother. Other people would write me on her behalf.

I was so anxious to get my B.A. from college. I knew that I needed it, but I really wasn't happy with the courses I had taken. I kept on thinking about what I should do after graduation and I decided that I ought to take Civil Service exams and get some kind of a Government job that might be open.

Although I enjoyed being among Jews while I was in the Army, I had never had anything to do with the Jewish chaplain. I never attended services, nor did I go to any U.S.O. I just didn't care for those things.

After graduation I got a job with one of the social service agencies in the city. I was a welfare worker, and I have been on that kind of work ever since. I have been advanced in rating, but, always, I have found the work quite interesting and satisfying. When I began I used to investigate welfare cases, their financial needs and their resources. I guess you would say I was a "caseworker." I was the one who had to decide upon whether to recommend assistance or withhold assistance.

This job had a strange effect upon me. I went to work with a great deal of feeling for all men. Strangely enough these contacts used to aggravate and irritate me. I think I became quite prejudiced because of it. The Negro homes I went into, with what I regarded as this constant pattern of promiscuity and dependency and the subsequent throwing of the responsibility for support by these people upon the community, caused me to react with deep resentment. I kept on seeing the increasing tax bill. I saw the average tax rate being increased out of all proportion because of this particular group. At least this was the way I looked at the situation, and it was most disturbing to me. I felt that this was an antisocial group who were content to throw themselves on the taxpayer and milk the community. As time passed, however, my view changed. I began to realize that either I was going to be adopting a kind of Hitlerian view, that there were superior races and others that were inferior, and say that all this had to do with the genes of some races and not of others, or I would have to look elsewhere for a proper explanation of what I was seeing. These antisocial traits and characteristics were, I came to believe, the result of the discrimination that had been practiced against them. The three hundred years of constant and deliberate effort to degrade this people and really make them inferior had been all too successful. For our society had really degraded them. They were, then, not inferior in some genetic, biological way, but in a societal way. If this was so, then the course of events could be changed if we really worked at it. So, you see, instead of quitting the job I came to see that I had an opportunity to really help these people, not so much by financial aid as by other cultural means. And I have really tried to do that through these years. Now, I enjoy my work very much. Now I am on educational leave from my job and I am studying for a Master's degree so that I can be a better social worker. I hope that, as a consequence, I shall be able to deal not with patterns of dependency but with these people's real problems. We certainly need to know more about human behavior—what makes people tick and what their needs really are—even more than we need to help them with relief checks. I find my college work most interesting, most rewarding.

Through these years, I have been pretty much alone. I'm not a youngster any more. I shall be forty-five on my next birthday. I have never married. I am not now going steady with any girl. I used to go out a little, but really I haven't any desire to do so.

I became interested and quite serious about religion about ten years ago. I had been out of the Army and out of school for quite some time. I found myself getting more and more concerned with spiritual matters. I can't say exactly what caused this change in me, but I can tell you about my thinking along these lines.

I believe that the world consists of finite things and all this can be grasped by the senses. In what is all the finite world contained? It *has* to be contained in something. But in what and by whom? I found that one is intellectually driven to the assumption of an Infinite, some way or other. The All of Nature *must* be encompassed in some kind of Infinite because the minute you come to a boundary you imply the beginning of the existence of another finite world. So, I found no satisfaction with this kind of an answer. I never really discussed my ideas about the Universe with anyone. First of all, most of my friends at that time were of atheistic inclination. You just don't discuss such questions with these people! So I just tried to reason things out for myself.

I found that none of the atheistic arguments about the nature of the Universe helped me one bit to understand the meaning of Life and Human existence. Gradually I began to feel that there must really be some order in the Universe. That was only another way for saying there *must* be a God. I called Him all sorts of different names, at first. I spoke of Him as the Infinite (with a capital "I"). But ultimately it all came down to the word "God." The Infinite cannot be anyone other than God. It was then that I realized that I could no longer deny His existence. So if I want to be honest I must accept Him and not try to fight Him. I began to see that, all through the years, I had really been fighting Him and acting as if I had some vested interest in so doing. So I finally said to myself, "I had better be honest enough to admit what I have been doing. It is better than going along with the kind of illusion I have accepted all these years."

That was about as far as I got in my reasoning for many years. But within the past five years, it began to occur to me that—well, if you believe in God, then certain steps logically stem from this. One ought to avow one's belief in a religious group. Naturally, I turned to the Jews, not only because they are my people but because they are God's chosen people. They are the vehicle apparently through whom the message was conveyed. So I turned to the Jews. But after all I had little education about Judaism, in fact, none at all except what I had picked up through the years. I found myself believing that God had chosen the Jews to convey a message to the human race. It seemed strange even to me that I would ever think that there was a God and further, that I would be saying that He had a message for all humans; and I could no longer deny that God had the power to do this. He is, after all, the Infinite, the Perfect. He is able to transmit His message however He wants. It was not beyond the realm of possibility that God was saying to man that He had a message and, further, that He was conveying the idea that there was to come a Messiah who was going to change the course of human events on God's behalf. Then I began to wonder: "Where is the Messiah?"

I was suddenly struck by a strange thought. I couldn't understand why, for two thousand years, God had made contact with the Jewish people and that there had been a very active interchange between the Jews and God, and then, all of a sudden it came to a stop. This struck me as very strange. That could only be attributed to one of two reasons. Either God was a hoax and it was only a group of clever Jews who had said there was a God, or God had actually completed His message to this people who either hadn't understood it or didn't want to understand it. If the Jews didn't accept or understand Him then God must have given His message to the human race through some other people.

I will say that I tried to study the Bible. I scanned it from cover to cover. I never really studied it as a true Bible expert would. I never turned to any learned Jew for his views on the questions I raised or the problems about God and His message. But the more I thought about it the stranger it seemed that God would have been in constant touch with one people, the Jews, for two thousand years and then, suddenly, there was no more relationship between them. There must have been some reason. Perhaps the fragmentation among the Jews was making it impossible for them to hear God.

It was about that time that, I remember, one day a co-worker, a young girl, invited me to attend a Catholic lecture. I said, "No, thank you," and I can remember feeling almost threatened by her invitation. I was resentful, at first—as if someone was trying to encroach upon me. Here I was just fresh from atheism and this girl was inviting *me* to a *Catholic* lecture. Here am I, a Jew, invited to listen to a *Catholic* lecture!! "Some nerve!" I said to myself. Then I began to see a little more to it, and I said to myself, "How did it happen that, of all the people she knows, this girl asked *me* to at-

tend this lecture? Is there some special meaning to the fact that I
was singled out for this Catholic message?" As I thought about it I
had the feeling that there was *really* some special significance to this
strange event. I felt that I really had no right to feel indignant with
that girl. I should not have been offended. Perhaps I ought rather
to thank her. Certainly there was nothing offensive that she had
done. I had acted as if my Jewishness had somehow been in-
sulted. The girl meant nothing. She had approached me openly
and I had acted so antagonistically.

I remember mulling it over and not coming up with an answer
right away. But I kept on mulling it over and over again. That event
was a strange one for me—an unusual one. It left a kind of a de-
posit or residue on my mind, and every once in a while that event
popped forward in my mind. Later, when I was considering joining
some religious group, this thing kept on coming back. Was there
something behind it all? Was there Some One behind it all?

I had the feeling that I should join some religious group. I felt
this great need. I thought, of course, about joining with other Jews
in the Synagogue, but, always, I had the feeling that there was a
certain incompleteness with the Synagogue religion. Again I thought
about why it was that prophecy had ceased among the Jews—about
why the Christian religion had to be established so that God's promise of a Messiah could be fulfilled. That is what I mean when I say
that Judaism seemed to me to be incomplete. It was then that I
said to myself, "You must face it. Distasteful as it may seem to you,
if you reject the Synagogue you are going to have to look at other
religions—and at the Church!" This was difficult for me to acknowledge because I sensed that, to some degree or other, examining
the arguments of the Church was, as with all Jews, a real threat.
But my search for truth in religion made me do just that.

I began to go into church buildings and look at the tracts of various kinds that are usually found in the church lobbies. I went into
Protestant as well as Catholic churches. I said to myself, "Now
that you have decided, after you have looked at the great Jewish
tract—the Bible—that the Jews have somehow gotten off the track

or that it is incomplete, now is the time, then, to really examine the Church's claims. What impressed me about the Church was its certainly that the Messiah had come, and He had established His Church and this Church is the direct lineal descendent of the Jewish Temple. All that the Jews had said would happen *has* actually happened only the Jews did not understand it. They did not *see* it."

All this didn't germinate over night, of course. It all took time and lots of serious thought. But one thing I did see clearly and that was that the actual continuous line from Moses to the present was through the Jewish Temple on through the Church. By some strange trick of history, the Jewish people had been "derailed."

At the beginning of my search, I had some rather naïve notions about the Messiah and what I expected of Him. I rather felt that when the Messiah comes everything will be hunky-dory. There won't be persecution. There won't be hatred. There won't be wars. Everything will be sweetness and light. But now I feel that such a view is rather naïve. Nature doesn't change that quickly or magically. I certainly can't see God raising a magic wand and saying: "O.K. I now will make you all good!" But I *can* see Him saying: "Look, I am laying down these prescriptions for you and it is up to *you* now." It seems to me that in the Jewish religion there are certain mistaken notions about the Messiah, about His coming. I don't believe that God works with people, sort of taking everything into His own hands like that. I think that He leaves the burden with the people. The decision making is left with *us*. That is what it means to have free will. It seems to me that Christians have a valid point about the nature of the Messiah.

I began to feel, then, that the Church was speaking the truth. But the question was: which church is the valid Church? Which one was created by the Messiah? Well, it came to me that the *one* church that had maintained continuity with the beginning was the Catholic Church. And this wasn't an altogether attractive conclusion to arrive at because a lot of the Catholic Church's history is, I think, most unattractive. Then I began to sense that the only explanation for these things that still disturbed me about the Church could be explained if there was a separation between the *human* nature of the Church and its *divine* nature. If I were to go purely on the human nature or actions of the Church, this would be the last group I would join. I began to sense the real truth about the Church. It has transcended human foibles and anti-Semitism and all kinds of other things that were definitely wrong. I believe that there is nothing that you can find in man that can't also be found in the Church. But it is the *divine* nature of the Church that is really above all that sort of thing. I am very happy today because the Church itself has now come out with a statement against anti-Semitism. The Church is correcting its views, and I hope that it will go on until it corrects other of its views that are the result of incorrect thinking on the part of man.

I accept Jesus as the Son of God intellectually because it seems to me that it is not so much a question of His miracles or prophecies but rather that, if the Old Testament is to be taken at its face value, He is the one transformed and fulfilled. He actually filled in the great gaps. I don't think of Him as, literally, the Son of God—not in a human sense. Nor was He fathered by God in a physical sense. But in a spiritual sense, I would say: "Yes, He is the Son of God. I think of Mary as having immaculately conceived Him. I accept that. It seems to me that the human vehicle that was to bring the Messiah into the world would, in some sense, be more perfect than the rest of the human species. Mary was the vessel for this very special happening."

I began to attend various parish Roman Catholic churches. I never took any definite courses in any of these churches. I just dropped around. But once, when I heard that evening lectures were being given on Roman Catholicism, I decided to attend. I was encouraged to do so by a certain number of priests I had met, all of whom seemed like nice fellows.

I was apprehensive at first because I realized that there are plenty of "kooks" in the Church, but I went anyhow and discovered a fair number of nice people in the churches who, accepting me as a Jew, treated me nicely and didn't try to force their ideas upon me.

If they had tried to do that I would have picked up my hat and taken a walk for myself. If I had run into any hostility . . . But I didn't. I didn't.

I continued to attend lectures in the various churches over a period of two years. I always went alone. (I'm a lone wolf.)

After taking those courses, I found no intellectual impediment in Catholicism. There was only an emotional one. I tried to analyze my feelings on this score. The only real impediment to my joining the Church was that this was a predominately Gentile group. They were not my kind. They had a long history of anti-Semitism. Their ancestors had done injustices against Jews and had a lot to live down. I felt that I had to reconcile myself to these facts. I felt that I would have to accept what my intellect told me, because to deny one's intellect is some kind of idiocy. As a matter of fact, my emotional reservations were dissipated, much to my surprise, when I met a lot of nice real people and, particularly, priests in the Church. Of course, I met some of the other kind too, but by far the great majority were warm and friendly, so that helped me to ameliorate any feelings that I had on the emotional basis.

I finally made up my mind to be converted to Roman Catholicism and I first spoke to the parish priest who had given the course about the matter. He asked me then to take another course with him. I remember that I had instruction along with another Jewish person who was being converted. This course lasted about six months. I attended about once a week. I was formally baptized about three years ago. I took my first Communion immediately thereafter.

My conversion, as I recall, seems to have been quite empty of any kind of emotional feeling. It was the right thing to do because it met the needs of my intellect. I had hoped that this religion I was adopting would fill a large void in my life. The gap was one of needing a general world outlook, something that would answer the great and all-important questions. It did not settle any personal fears. It made me more a part of society because I felt before, as an atheist, that I was kind of downgraded.

I observe certain precepts of the Church. I go to church every

Sunday. There are, however, actually very few practices of the Church that I observe—I *do* observe what is of obligation. That means mass every Sunday and seven or eight days during the year that I observe. That is really about all. Oh, yes, there *are* other things that I don't seem to find very demanding on me such as not eating meat on Friday. A Catholic has nothing to complain about in the matter of observance, especially if he knows about how much more ritual observance Judaism would expect of him.

I have, since my conversion, joined a society all of whose members are Jews who have converted to Catholicism. Somehow, being with Jews whose religious experience has been so much like mine gives me a good feeling.

As a consequence of my conversion, I feel that I have become a better man. In my personal life I maintain my personal purity. In my relationship with other people, I try to think always of what my religion expects of me and I try to live and act that way. The doctrine of the Church, the teachings of the Church, mean a great deal to me. I feel at one with God. I have a sense of comfort that derives from the Church, but I never feel emotional about my religion.

As for this Society of Catholic Jews or Jewish Catholics, however you want to put it, we have meetings and functions that demonstrate the kinship between Catholicism and Judaism—the fact that Catholicism derives from Judaism, the fact that Catholics are spiritually Jews and they all ought to know that. There are a number of Jewish converts who run into problems at home or with their associates or in the community. We, the other members, try to help them with whatever supportive work we can.

I never did disclose the fact that I had converted to Catholicism to my brother or father. They would have sneered at me. It wouldn't really mean anything to them. In fact, I could respect them more if they *resented* my becoming a Catholic. But they wouldn't resent that as much as the fact that I believe in God.

If I ever met a Jewish girl whom I wanted to marry I would love to have her be a Jewish Catholic. It would be a genuine impediment if she were not Catholic. I see marriage as requiring faith and a kind of harmony between two people. If they disagree on politics alone there can be trouble, let alone on such a basic thing as religion, which involves their view of all of life. I would want my children to be reared as Jewish Catholics. This is important to me.

My friends do not know that I have been converted to Catholicism. Their view of life seems objectionable to me. If they had been religious Jews, I could have liked them more than I do their atheistic and leftist learnings. At present I have been getting myself a new group of friends. Some are Jewish and some are not. But even these Jewish friends have not been told by me of my conversion. I think that they would regard the act of conversion as a kind of desertion—a kind of a slap in the face of the Jews.

I am really basically happy with what I have done. I have no sense of regret of any kind. Conversion to Roman Catholicism has cut me off from some people, but I feel that I have made the right decision. But there are still some points I haven't yet resolved.

Phyllis Mitropulous

I am an only child, born to Catholic parents who wanted me to be a good Catholic. My father had been a Protestant—to be exact, a Baptist—until he married my mother and then, because of her, he turned Catholic. But, as far as I can remember he was never a really religious man. He did it because my mother wanted it and for no other reason. He hardly ever went to church as far as I can remember. My mother was an Irish Catholic. She was born and reared in a small town in northern Massachusetts. Her family had come to the United States during the latter half of the nineteenth century. My father, who is a carpenter, is a fine man. He was always lots of fun. But he never really earned a good living. He came from a large family. He has four sisters and a brother and each of them married a person of a different religion. One married a Greek. Another married a Baptist. Still another married a Congregationalist. His oldest sister married a Jew, and his brother married a Catholic. You'll agree that's quite a variety. And they all get along quite well. Most of them live in this area, so we see them fairly often. The one who turned Catholic converted, as did the aunt who married a Jew and the one who became a Greek Orthodox. So, you see, conversion is no new experience in my family.

I guess my father's conversion to Catholicism didn't mean much to him, but it made my mother and her family happy so that was all that really mattered. We were all used to the idea of conversion within the family so it really didn't mean too much to any of us.

I attended a Catholic school. That had been agreed on by my parents. I went to that school for twelve years—from kindergarten through senior high school. I remember that when I was in high school I was allowed to date and that not all of the boys I went with were Catholics. But there was never any objection from my parents. I do not remember their ever getting worked up about it until I told them that I wanted to marry Jim, who was of the Greek Orthodox religion. And that's about when all hell broke loose.

I met Jim when I was a junior in high school. I had gone to a lawn party and I was with a group of my girl friends. I happened to notice the fellows he was with and he knew the girls I was with but he didn't know me. That's how we got acquainted. Naturally my girl friends knew these fellows. We all got to talking, and through that, we got introduced.

I dated Jim off and on. You know how things start like that? I was seventeen years old at that time. I had planned to go on to a secretarial school following graduation. Even during my senior year at high school I was taking secretarial courses.

When one of the Sisters, a teacher at the high school, heard that I was dating Jim, she spoke with me about it and told me that this was not the right thing to do. You see, they gave a marriage course at the school. I recall that two of the girls in my class went into a convent, planning to becoming Sisters, but both of them came out, and, later, they got married. There were several other girls in my class who married outside of the faith. Both married Jewish boys and they converted.

Most of the discussion about marrying outside of the Church took place in class. It was a class in religion. The Sisters would talk and say that we shouldn't be going with boys of different religions because it was going to lead to trouble. But, of course, we all thought at that time, "I'm having a good time, now. This isn't really serious." That certainly is the way I felt at that time. I continued to go with Jim, off and on. I dated other boys too but it *did* become serious.

Jim was in business with his father. He lived in a town not far from mine. Jim was learning the business. He was a toolmaker. He had gone to high school but didn't graduate because he was more interested in his father's business and it was too hard to try to work and go to school at the same time.

Jim's family are all good church people. He has three sisters and a brother—almost like my own family. All the members of his family married Greek Orthodox people. They were all quite religious. Jim attended church regularly every Sunday. He was a choir member, and he belonged to the Church Youth Group. They all felt close to the church and to the other Greek people in their town. There were many Greeks in that town, and it was all like one happy family.

Jim loves his work. He gets along very well with his parents and his sisters and brother. It's all quite wonderful to see how happy they are together. The whole family—uncles, aunts, cousins, brothers-in-law, and sister-in-law—all get along fine. It couldn't be a better family, and I really mean it.

At the beginning, we dated about once a week—sometimes it was two weeks or so before we would see each other. It was about six months after our first date that we started more or less to go steady. It was about that time that Jim went into the Army. That was after we had started to go steady.

My mother and father knew that I was seeing Jim and that I liked him a lot. I knew they were upset about the difference in religion, but they didn't say much at all. I don't think that they thought that I was that serious. They must have thought, if they pushed me, I would get married to Jim. If they said, "You can't go out with this particular boy," they would only bring us closer; but I don't know for sure what they were really thinking at that time. Then, I really fell in love with Jim and it was too late then for them to do anything. I don't think I was the type to listen anyway. Even from the beginning I was that way. If they had said, "You can't go out with him," I would still have done what I wanted to do. Even when they knew that I wanted to marry Jim, they tried to get me to change my mind. It wasn't that they really had anything against him. His character was good and they knew it. They objected to his religion. My mother especially was all worked up about it.

I had always had pretty much freedom. My parents always thought I had pretty good judgment. They knew that I didn't go for the type of fellow that was a bum. They realized that from the company I was keeping. All the fellows that I ever went out with I was allowed to bring home. I used to invite Jim to the house. I remember that, at the beginning, I invited Jim to have dinner at home, and they asked me his name and about his religion but they probably thought this is just another one of the lot I was going with.

Just before I became engaged—you know how you go about those things—softly. You just don't walk in and say, "Hey, Mom and Pop, I'm going to get married." You kind of hint around and look at your mother's diamond ring and say, "Isn't that a beautiful diamond," and all sorts of things like that. So, I think, Mom sort of knew, and she tried to talk to me about it. She said, "This is wrong. You couldn't possibly have two religions in the same family. One side would have to give." Of course, she was a good Catholic. She only knew one narrow path. She wasn't broad-minded when it came to religion at all. She had expected that I would be married to a Roman Catholic and be married in the Church. If Jim had said that he would be converted to Roman Catholicism that would have been fine with her. In fact, she said exactly that.

I never discussed Jim or the possibility of his conversion with any priest or with the Sisters. I knew, naturally, from going to the Catholic School, what the answers would be. I knew how I'd be approached and told why I shouldn't do that. I did talk to my girl friends and a lot of them tried to persuade me not to marry Jim. Some of my girl friends were also going with boys of other religions so they couldn't say anything.

But how is anybody going to prevent people of different religions from meeting? In this modern world we meet all kinds of people. It's a very natural thing for people of various religions to be thrown together as we were. We're bound to meet all kinds and all religions. Some years ago, the Greek people married only Greeks. They all came over from the Old Country and they knew them best. The Irish Catholics married only Irish Catholics. This sort of thing went on for a long time. But nowadays the world is too modern for all that sort of thing. Marriage between people of different religions can't be helped. What matters is that the fellow and the girl should be honest, and they should come to an agreement before they are married on the one religion they are going to have. If they do that, I think it is good. Either one way or the other, insofar as religion is concerned, and not with one side saying, "I'm not sure if I can do that," and the other side saying, "I'm not really sure I can do this." In that way they will both be stepping into something that is way over their heads. Life is hard enough without having another problem like that. Especially religion. It is something that should be holding a marriage and a family together and not pulling them apart.

I am expecting my first child shortly. (We've been married close to four years.) I feel a sense of satisfaction in knowing that the child is going to be of the same faith as his father and all his family. I'm glad, mighty glad, that I converted to the Greek Orthodox religion.

My husband didn't force me into conversion. He didn't say, "You've *got* to change or I'm not going to marry you." He just said, "This is a problem, something that you and I will have to work out together. We have got to decide what to do about it." You see, despite all my Catholic schooling and upbringing, I wasn't that strong in my religion to insist that I was going to remain a Catholic. I guess I never was a strong Catholic. I started, years ago, to think different. Like when the Sisters said, "You shouldn't do this and you shouldn't do that." I didn't have to give up my belief in Jesus Christ in order to become a Greek Orthodox. That's the same for both religions. I had been baptized. That, too, is the same for both. In fact, I didn't think that I was giving up any of my religious beliefs that meant something to me. All I would be doing by conversion was to accept different church forms, different ways of doing things *in church*. I just really didn't have to adopt new ideas. There were really no great changes that took place.

I think that I first began to think about the Greek Church after Jim and I met. I began to ask questions about it—and I read a little about it too. I really didn't have an interest in it all until there was a cause—and the cause was Jim.

After my talks with Jim about religion, I could see that his church meant far more to him than my church did to me, so I decided that it was I who ought to convert. Also his family was so close. They were such good, happy people that it meant that by conversion I would keep him close to his family and I too would be close to them. Remember too that Jim was working all this while with his father in business. And some day, Jim would be the owner of that business. My parents are nice and good people, but I didn't feel that I could give up Jim. He meant most to me. It was then that I went over to see Father Stuart of the Greek church to find out from him about Greek Orthodoxy and what I would have to do to be converted. Of course I told him I loved Jim, and he, knowing Jim, wanted to help us to get married properly.

I told him that I wanted to investigate first. I thought I wanted to convert, but I wanted to make absolutely sure. I didn't want to make any mistake on something as important as this. I took a series of about twelve lessons from Father Stuart. He gave me many books to read and study. Of course, we discussed these lessons and books very carefully. And I then began going to Jim's church regularly each Sunday. I became acquainted with the church too. The Greek church is really a very interesting place. It is quite different in many ways from the Roman Catholic.

Jim's mother used to invite me over very often. She is a very important and honored member of the Greek community. They in-

troduced me to their friends and all the relatives. They liked me
and I liked them a lot. From the very beginning my mother-in-law
responded well to me. And, because of her, the whole family and
the whole Greek community did also.

Jim came to all my meetings with Father Stuart. I think that it
is a good thing for two people like us to meet in order to talk about
religion. That brought us together even closer. It strengthened the
bond between us.

Of course this was not an easy time for my parents. They knew
that I was going to marry Jim and that I was converting. Each and
every night there were tears. My mother would say, "Oh, how can
you do this after you've gone to Catholic school and church all
these years?" My father stuck with my mother. I couldn't really
understand him at all. I asked him, "Why was it right for *you* to
convert from Protestantism to Catholicism and why isn't it right
for me? Why are you condemning me for doing something you,
yourself, did when you married Mother?"

Neither my father nor my mother would have anything to do
either with my formal conversion or with our wedding. They didn't
go to either. On my mother's side of the family nobody came, but on
my father's side, like I said, they had all married people of different
religions, so they all came. Up until a few months ago, I never saw
my parents. They wouldn't have anything to do with me.

Just two months ago, Jim happened to meet my mother on Main
Street while shopping. My mother said, "How's my daughter? Why
don't you bring her down some night?" So my husband hurried
home and told me, and, a few days later, he took me down there.

During all this while I had tried to keep from feeling lonesome.
I tried not to think about it. I kept myself busy and if someone
asked me personal questions about my parents, I would just avoid
answering and try to put it out of my mind. But it was, naturally, a
real problem.

My "in-laws" never said anything to me about my parents. They
felt badly about my parents not going to the wedding, but they
accepted it.

I was converted about six months before the wedding. It was a beautiful church wedding. Jim's folks arranged it all. Their many friends—and they know just about everybody—were all there. These Greek people feel more for people, I think. Like if you have a problem, it's not just a problem you have to face yourself. The family joins in and helps you. They give you their opinions. They try to help you reach an agreement. They don't say, "Do this" or "Don't do that." Rather, they say, "We'd like to help and it might be nice if you would do this or that." They *really* help you.

The conversion ceremony was really very simple. I can't say that I felt any great change come over me. The greatest change was in having such a wonderful family as Jim's parents, his sisters, and brother. In fact they have made me feel like a Greek because they are so wonderful to me. I get along very well, wonderful, in fact, with them all.

Father Stuart has helped me too. He has been very kind. He explains things to me when I ask him. I find that the great change in my religion is that now I go to the Greek Orthodox church rather than to the Roman Catholic. My religious beliefs haven't changed. It's only the service in the church and the kind of people I meet there that have changed. But more important than all this is that Jim is happy and proud that I am now Greek Orthodox. *That* is the most important thing.

If things had worked out the other way and Jim had converted to Catholicism, I suppose his folks would have been quite like my parents. But even that I doubt, because they are just different people.

There have been no tears by my mother and father since we got together again. They still think I did something wrong, but I said to them, "Let's not talk about the past. Let's look ahead to the future." They know how things are now and there is no use looking back. I know we will never see eye to eye on what I did, but I know that they still love me. If we look ahead, all of us, we'll be better off.

I have never had any feeling of regret for what I did. I had thought it over very carefully before I did anything. The Greek Orthodox

Church has really not changed any of my beliefs. I keep an Ikon in my home like all good Greek Orthodox people do. My conversion has not brought me especially closer to religion, but it has brought me closer to a wonderful family and to Jim.

I don't think I could have married a Jewish person because there would have had to be great changes in my religious beliefs. For instance, I couldn't believe in Jesus, etc. I couldn't observe the same festivals or go to church on Sunday.

You ask me what I might do if some day after this child I am now carrying grows up and wants to marry a Roman Catholic after having been brought up in the Greek Orthodox religion?

I think that I would explain to him my position, how I felt and why I felt as I did when I was converted. I would say, "As long as you make sure this is what you want before you jump into it, I am satisfied."

How could I turn around and say to my son or to my daughter, "You can't do this. You have to marry someone of my religion!" Even if it was a Jew my son wanted to marry, I would say the same thing. I would want my children to please themselves—not me or my husband. My husband would, I think, go right along with this thinking. It is love that *must* come first. I married out of love. I converted out of love for the man I married. That is the most important reason I can think of.

Enid and Arthur Weston

ARTHUR: I am an Englishman, brought up strictly in the Church of England, born just seventy-five years ago. I think I am old enough to make up my mind about things without having to trouble myself about the opinions of anyone other than my wife, Enid. Because I finally reached that stage when I could declare my complete independence without having to account to anyone other than Enid I made a choice with respect to religion that I should have made years ago. About ten years ago I formally converted to Judaism. Just two years ago Enid also became a formal convert to Judaism. All the usual reasons for which people convert didn't apply to us. We converted out of sheer honest conviction that Judaism represents the truest way of life we know. God is One. We believe, Enid and I, that God made a covenant with the Jewish people that is as meaningful today as it ever was.

I was born in a little town not far from London, but living there as a youth, I can think of very few people who ever made the journey to London. Roads were not good and distances meant much more in those days. Our little towns were quite independent of each other.

Enid also was born and reared in the same town. We were both members of the Church of England and we were brought up strictly, very strictly. At least so it seems to us now. When I was a youngster I was a choir boy and all the rest that went with it. I had three brothers and two sisters, and they received exactly the same kind of upbringing as did I. It was precise, exact, and rigid. You listened to your parents and you obeyed them without question— quite a far cry from the problems parents speak about today. There was church attendance and Sunday school and observance of the Sunday in a certain way. I accepted all the regimen without question until I was about twelve or thirteen years old.

I remember one incident which stands out very clearly in my mind. It had to do with the Athanasian Creed. At that time I was a choir boy. As you know, while saying the creed, everybody is obliged to turn East and repeat the creed. Now something struck me about that creed that made it impossible for me to repeat it. I suddenly realized that I didn't believe that creed. I could not say, "I believe in God the Father, God the Son, and God the Holy Ghost." I simply did not believe it. I am afraid that I was rather closemouthed in this respect. I kept my feelings to myself. Now please don't misunderstand me. It was not because I was irreligious, nor have I ever been, but it did have an effect upon me. I could not then, nor now, use any word other than to tell you that I "revolted" against this particular form of worship.

One day, as I recall, I was observed *not* repeating the creed in church. So I got into difficulty. It was during the service and I was in the choir. This feeling within me had gone pretty deep for me to take the chance of refusing to repeat a fixed part of the service. But that is exactly what happened. I was educated in private school. What it is called in England is a grammar school. It is a little difficult to make comparisons at this point. It was a difficult system of schooling but a very effective one. My father was a master tailor and he employed several men. It was altogether a custom-tailoring business. I do not believe that my father had ever had any formal schooling, but he was by no means an ignorant man. He was a very religious man. He and his family were all Anglicans. His forebears had been farmers. My mother's background was quite similar except that her family had been chemists. I cannot remember whether or not my mother had any formal schooling. I am inclined to think that it was little, if she had any at all. She too was a religious person and both were disciplinarians. But then, most of the parents were, in those days. It was a good family. We children were reared in what must be called a happy family measured in terms of those days. My parents got along well together. There were never arguments, quarrels, or things like that in our home. They were highly respected citizens, but, apart from being regular attendants at church, I do not believe they played any special role in church leadership. We always had a morning and an evening service. The family attended both of these services on each Sunday.

Restrictions on Sunday were numerous for us children. We were not permitted to play. We were not permitted to take part in anything like that, at all. You couldn't do anything that a growing boy would love to do. Now actually we often did them, but all this was contrary to the dictates of parents and church. No chores, no work. Sundays were really days of cessation from any and all forms of work.

ENID: Although Arthur and I come from the same town our backgrounds are not identical. For example, I came from a very good home, but it certainly was not a religious home. Oh, my parents and all of us "belonged" to the Anglican Church but we did not attend very frequently. I recall that my father attended only when he thought that the preacher would be unusually good that Sunday. When he went on those special occasions he usually took me along. My two brothers, two sisters, and I were not given the kind of religious training that Arthur had. We were allowed to go to church or not go as we chose. Sunday was not the formidable day that was for Arthur. It was a beautiful day. It was a happy day with the family all together. Often members of the family who lived in nearby towns would visit with us. All in all, it was the kind of home and life that one can recall with pleasant memories. I recall that my grandfather, Father's father, did not attend any church. He was really an irreligious man; he was a good man but he didn't believe in Jesus Christ. That's what we all knew about him. But he was beloved by us all. We loved and admired him. There were stories about my grandmother too. She was said to have come from Russia. Even though there wasn't much talk about it I remember that, from time to time, someone of us would ask, "Is Grandmother a Jew?" We never knew for sure but we just assumed that this was so. Not that I had ever met a Jewish person. There weren't any around there, but it made Grandmother into a romantically mysterious person.

My parents were friendly people, and they were well received in the community. No one really spoke about our eccentricities with respect to churchgoing or our choice of churches. Sometimes it was the Methodist Church and, at others, the Anglican or some other. There was always a choice that we could make.

ARTHUR: The point Enid has raised with respect to her grandparents makes me remember that my parents had always said that her grandfather must be a Jew because he didn't believe in Jesus Christ, and they said too that Enid's grandmother was a Jew. That was what the townspeople really believed.

ENID: Be that as it may, I'll get back to what I know best—my own story. I attended private school in my town and went through the equivalent of high school, and the rest of my training was associated with the arts of the household. My mother became my teacher. It was while I was at high school that I really got to know Arthur. Of course I had seen him in town when we were very young. Our families knew each other, too, but it was when Arthur was about eighteen that we became friends.

ARTHUR: That was about the time I started to take a special course in engineering. The school was a short distance from town and at the opposite end from where my mother lived. My father had died a few years earlier. It was a sad blow for us all. We had been a happy family despite my religious rebellion. I remember that my parents spoke with me about my failure to repeat the creed but they did nothing more. There was less open rebellion on my part, and when my voice broke and I could be released from the church choir I was pleased. I had been confirmed in the Church of England when I was about fourteen, but I didn't take it all too seriously. Following confirmation it was required that one attend communion. I attended once and only once. I think then my feelings against the Christian religion began to mount. I began to take a thorough dislike to the communion service. The Sacrament—"this is my Body and this is my Blood"—I didn't like that. There was something so obviously wrong with it that I didn't want any part of it. It was too much like a pagan belief. From those early years on I tried whenever possible not to have any association with the Church. As a matter of fact, when Enid and I got married I insisted that we be married by a Justice of the Peace and not by a priest or minister.

ENID: My husband really objected to them or even to being married in a church.

ARTHUR: I was then planning to come to the United States. Arrangements for the ceremony were made hurriedly. Only my wife's family knew that we were to be married. About five days after the marriage ceremony I left for the States, but Enid remained at home until the following April. I managed to get a good position almost the day I arrived. I lived with a brother in western New York State. When Enid came that April, we got a very nice apartment and enjoyed life in that community. We have had a good life. We have two children, a son and a daughter. They were born in that town. Our children have grown up and gone to college. Now they are both married, and I am happy to say we have seven grandchildren. And for most of these years Enid and I got along without any formal attachment or affiliation with any church. Some years ago I joined the Masonic order and later became Master of my lodge so it became necessary for me to attend church services, but that was the extent of my association with a church. Now my children, when they were little, went to an Episcopalian Sunday school, but that's only because this church was located nearer to where we lived. Later, when my daughter and her husband moved to Connecticut, they attended the Congregational Church because her husband was a Congregationalist. But here again, I would say that this was almost like taking out a social membership in a golf club. I guess that the grandchildren have all gone to Sunday school, but it really isn't of much concern to me or to their parents. The formalities have been observed. I don't think that it is more than that. Yet I think that they are all religious people, as I am. It's just that my definition of religion—and theirs—is far less formal than the Church. A good man who believes in God, not in Jesus, and who tries to live in accordance with what he conceives to be God's ways for man, is a religious man. Such a man doesn't require a church or a belief in Jesus or all the trimmings of Christianity.

ENID: Strangely, although it was I who came from a nonconformist family, I did not like the idea of disassociating myself from the Church. It was Arthur, not I, who made the break. I did not convert to Judaism until about three years after Arthur. When I converted, I did so because I wanted more unity between my husband and myself.

ARTHUR: The real story of my religious life began about ten years ago in a very peculiar manner. I was never irreligious. I think it would be unfair to regard me as irreligious. About ten years ago I received an invitation from someone I knew, a Jewish business friend, to attend the High Holy Day Services with him at the Reform temple where he belonged. He and I had discussed religion many times over a period of years. Well, I was tremendously interested and curious to a degree, so I decided to take advantage of this invitation and attend. I was about sixty-five years old then. The service was most impressive. I heard the "Shema" repeated. I did not understand the Hebrew, but I certainly understood the English. And it made me think. It made me do a lot of thinking. Then too, I did not see certain symbols that had always troubled me. But the last words of the "Shema," "God is One," made a great impression on me and I didn't forget it. Thinking this over many times, I began to realize that this, perhaps, was what I had been looking for for many, many years. There was no discussion of the Trinity, no splitting of the Godhead. The Jewish religion was really very simple, a beautiful religion without complications. This was really the turning point.

I thought about this for some weeks. Then I decided to visit the rabbi at whose temple I had attended the inspiring High Holy Day services. That first time I came to see him I might say that I wasn't altogether without fear. But I told the rabbi of my possible intentions, and we had a long and pleasant discussion on the nature of Judaism, what it expected of its adherents, and what should be expected of Judaism by people like myself.

Enid and I had, of course, discussed all this from the very outset. She used to come to the synagogue with me on the several occasions when I wanted to see more of the Jewish service. But Enid was not inclined then to consider conversion as I was contemplating.

ENID: However much all this meant to Arthur, it certainly had not taken on all that meaning for me. I was quite content to let things remain as they were. I didn't feel that I really needed any new church affiliation. I was already a middle-aged person and had gotten along very well to this point. Why then bother with something new?

ARTHUR: The rabbi seemed to wonder as to my sincerity, at the outset, but, soon, he accepted me wholeheartedly. He directed my study of Judaism, recommended some important books for me to read and study. I remember Rabbi Milton Steinberg's *Basic Judaism* especially. It was a very wonderful book. I read Dr. Sachar's *History of the Jews* and many others, but these two stand out in my memory. I was quite familiar with the Bible. Obviously I had read and reread it many times. This study and discussions with the rabbi continued for almost a year. During that time, I attended synagogue services regularly with Enid. It was all private instruction with the rabbi and, for that reason, was especially helpful and meaningful to me.

I was converted in the rabbi's study. It was a brief and formal examination of my beliefs and attitudes. I don't recall at all very clearly now, but the rabbi proclaimed formally that he was satisfied with my qualifications. Oh yes, I was given a beautiful Hebrew name, "Hillel." He was the great and gentle Hebrew sage whose Golden Rule was "Do not do unto others what you would not have others do to you."

My conversion took place about ten years ago. I was already in my "sixties," a mature man and certainly not given to snap judgments. When I made a choice like this you may be sure there were no ulterior motives involved in my conversion. I was seeking a faith that would satisfy me intellectually and emotionally as well, and I know that I found it.

My children, who were grown and had families of their own, were, of course, not directly involved in what I was doing, but I know that they were aware of it. There were, however, no real discussions concerning it. After all, they *were* grown up and they *were* married. Neither Enid nor I felt that it was really necessary to discuss it. They were already established in their own churches, and it didn't seem necessary to go into detail any further. Enid and I did discuss the matter.

ENID: Yes, I told him if this would make him happy, this was the thing for him to do. I remember attending Arthur's formal conversion ceremony and I said to the rabbi, "This is what Arthur wants and I am happy about it."

ARTHUR: Since then, Enid and I have come to every Sabbath eve and Sabbath morning service every week. I kindle the Sabbath candles each week. I have studied the Hebrew language. I know the Hebrew prayers very well. I did all that after my conversion because I felt it was important for a Jew to know the Hebrew of the prayer book. I also attend services that are held in the temple each evening—well, almost two or three times a week. The Jewish community seems to accept us as Jews. There is a very fine relationship between us. Of course there will always be some who will question why I became a Jew, but that is reasonable and understandable. But most people respond as the rabbi does. He once said, "Arthur, we don't regard you as a convert, only as a fellow Jew." This is very meaningful. This made a terrific impression on me. It was wonderful to know that the rabbi feels this way about me. And the truth is that I feel that I am part of the totality of the Jewish people. I don't feel that I am only a Reform Jew just because I was converted by a Reform rabbi. I love the Jewish people and feel part of it all. Enid and I love the Jewish people. We just love to be with Jewish people, and I might say that, strange as it may seem, I myself am at home among Orthodox Jews too. I am at home in an Orthodox synagogue as well because I know the Hebrew prayers. If, some week, it isn't possible to come to the temple, Enid and I go to a Conservative or Orthodox synagogue. It is all the same to us because we feel Jewish, not Reform or Orthodox or Conservative. We subscribe to Jewish Philanthropies, belong to Temple Men's Club, and try to do everything that good Jews should do. I do not observe the dietary laws because, as a Reform Jew, I am not required to, but I have great respect for those who do. Frankly, I am thoroughly happy about being a Jew. If I had it to do all over again, I would most certainly do it.

If all this had happened when I was much younger and, as a consequence, my children were younger, and if a son or daughter came to me and said, "I want to marry a Christian," or any one else, my feeling would be one of no interference at all, excepting that I would have hoped it might have been a Jew. There certainly would be no interference of any kind or any objection from me. This sort of thing, in my view, is a personal matter. It must be decided on a personal basis by the parties directly concerned.

ENID: I agree with Arthur on this matter. I think that children should make up their own minds. You will notice that Arthur made up his own mind about his conversion, quite independent of me. He didn't feel that I had to do what he wanted in this respect, and I felt that he ought to go ahead whether or not I converted. His life is his own. I have no right to interfere. He didn't insist that I convert to his new religion. But when I was ready, and without any pressure whatsoever, I converted on my own. I felt that this would make for even greater family unity. I must confess that when I finally came into the Synagogue I felt that I was coming home. There was a sense of satisfaction, a sense of pleasure. The rabbi has influenced us greatly. There is no denying it. He is a most unusual man. If we have any regrets whatsoever it is that these conversions didn't happen when our children were very young. We might have given our children something more than we did in the matter of religion. Religion might have played a much more important role in their lives than it does.

ARTHUR: We feel that our conversion to Judaism is really the greatest, the most important thing that has ever happened to us, and we feel that we are fortunate to have discovered Judaism before it was too late.

John Cullen

We're a very mixed lot, my family. I have German, French, Swiss, Scotch, and Irish ancestors. Actually we're a kind of melting pot, so characteristic of many American families. My father was born in the Swiss Reform Church. My grandfather had been a minister in that church. My mother too came from that church background. Both of my parents were reared in Ohio. Later, they moved to New Jersey, just a few years before I was born. My father was a schoolteacher, and my mother was a housewife. Both of my parents' families had come over to this country in the eighteenth century. So, you see, we are old-line Americans. My parents, both father and mother, were college graduates. The importance of education and learning was always paramount to my people.

My parents became Episcopalians long before I was born. There were few Reform churches in the area in which they lived and apparently none whatsoever in their immediate vicinity, so they joined the church that was both closest and most pleasing to them. That is how they became Episcopalians. They believed that this church was closest to the Reform church in terms of doctrine. And they both became quite active in their church. My parents were churchgoing people, and my brothers (I had two older brothers) sang in the church choir. As a matter of fact, at one point my father sang in the choir too, and my mother played the organ in that church.

The ties to the church were so close that when I was about ten years old, I went away to the Cathedral Choir School. I sang with that choir group for a year, and, from there, I received a scholarship for a prep school from which most of the boys went on to Yale University. That is how I finally went on to receive my higher education at that fine university.

My brothers all attended church regularly as did I. My youngest brother was a very brilliant man. He became a very well known writer on some of the most widely read magazines of our day. My older brother was also a "brain." During their childhood and early youth, I would have classified them, more or less, as agnostics. Both boys were skeptics and freethinkers. They went on to excellent universities and did extremely well. Religion, for them, was something to be argued about, and, believe me, we all argued with each other on religion and other subjects, heatedly.

We all loved to read. Books were very important in our family. Aldous Huxley, D. H. Lawrence, and the early Evelyn Waugh were our favorites. That was the kind of intellectual environment in which we were reared.

My parents, knowing of the scholarship connections between the Cathedral Choir School and the prep school, hoped that I might be fortunate enough to win one of these coveted scholarships if I attended and participated in the choir school. I loved to sing, but I was not particularly religious. But I wasn't irreligious either. I think I went along with the faith but without any great enthusiasm or devotion.

My first really religious experience came about during my years at prep school. I would say, to be more exact, that it occurred during the summer before I went on to Yale—just after I had graduated from prep school. I was working at a summer job as a tutor companion to two young boys. I spent that summer at the boys' home and came to like the boys' father. He was a highly intelligent man. I remember my most interesting conversations with him many an evening, after the boys had gone to bed. He was a devout, religious man. I can remember that he definitely stirred an interest in religion for me. He was an intelligent man. His interest in religion helped to deepen my own interest.

My parents were especially pleased with me because I had done so well in prep school. My father was a most interesting man. He was extremely strict and a disciplinarian. I can't say that the relationship of us boys with him was perfect. He was a stern man and a little on the cold side. His favorite word was *responsibility*. He had a strong sense of responsibility himself. He was, I thought, not really a believing Christian himself. He was a kind of humanist. Yet he was always active in the Episcopal Church—even after he retired and moved down South. I know that for a considerable period of his life he did not believe in the basic tenets of Christianity even though he went to church. But that is, of course, true of many other "active" church people. They more or less take this and leave that. There was a great deal of the creed that was recited every Sunday by everyone, which a great many of the congregation did not accept—my father was one of these. I became very much aware of his religious views at about the time I was converting to Catholicism. We had many religious discussions. There were many arguments too, both with him and my brothers. They were trying to persuade me—all of them. My mother, who did not enter into these discussions, was made quite unhappy by the heat of the arguments. And she, although she didn't get mixed up in them very much, was kind of a believing Christian. She died just after my conversion. I don't think that she was very much upset by my conversion. But she was unhappy because it made my father unhappy. It created certain tensions and conflicts in the house.

My brothers and I used to argue about my religious ideas. We argued very loudly and heatedly, and it was this, I think, that made my mother unhappy. I'm sure she wished that I had not become a Catholic, simply to avoid arguments.

Before I went on to college I think I became somewhat manic-depressive. I was so stagnated with the prep school atmosphere (I was just marking time, really) that I began to think too much about myself and worry about myself. Also, a rather extraordinary thing happened which created additional tensions in me.

I belonged to a class in school all of whose members were very much older than I. I remember very vividly that we had what the boys called a "purity contest." Each of the boys talked about himself and his sexual exploits. I can remember that I regarded it as a personal disaster when I got 100 percent in the purity contest. For some reason at that time, I had never kissed a girl. As a result I got that 100 percent mark. Well, this was fatal. They held me up to ridicule, and because my initials were J.C. they began to call me

"Jesus Christ." I know it shouldn't have bothered me, but, quite obviously, it did, and it continued all through that last year. I became somewhat introspective, somewhat manic-depressive, so I think it laid a kind of groundwork psychologically for an act of seeking something outside myself, stronger than myself, on which to rely, to compensate for the hurt. I had a great need for emotional security. You see, I had been away from home a great deal. Although I went home for my summers and we had a strong family life during those summers, I really felt emotionally insecure. Again, I stress that the relationship with parents and brothers was good. We were very close. We were truly fond of each other.

When I started Yale in the fall of that year, I found myself under the strong influence of an instructor, in short order. I had picked a field of concentration (in my case it was history). This instructor had many conferences with me. I think they took place about every couple of weeks. This man was not a Catholic at that time although, at a later date, he became one.

During those first two years I had fallen in love. She was a pretty young thing. It was a summer romance between my freshman and sophomore years. Somehow we got to talking, the instructor and I, about love. He tried to point out the relative importance and difference between carnal love, human love, and divine love. I can remember that this particular session was a kind of a turning point for me.

While at prep school I had shown a considerable interest in my studies. I enjoyed music and art. I loved poetry too. But I had an all-round career then. I played on three different athletic teams also, but my interests in these other things put a label on me. I was "different." These boys simply could not comprehend the possibility of my enjoying music, art, or poetry. Oh, they were decent boys all right, but they looked upon me as rather strange.

When I went on to Yale I was released from this type of atmosphere. The life of the intellect became respectable. The intellectual tradition was stressed. Even the so-called "playboys" were interested in art, music, or literature. So Yale was a real blessing for me. I found release for my interests. I began to come out of my unhappy moods. I no longer felt alienated from my fellows.

At any rate, this instructor at Yale had a very great influence on me. He counteracted not only the boys at the prep school but my own brothers. They had made me feel that religion was passé! They felt that there could be no reconciliation between faith in the supernatural and the recent developments in science as well as the growing education of mankind. Religion, for them, was, in effect, a superstition that only simple, peasant types could buy. The instructor started the countermovement for me. He encouraged me and introduced me to the works of the great Greek philosophers. I became very fond of Plato and read all the Dialogues. I was struck by the fact of how much religious faith there was in Plato. Many of the basic principles of Christianity are, I think, duplicated in Plato. I was introduced to the works of St. Thomas Aquinas. I began to see that one could be a first-class intellect and, at the same time, have a religious faith.

There were several others, too, on the Yale faculty who impressed me, not alone with their rich knowledge but with my own potentials. I remember that during my college years I read voraciously. I discovered that there were many first-rate minds who were also Christians—believing Christians. I found myself deeply influenced by great teachers and great books. As time went on, I found myself reading and appreciating the works of the early Church Fathers. More and more, religious belief came to have meaning and high significance for me.

My two roommates at school were Protestant and Catholic, respectively. The Protestant—Arthur—was one of the quietest men I ever met in my whole life. He seldom spoke unless spoken to. When we talked it seemed that it was generally about religion. We would discuss such subjects as "Grace" and "Predestination." I remember going to the library and looking up the Catholic Encyclopedia in order to read the articles under these headings. The two articles were both written by the same man, a German Jesuit Father Pohl, I believe. At any rate the article on "Grace" brought out that all men are given sufficient Grace to be saved. And *that* relieved me. I read the article on "Predestination" and I came to a section where it distinguished between the two doctrines about Grace, the Calvinist doctrine and the Catholic doctrine. And all of this had special meaning for me. It greatly relieved my mind. For I saw in all this a view of God and His relations to man. I saw that God foresaw how man's free world would react to the temptations and the opportunities for life. Then, having foreseen it, He predestined where man would be saved or damned, and this, of course, left room for man to operate freely. All men were given of God's grace. I seemed to envisage God as a sort of man in a balloon over a river. He had a view of the entire river and saw a man going down the river in a canoe. God, the man in the balloon, stationed up there over the river, knew precisely where all the rocks were and the strength of the current, and He could look into the mind of the man in the canoe, see into his reflexes and nerves and muscles, and know exactly how he would react to the current, the rocks, the river, and He knew how that man would get down the river. Although it was kind of childish, it helped me considerably. My reading of these and other articles in the Catholic Encyclopedia relieved me so vastly that, almost immediately at that point, I started instruction in the Catholic religion. You see, I had done a lot of reading over the past several years so I felt that I was ready to accept the Catholic faith.

I never felt the need to discuss this matter with my family before I made any move. When I went home I talked about it, but I didn't really do more than listen or, if you will, tolerate their positions, which were not too friendly to my point of view.

I took my instruction in New Haven. The priest was a young man, a fine man—not the most exciting man in the world but a good man and he gave me instruction.

My father was the one who reacted most violently to the news that I intended to become a Catholic. He was very angry. He was so upset and so disturbed that he wanted to complain to the University authorities about the instructor whose influence had led me to the door of the Catholic Church. He wanted the instructor discharged, or at least to be severely reprimanded. He told me that if I became a Catholic he would take me out of Yale, as if this whole thing had been a waste of time and money as far as he was concerned. Although my father had many Catholic friends and got along well with them, he had always typed Catholics as the equivalent of Tammany Hall politicians, all of whom he really despised. He never did say that if I went through with it, he would cut me off from the family.

Although he shared the same religious doubts with my brothers, he never fought me on grounds of his agnosticism or of atheism. But he did fight me, insisting that I was not to become a Catholic until I had completed my college education. I went along with that, and I deferred my admission to the Church until I had graduated.

It is very difficult to say to what extent I was looking for something when I began to study Catholicism or to what extent I had found something I could not very well reject with intellectual honesty. It is difficult indeed to distinguish between one's emotional needs and the psychological and intellectual needs. In my case, I believe that all of these needs were satisfied then and continue to be satisfied by Catholicism.

I know that there was a psychological drive compounded by the sense of inadequacy which, to some extent, had been highlighted and dramatized during the years. As the youngest child in an intellectual family, as the winner of the "purity contest" in prep school, as a youthful lover—these and other factors were met and answered by my conversion. Coincidentally, by the providence of God, I ran into a man, that instructor at college, who presented to my mind a strong case for a supernatural faith and in Christianity. All these seemed to direct me toward conversion to Roman Catholicism. I found a religious system—a way of life—I could not reject.

During all my years I have read the Bible. I look upon it as the word of God. Yes, there *are* some things that are difficult for me to accept in the Bible, such as the miracles, but the over-all position I take is that the Bible *is* the word of God.

Neither of my parents was present when I was received into the

Church. I had fulfilled my agreement by not converting until after graduation from college. They both knew not only that I intended to convert formally but also *when* I would convert. There was no secret about it. My father had by this time resigned himself to the idea. He didn't lament or bewail. My mother would not have attended out of regard for my father. As for my brothers, they simply ridiculed me. As I have indicated, I always had felt insecure in the presence of my brothers. I was always made aware of my inadequacies between what they knew and what I knew. One brother was certainly the intellectual of the family. I may say too, he was the dominant one. And yet we were very fond of each other. Always have been. My mother was always very warm and very close to us. She was a wonderful, sweet woman. She was not intellectually as strong as my father. Yet, he mellowed as the years went along. As we became older, we became closer to him and he, closer to us.

I don't recall that any great change occurred within me as a consequence of my conversion to Catholicism. When I went over to the Catholic Church I gave up singing regularly (for pay) in the Episcopal Church. I didn't feel that I should attend services there. As you know, in those days the Catholic Church was more strict than it is now. It was frowned upon to have Catholics singing in a Protestant church. Being part of a church was not new. I don't recall any great sense of relief or consolation or comfort or anything. Yes, it was good, but I don't recall anything very deep or very strong.

My first job was as a newspaper reporter for a New York paper. I enjoyed the job immensely. During this period I was attending church regularly, of course. One day I happened to buy a copy of a liberal Catholic paper. I got to reading it and became very much interested in it. But I was beginning to feel a bit isolated as a Catholic. My family and most of the other friends I had acquired over the years were Protestant. I decided to visit various Catholic churches. I really didn't feel that I was a part of anything very much except of the Church Universal, and even that is pretty hard for a single individual to feel. I was sort of looking for something *within* the church to which to attach myself. I believe that is why this Catholic liberal paper appealed to me. It was concerned with the lot of the laborer, with poverty and slums and the like. One day, the noted Catholic, Dorothy Day, came to speak at one of the local Catholic meetings and I went to hear her. I can recall being so impressed by her, so persuaded by her eloquence, that by the middle of her talk I decided to try to work for the liberal Catholic paper. I was fortunate and landed a job a few months later.

I think that the several years I spent with them were certainly among the most rewarding, the most exciting of my life. There was so much to write about and so much to do to help the poor, to run bread lines and do any and all things that were required at the time. I became interested, as a consequence, in the union movement and worked with the Catholic Trade Unionists. All this time I came to feel that Catholics should know more about the teachings of their church, with regard to the trade-union movement and the rights as well as the responsibilities of workers. I found myself more involved in these liberal movements as time passed. I felt that these movements could be reconciled with the Christian point of view, the *religious* point of view.

It was about that time, when I was so deeply concerned with the Labor movement, that I met my wife. She had been working in New York City, and she was a Catholic. It was a swift romance. We were married about fifteen years ago.

A group of young liberal Catholics, of whom I was one, decided to publish a new Catholic journal. For years I wrote for that magazine. Later, I moved on to other Catholic papers and participated, as well, in Catholic Social Action Conferences. Whatever I did was the result of a sincere desire to make Catholicism a way of life not only for myself but for Catholics everywhere. For a while, I undertook a rather important post outside of the country, but always I kept my standards with respect to the great needs for social improvement in the forefront of my thoughts. I tried, to the best of my ability, to *live* my religion. Now I have an important position involving youth.

I think that I can say, in all truth, that my religion has influenced both the nature and the quality of my work. It has deepened my interest in works of mercy. The social aspects of all my work through the years has never been forgotten by me. There was always a Christian point of view, a religious point of view, that I brought to everything I have ever done.

The act of conversion has had a genuine influence upon me. I don't think that I could have felt this way without that formal act. I have a genuine sense of concern for people and their welfare. I derive hope, strength, and comfort from the Catholic Church. I have a very strong need for it.

I have been fortunate in marrying the kind of girl who felt as I did about Catholicism. Dorothy has a strong religious sense. When the going was rough for me both financially and health-wise, she was always, and is today, a tower of strength. I have a fine family of three children—two boys and a girl. My daughter has a strong religious sense. I think that the others will acquire it, in time. But it seems that everyone has to reach it for himself. As they grow older, I hope they will acquire it.

If my children were to decide to convert to another faith, I suppose it *would* upset me. But I would try to be as understanding as possible. I know from the way my father reacted to me that he didn't stop me from converting to Catholicism. When he threatened me, I reacted against his reaction. The more strongly he was opposed to it, the more strongly I clung to the idea of converting to Catholicism. I would hope that my children would always remain Catholics. I would like to see them in the Roman Catholic faith. Yet, I would try very hard not to become belligerent about it.

I think that my values have changed since I became a Catholic. Before I became a convert, I felt alone and I was highly dependent upon myself. I just didn't feel that I had sufficient strength of my own really to be happy. Since I have become a Catholic I feel there is strength to be gained from Grace and the Sacraments. I feel that very strongly. I have a very strong and continuing sense of the potence of God, and this has been a great comfort to me.

God has been extremely kind to us. Things have worked out well for me and my family. I have been fortunate in my family, my wife, and the children as well as in the jobs I have had.

Karen and Stanley Goldman

Q: As the daughter of a Baptist minister who has formally converted to Judaism your story is of particular interest. It becomes especially significant because you, shortly thereafter, married a Jew whose career as a college professor is directly associated with Hebraic scholarship. How did it all come about?

KAREN: Yes, it's true. My father and his father before him were Baptist ministers. Mother's parents were both Presbyterians. Both sides of the family were devout Christians, and this includes uncles and aunts as well. They all seem to have enjoyed a fine reputation. Many members of the family were businessmen. There were a few in the professions. My grandmother on my mother's side was very active in one of the circles of the Presbyterian Church. She was always regarded as one of the pillars of her local church. Mother's family lived in Buffalo, New York. Mother and her several brothers were born and reared there. Grandmother was a matriarch. Her home was the center where we, my two sisters and I, always went for the holidays. It was a good family. Relationships between us all were excellent. It was a good and happy family, all through the years.

Father was born in Portland, Maine. His father had come over from England. He and his parents had come to the United States when Father was just two years old. My grandfather, a Baptist minister, was called to serve a church in that community. He was, I am told, a fine man. I did not know him or my mother's father; both were gone before my parents were married. But, on the basis of what both my parents have said, their home lives were exemplary. There was always a great deal of respect and love and admiration in their homes. My grandfather, on my mother's side, had been a businessman. He had owned a small foundry. I know, too, that both families were devout Christians. They were regular attendants at services, and they lived their lives on a high moral and ethical plane.

Dad's family was very interesting. This was a Baptist family from way back. He was a New Englander, born and bred. Some members of his family had been in the country before the American Revolution, and, according to family records, played important roles in those revolutionary days. Apparently there was always a great concern for the Church and in scholastics. One of the noted New England colleges was served by my uncle as its president. Another uncle, my father's brother, became the president of a noted Baptist theological seminary. Both my uncle and my father became Baptist ministers. When my parents married, Mother became a Baptist. She always resented the fact that the Baptists insisted that she be baptized and immersed. They wouldn't accept all her good Presbyterian upbringing; she had a great sense of humor but—and this really galled her—she was indignant because she had to be baptized to become a minister's wife.

Q: How would you describe your home life?

KAREN: Ours was a happy home. The relationship between my parents was excellent. As for our religious life, it was about what you might expect in a Baptist minister's home. On Sundays, for instance, we played paper dolls or read. Even knitting was frowned upon. For us it was really a day of recreation. But Father didn't stay in the ministry. He had developed a throat ailment and could no longer preach, so he gave up the ministry and went into business. After years of study and training at an Ivy League college and, later, at the seminary, it was a difficult moment for him but there was little else to do. A preacher who could no longer preach just *had* to make a change.

Luckily, Dad did fairly well in business. He was quite shy, but people who made contact with him knew he could be relied upon so he got business. He was a completely trustworthy man. Even though he gave up the ministry, he became a deacon in the Baptist church; he also taught a Sunday school class.

It was always taken for granted that my sisters and I would be going to college. It was quite a financial struggle for Dad to put us through, but he did. My parents were determined to let nothing stand in the way. One of my sisters went to Ohio State, but she fell in love before it was over and she didn't finish. A younger sister got her A.B. degree. She was interested and majored in archeology. We had, of course, all gone to the local high school, but I think my major activities were most closely associated with the church. There was the young people's group, the girls' missionary society, and I also sang in the choir. When I went on to college (I chose a major girls' college in New England), I became very much interested in subjects like economics but, most particularly, in social action, in helping to bring about a more equitable society. Coming from a fundamentalist Baptist home, it wasn't always easy to get my father to accept my views. I remember once talking about some current issue, I have forgotten now what it was, I said, "Just as people used to believe in the Virgin birth——" and Dad quickly said, "I still believe in the Virgin birth!" I hadn't realized how our ideas with respect to religion were beginning to differ. Now neither Mother nor Dad insisted upon my following their ideas, although they would have been pleased if I had, but the difference between the point of view of the generations was beginning to manifest itself. My view of religion was clearly one that involved social action, the direct application of religious principles to life itself. One of my sisters has remained quite conservative in all things. In fact, I'm tempted to use the word "reactionary." She seems to be opposed to change in any form. The other sister married a young Baptist minister who has, since, become a professor of theology in a Baptist seminary. You see, we have always had close ties to the Church, but, for me, religious life was always more fully to be lived through the application of religious ideals to the current issues of the day.

Our home always was visited by ministers who visited our community. We children used to listen to the conversation and I know I gained much from the discussions. I think that my views with respect to the role of religion in our day was very much influenced by these exciting discussions led by such people as Sherwood Eddy and other noted evangelists. So many of these people were ecumenical in spirit, and their liberal philosophies excited me greatly.

Q: What were your fields of interest at college?

KAREN: While at college, I found myself drawn to the study of sociology in addition to economics. These two fields fitted in with my interest in social improvement. I became a member of the Debate Society and International Relations Society among other things. My college years were both happy and exciting. For me they were really years of growth and development, so much so, that I determined to go on to graduate school in New York City in order to get an M.A. in social work. But because I didn't have the money and my parents could provide only a small portion of what funds I needed, I took a job as a secretary in a social work agency for two years.

Oh, yes, I forgot to tell you about another significant influence in my life. During my college undergraduate years, I attended the college church, which was a kind of Protestant, nondenominational arrangement. We had wonderful speakers who came from all over the world to address us at this chapel service. I would say that this was a great intellectual and religious experience for us all. Certainly it was for me. Chapel attendance was compulsory, but it needn't have been insofar as I am concerned because of the caliber of the speakers and their insights. I gained so much from it all.

My views were reinforced too by my teachers in the sociology department of the college. They were excellent, forward-looking people whose views with respect to world events, the growing emphasis upon unionism, and the like, helped me to clarify my own thinking. One summer I was chosen to attend a school for industrial workers so that, meeting with these people, asking questions, and entering discussions, I really gained a great deal.

My parents knew all about my interests. At first there was some degree of consternation, but they softened as time went on. My mother, who had always voted a straight Prohibitionist ticket in national elections, actually found herself voting for Norman Thomas for President. These changes came about gradually, but they actually took place. My mother was revolted by Hitler and what he was beginning to say and do. There was a genuine interest in the foreign-born and, later, in the refugees from Hitler. Mother was more than sympathetic. Never had I sensed a feeling of looking down upon the foreign-born or even of regarding oneself as superior to them in any way. Rather, my mother was way ahead of her time in wanting all minority groups, racial and religious, to be given equal treatment as Americans.

I can recall when an Italian family moved into our neighborhood and their distress when there was some discrimination on the part of some neighbors. Yet, my mother would not accept this sort of thing. She visited each neighbor and clearly and unequivocably expressed her indignation because of their attitude. What is more, she prevailed. The neighbors just changed their tune. There just was no feeling of superiority vs. inferiority on my mother's part. She was a tower of strength all the while. That is true until I met Stan and the problem became more personal and immediate.

Of course, Mother hoped that Stanley would really see the light. But when he didn't she became much more understanding of Stan and his religion. She was pleased, I think, because he had such a positive view of his own religion.

I had been working at a secretarial job but about one year later, I was asked to take a position in the work of the Y.M.C.A. for the National Board, in Belgium. Well, it was here that I, for the first time, really became aware of the Jewish people. Hitler was already in power in Germany. My attitude toward the German situation was much sharpened during that year. I got to know these

German Jews intimately. I was very much involved with them. I understood the horrors of the situation and, personally, I became very much involved in the lives of these people.

Q: Stanley, your background appears to be very much different from that of Karen's. Tell me about yourself and about your parents and family.

STANLEY: I was born of Orthodox Jewish parents in New York City. I think that the very idea of marrying someone who would convert from their religion to Judaism because of me would have been quite disturbing, even revolting, to me at one point in my life. Yet, when it happened, it became the great climactic moment of my life.

I have five brothers and sisters. Three are younger than I. The others are two and three years older.

My parents were very Orthodox. They had come from Russia, both of them. There had been rabbis in our family. And this, my mother pointed out, was a sign of the importance of learning and the reverence for Jewish tradition that characterized our family. The family I come from was a really Orthodox Jewish family. Kashruth (the dietary laws) was observed; the Sabbath was observed. I can, in fact, think of nothing in Orthodox Judaism that was not meticulously observed. My father was a tailor. He was a devout and learned Jew, but, in order to earn a livelihood, it was necessary for him to become a tailor.

My father had come over to the United States earlier. He had worked hard, and, as a consequence, he made it possible for my mother and several children to come to the United States. They all lived on the East Side of New York City. We kids all worked hard to supplement my father's earnings. We all sold newspapers. And sometimes my father would supplement his earnings by taking orders for a grocery store in the neighborhood. It was a precarious kind of living, but it certainly meant life to us.

I was about seven years old when we all moved from the East

Side up to Harlem. Harlem was then a fine Jewish neighborhood. We had done well, and we were delighted that we were able to make this move.

All those early years, my father and mother were quite certain that I was going to be a rabbi. Of course it was not really a matter of consulting me. It just seemed natural that I would be the one to become a rabbi. I was devout. I followed all of the traditional practices. There just was no reason to even question this. I had attended the Talmud Torah and had the knowledge of Judaism which seemed to prepare me for the Orthodox rabbinate. But, when my parents tried to enroll me in the school that might head me on to the Orthodox rabbinate I was, fortunately, turned down, because I was too small and too young.

I had an uncle who was a real scholar. He was a truly devout and good man. He was very much upset because I was turned down at this school. He, therefore, wrote a letter, complaining because a child who wanted to study Torah was turned down, and he regarded this as a real violation of Jewish tradition. Much to his and our surprise, I was accepted for the Uptown Hebrew Talmud Torah. Here I really did learn a lot. I got so much out of this that I really cannot begin to tell you how much I acquired. I can say that it all made me more devout and even more a member of my people.

All this while I attended public school and from there I went on to high school. But while at high school, I attended an afternoon Hebrew high school. It would have been unthinkable that I should have concluded my Hebrew education at age thirteen, the time of my Bar Mitzvah. When I graduated from public school, I went on to high school, and, from there, I went on to C.C.N.Y. My family supported me in part, but I also worked after school hours and I earned enough to put me through college. I never really worked at extracurricular activities. I worked outside, in such places as the Post Office Department, as a clerk, as a subway attendant, in fact, in many different jobs, all of which could and did provide me with the funds necessary to get an education. It was always a matter of working. I taught in a Hebrew school too, but that was already in my senior year in high school.

I was still quite observant at home but I had ceased to observe the dietary laws outside of my home. But I must confess, to this very day I still am not happy about mixing milk and meat, which is a violation of Orthodox Jewish standards. My parents, all this while, were still very certain that I was going to become a rabbi. This, in fact, became a great objective, a great goal. The idea that I would become a rabbi meant more to them than I could even imagine.

My college years were good years. I had some really great professors, and I was absorbing learning like a sponge absorbs water. But all this while, I was thinking about my future. My decision was that I ought not to become a rabbi but rather that I ought to become a Hebrew scholar, independent of the rabbinate, and perhaps teach in a college or university. When my undergraduate work at college was completed, I broke the news to my parents that I wanted to go on to graduate school but not prepare for the rabbinate. Of course they were quite disappointed, but there was a degree of consolation in that I was going to become a scholar in some phase of Semitics.

All this while, of course, I was working at odd jobs, late afternoons and nights, to pay for my schooling. It was a difficult thing to do, particularly because my scholastic load was becoming even heavier. But I was quite determined. I felt that an advanced degree from New York University in New York City would help me. It was there, in one of the graduate classes in sociology, that I met Karen.

Many of the people taking this course would go out to lunch together. Oh, about six or seven of us, and, in that way there was a very warm relationship that developed in the class. Actually it was all very informal.

KAREN: I was attending this class in partial fulfillment of my M.A. requirements. Stan and I came to be good friends in a very nice setting, what with the classes and these lunches so many of our classmates joined in. There was always much discussion and much bantering, too. It was all really most pleasant.

One day Stan asked me to go out that evening. Of course, I said "yes." He was such a nice guy. Oh yes, I knew he was Jewish, but that certainly didn't make any difference to me, not at the beginning. It is only when it came to be serious that I got a bit concerned. At first we were going out together a couple of times a week. Then it became a fairly steady thing where we were seeing each other almost every evening. We were both living in New York City.

But it all didn't go so easily for us. We were going with each other for about two years before we finally decided to really be serious. It was another two years before we finally decided to marry. That makes four years in all.

Q: Why did it require so long a time for you to make up your minds?

KAREN: Decision making in this case was not easy for either of us. We both came from families that were religious and very serious about it. Each of us associated religion with the highest ideals and standards. My family had really had no association with Jews. I have noticed however that it always seems easier for Christian families who have been reared on the Bible to love the Hebrews but not especially like the Jews. There too, Stan was planning his career around Semitics. He wanted to be a college professor, but the subjects of his choice were most directly associated with Jews and Judaism. Further, Stan had a very strong feeling of identity with the Jewish people. As I view it now, I would say that it was less hard for me because, by this time, I had been very much imbued with a liberal interpretation of Christianity. I was working in a liberal environment in which there were many Jewish girls. I was not really strongly affiliated with a church, although I attended Riverside Church quite often. My interest in social action was broad enough to permit persons of all faiths to work in this same area.

My parents heard about Stan, and although I could see that they were not highly pleased about it all, they did and said little. It was only just before the decision making time for me that it became very serious. Then Mother suddenly became very conservative. She began to be very worried about it. She argued against the marriage on the basis of faith and the need to preserve what was so precious. Then too, she was motivated by her desire to keep me from getting hurt, by which she meant that a marriage between people of different faiths meant that such a marriage must end in divorce or separation, and that would, of course, hurt me.

STANLEY: I was having a difficult time of it too. Not only because I had never in my life thought that I would fall in love with a Christian girl and here it happened. I was aware, too, of my special scholastic interests that associated me so very closely with Judaism and the Jewish people. Things would be more difficult for that reason. Further, I was really a devout Jew. Judaism meant so much to me, what would happen to all that I treasured if my wife and I didn't agree on matters religious? How could she, who herself had such a fine heritage, give up any part of it or all of it in order to marry a Jew? How could I marry Karen unless she voluntarily converted to Judaism? I could not possibly conceive either of my giving up my faith or of marrying and having each of us maintain our separate religious ways.

In the meantime, my father had died, and there was Mother to be concerned with. When Mother found out that I was going out with Karen, she was really upset at first. I think it can best be described as a very grave shock. Even when she heard later that Karen was planning to convert to Judaism, she was not satisfied. It was about then that I was on the verge of giving up my idea to become a scholar in Semitics. But Karen was determined that this must not happen. She really worked away at me so that I came to my senses and stayed with my original plan of study.

KAREN: During this long period when we were in the process of arriving at some decision concerning our lives, I had already concluded that, if Stan would marry me, I would convert to Judaism. This was not really a great wrench from the family tradition because I had really already made that break. I certainly was no longer related to the theological ideas of my parents. The idea of the divinity of Jesus had long ceased to have meaning for me. Ideas like the Virgin birth had no significance for me whatsoever. God, for me, was One. Really, the gap between the ideas of my folks and myself had widened so, over the years, that there just was no point of contact between us any more. Of course, it is one thing not to believe in or accept the conservative Christian approach and quite another to really accept and understand the nature of Judaism, but I was doing my best to bridge that gap.

Stan and I decided that we would get married after I had converted to Judaism. So, the next step was to talk it all over with some rabbi. In Stan's work, he knew many fine rabbis, and so we went to one who was most solicitous and helpful. I studied with this rabbi although the rabbi relied very much upon what Stan told him that I knew about Judaism.

STANLEY: The difficulties increased with my family. I began getting the silent treatment. They were all very much upset. They would have been very happy if I broke the relationship with Karen, but I think they saw my career as a Hebrew scholar going down the drain.

Q: Did both of your parents accept Stan without reservation?

KAREN: I was really amazed at the way my father accepted Stan. I had expected that my father would have been distressed and my mother would have accepted it, but it was very much the reverse. I think that my sister and brother-in-law, who had met Stan on several occasions and who also had an appreciation of his scholarly work, were the ones who helped to bring my father around and who softened the opposition. They even came to accept the idea of my conversion to Judaism. They felt, as did I, that family unity was most important, and they recognized that it would have to be in Stan's direction. They knew that I was certainly no longer an orthodox Christian. I had long before recognized that our problems would center more about home ceremonies like the observance of Christmas and Easter than about theological matters. Insofar as I was concerned I was determined to make Hannukah something very special so that my children would never miss Christmas. But later, after our marriage and the coming of children, it was still a problem because my parents did, of course, celebrate Christmas. I remember one occasion when my parents had one of the neighbors dress up as Santa Claus and give gifts to the children when we came to visit them during the Christmas holidays. It was all very beautiful, but it was, nevertheless, difficult for Stan to take.

STANLEY: After we were married, I accepted a teaching post at a state university. We were far enough away from our families to try to make the necessary adjustments in our lives. Karen had been converted according to Reform ritual. She received a Hebrew name and promised to rear the children as Jews. There was no immersion ceremony. My friends generally accepted Karen. The new friends we made on the college campus accepted us without question. We became members of the local synagogue, and Karen participated in its affairs. She was especially active in its sisterhood. Every once in a while there were repercussions, like the time when the father of one of my students complained that my example would only hasten the intermarriage situation on the campus because Jewish boys and girls, seeing Karen and me happily married, would cite us as proof that intermarriage always works out well. From time to time such things happened, but they all quieted down and my position was never in jeopardy. Young people did come to me from time to time to ask my advice about interfaith marriage, but, always, I made it clear that such marriages depend in large measure upon whom one marries. I always refused to generalize.

KAREN: We have certainly tried to maintain a good Jewish home. Stan always makes the Kiddush on Friday night; I always kindle the Sabbath candles and make the blessing over them. We have three children, two sons and a daughter. The boys went to Hebrew school and were Bar Mitzvah. I regret that Stan's mother, who passed away just before we got married, was not there to witness these occasions. She would have rejoiced, I know. She was quite ill before she died, and I tried to help her as much as I could.

STANLEY: And I know how much she appreciated Karen. We have been married for twenty-seven years. Our children are quite grown up. I think that things have worked out very well. When the children were young, there was an identity crisis every once in a while because they knew Karen's background and mine, and they knew our respective families. After all, the two families are really very much different from each other. One family seems alien to the other, but, on the whole, I think the adjustments have been made.

KAREN: Interfaith marriage is a serious matter. I would insist upon conversion as a prerequisite. If my children fell in love with a Christian, I would, above all else, want to know the kind of individual he or she was. Then, I would urge conversion to the faith of the minority member. If the interfaith marriage situation loomed and the other party did not want to convert, I would hope that both parties would sit down with us and let us help them to face all the issues. If then, they decided to get married, I would say to myself, "I can't live their lives for them." Yet, I would certainly try to maintain my ties with them. After all, these are my children.

I think that conversion can work out very successfully. I feel that this is certainly true in my case.

* * *

INTERVIEWER'S NOTE: At the conclusion of this interview, the daughter of Karen and Stan entered the room and, in a highly emotional manner, turned to me and said: "I heard the entire interview and I feel that I must add something to what has already been said.

My mother may feel that she is a successful convert to Judaism, but I don't. I feel that she is not now nor has she ever *really* been Jewish. I do not regard her as a Jew. The conversion didn't make her Jewish, nor does marriage to my father. One has to be born a Jew, live in a Jewish home, and understand and accept the nuances of Judaism. Being a Jew is *more* than just a matter of rejecting Christianity. It is more than lighting Sabbath candles. It is *feeling* Jewish and I do not feel that my mother is that kind of a Jewess." As abruptly as she had entered, so, she left the room. Karen and Stan offered no further comment.

Saul Miller

The Midwest is my home territory—Chicago, Illinois, to be exact. I was born there a little over forty years ago. All of my early schooling through high school was acquired there. I went on to the University of Chicago as a science major and graduated after only three years' work. My interests were always associated with such subjects as math, physics, biology, and chemistry. It was only after I received my first degree that I switched fields. I am a social scientist today. I have a Ph.D. in that field. All of my graduate work was done in New York City, at Columbia University.

My parents, both of whom have died, came from the Midwest. I can't say that I ever felt that there was very much affection displayed in our home. The relationship between my mother and father was a rather shallow one—it wasn't an affectionate relationship at all. Their respective families had come from Russia in the eighteen-nineties. Both Father and Mother spoke English well. They were, in fact, both college graduates. Father was a chemical engineer. My mother was an orthodontist. Each had special interests and concerns. Of the two, Mother was the more affectionate, but my father was kind of a cool cat. I have a married sister who lives in upstate New York. I haven't been in touch with her for a very long time. I really know very little about her. She is considerably younger than I. We really lived in two separate worlds both as children and now.

I teach social science in one of the nearby universities, but I do other things as well. I happen to be good in languages, so I do a considerable amount of translation work for a federal government agency. I also have a law degree, and I practice law in New York City. Books and learning were always very much a part of my life. Our home always had a good library. My parents always kept good books around, and I got used to them and came to enjoy them very early in my life. I have the feeling that books were more companionable to me than were my parents. Oh, I mustn't give you the impression that we hated each other, or, even, that we never got along. Actually we related to each other in very "proper" terms, but there was, I felt, always a distance between us. My parents were pleased, yes, even proud, because I was doing so well scholastically. There was always friendly concern, but we were never really warm or affectionate toward each other. It just wasn't that kind of a family.

My sister was also a college graduate. She is married to a scientist who works in a major lab. He is Jewish, as is my whole family. But I'm sure that none of us ever really had any affiliation with a synagogue, nor did we ever go to Hebrew school or even Sunday school. We *identified* with Jews but really did not participate in any of the religious ritualism that is said to characterize a Jewish way of life. We certainly didn't observe the Sabbath or maintain dietary restrictions, etc., that religious Jews generally do. But when Hitler began to oppress Jews or other forms of anti-Semitism made themselves manifest, we certainly felt as if these were *our* people who were being hurt.

I am married. My wife is of Austrian origin, and she was and is a Roman Catholic. I met her long after I converted to Catholicism. We have three children, two boys and a girl. My wife formerly lived in Connecticut. We rear our children as Catholics, of course. And I may say that our faith means a great deal to us. There is nothing perfunctory in our relationship to the Church.

I have already told you that my parents were not religious but I failed to speak about my mother's parents, who lived with us. They were religious to a certain extent. They went to the synagogue on the High Holy Days. I still remember that my grandfather used to spend the whole day of Yom Kippur (the Day of Atonement) in the synagogue, but my parents never did. I was never Bar Mitzvah. My sister went to a Sunday school for a few years but never was confirmed. I recall that she said that she didn't want to be confirmed because she realized that all her friends were just going for the purpose of having a big party afterwards. That disillusioned her so much that she dropped the whole business on the eve of the big splash. Neither my mother nor my father raised any objections because they too had an antipathy to hypocrisy.

I remember too that my father exposed me to the synagogue once. I was about thirteen years old at the time. I went along with him to a service after which he said: "Do you want to go again?" I said "No," and that was the end of that. Nothing more was ever said about it.

My parents had a few Jewish friends among their friends, and, I believe, we lived in what might be called a Jewish neighborhood. But we weren't especially close to them, or for that matter, to anyone else. We had people "in" from time to time, but, in the main, they were business or professional people who related to my parents in those terms.

I never really became aware of a lack of religious training. I never thought about religion at all except one time when I was in the Army. I had heard someone say that there were no atheists in foxholes. All this meant to me was that atheists ought to stay out of foxholes. No. I just didn't have any thoughts about religion either before or during my Army years.

I had gone into the Army just after I finished college. I served for a period of three years in France, Germany, Austria, England, and in the United States. There is really nothing unusual to report about my Army days. Generally speaking they were days to put up with and get out of as quickly as possible.

When I first came home from the war, my mother had died and

my father had sold our home. He was living in a room. He later moved out to California. So I was pretty much on my own. My sister was then living in the Pacific Northwest. There was an aunt and uncle whom my parents were fairly friendly with. But they meant nothing to me. So, I was really quite alone in a physical sense. (I had been pretty much alone in a spiritual sense for a very long time before I went into the Army.)

I then decided to go on to graduate school in New York. There were no family or other ties to prevent me from doing as I wished so I went East. I was living on the G.I. Bill in those days.

I worked hard as a graduate student. I received both M.A. and Ph.D. degrees. I remember that all my time was taken up with my schoolwork. I seldom went out. I do not recall having any dates. I was just anxious to do creditable work in my courses and seminars. But it was during that time that I became a Catholic.

During one year I took a course with a professor on the Soviet Union. He deplored all that was going on in Russia but didn't make it clear to me just exactly *why* he felt this way. I kept asking myself, "Why did he deplore it? Why is what is happening in Russia so deplorable?" I had heard that Monseigneur Fulton Sheen had written a very good rationale about it, so I went to the university library and found the article and read it very carefully. In that article he mentioned Gilbert K. Chesterton as a very thoughtful writer. So I took out a book by Chesterton, and I found it most stimulating. Well, I began to read many of Chesterton's books, and it was he who gave me my interest in the Church. Most of the books he wrote were written before he had become a Catholic. But my debt to him is great indeed.

Now, you will remember that my father had moved out to California. From time to time I wrote to him and received letters in return. But they were rather shallow—intended only to keep the line of communication open. Chesterton's ideas had intrigued me. I felt that I needed to talk them out with someone. But I really had no one locally to whom to talk. So I began to write lengthy letters to my father about how challenging Chesterton's ideas really

were to me. And that started a very voluminous correspondence
between us. I had always respected his mental ability, so, inasmuch
as all I was reading involved a mental problem, I felt that he might
help me toward an intelligent understanding of Chesterton's ideas.
We wrote long letters to each other. What I really was asking was
that he enter his objections to Chesterton's advocacy of Catholicism.
Basically, the letters centered on Catholicism rather than upon
Chesterton.

My father became pretty antagonistic. He reasoned—he wasn't
just emotional. He reasoned with me, but it was clear that there was
a great deal of antagonism to my ideas. He sensed that I was leaning in the direction of becoming a Catholic. Actually, I think I said
so. I wasn't hiding anything. But he didn't like the idea at all.
Actually he didn't care for any religion, and he only mentioned the
others, including Judaism, in passing. I sensed, of course, that he
really didn't have any personal convictions about religion. It just
didn't mean anything to him. Well, he wrote and wrote until he
died. That was before I got my Ph.D. degree. But before that I had
come to the conclusion that he really didn't have any good argument against Catholicism. There really hadn't been anything gained
by carrying on the correspondence with him.

The more I thought about Catholicism, the more convinced I
became that it wasn't enough just to have a good Catholic philosophy. I ought to be doing something about it. And, by "something"
I meant conversion.

I had become convinced that the Roman Catholic doctrines were
true. I had come to believe that the Church was founded by God.
Now up to the time I began reading Chesterton I hadn't really
believed in God at all. I thought of God not anthropomorphically
but as a Power, a Force. I saw in Jesus Someone who was Divine
and believed, then as well as now, that He had set up the Church.

I think it was Chesterton's approach to Catholicism that had
fascinated me. He didn't talk about emotions or anything like that.
He talked about historical facts and the explanation of these facts.
That was what appealed to me more than anything else. He was

talking about events and explaining them in terms of God. He showed how the miracles could only be explained as acts of God and how difficult it would really be to say they weren't.

I reasoned: if Christ was God and He had set this organization up for His purposes, then when the Church spoke it was with His authority; and from there on, I didn't have any problems with what the Church said because I regarded it from the point of view of His authority. His authority is what matters. When He spoke it didn't matter much what He said because He was the authority and the Church was His creation.

I never, during all the time I was investigating Catholicism, studied any other religion. This would have been pretty much a waste of time. I saw no point in checking on other religions when I was already convinced that the Catholic Church was the only true Church.

Despite these convictions of mine, I didn't do anything for about a year. I was absolutely convinced that I was on the proper course. But I realized that this was such a weighty move that I ought not to move too quickly, so I cogitated, I read—I was always reading but only about Catholicism. I never went into the Church until I had decided I could go, spiritually. This was a personal matter with me. Excepting for the correspondence with my father, I never discussed the matter with anyone. About a month before I made my decision—after the year of cogitation had passed—I found that I needed a sponsor, so I got in touch with an old Army friend of mine who was a Catholic and talked with him about it and asked him to be my sponsor, but otherwise, I spoke to nobody.

I had not examined the ritual of the Church until I decided to enter. I was perfectly willing to accept whatever ritual there was because of the greater Truth represented by the Church. I did not know what the ritual was going to be so I didn't know that they wouldn't fit me or whether they would. You know, I swallowed all that. I accepted something that was basic—the Church itself.

I had not felt insecure at any time. I thought that the doctrines of the Church were right. That was all that mattered. I felt that if I thought that what the Church, the *true* Church, had to say was true, I had to affiliate with it because that was part and parcel of the truth. I feel that Jesus is God. I really don't believe anything novel.

My contacts with the Church at that time were so limited that I had to use the telephone directory in order to pick some church and priest to which I could come with my request to convert to Catholicism. The priest I talked to had never seen me before nor I him. He satisfied himself early, after a few meetings, that I knew what I was supposed to know. It all happened quickly after I had found the true Church. I was then baptized and converted.

Following the conversion I got interested in a group of religiously active Catholic laymen. They had a program for volunteers so I offered my services once a week and sometimes on weekends. I got to be pretty active in that program. I worked in Harlem long before "Race" got to be very popular.

After I received my doctoral degree I was thinking about becoming a "religious," of devoting my life to the Church. As a consequence I went to live near Fordham University and got to be associated with some of the priests there. It was all informal, of course. But it was with a view of entering a religious Order. But that didn't work out. Fundamentally, the group that I had desired to join didn't want me. I had wanted to enter the Jesuits, and they didn't want me. I was really not upset about it, but I still was thinking seriously about devoting my whole life to the Church. It was about this time that I met my future wife. She had been a volunteer in the same organization of church people which I had joined some time before. She was a dental technician. She had come to work in New York City. As you will recall, I had not met her during all the time I was thinking about conversion. But it was a swift romance, about six months, I think, and we were married in her parish in New York City. I had met her family. Her father is a very hard-bitten man, and he thought I was making a mistake because his daughter was too independent. You see, she had left her home because she hadn't gotten along with her father. But he was wrong about her. Today, we visit them from time to time, and, I would say, the relationship is a good one.

I am living fairly comfortably. I work hard at a variety of jobs. I teach but that is not my first love. I wouldn't want to devote all my time to teaching. Research is really my cup of tea.

My children are being reared as Catholics. I am accepted as a member of the Catholic community, and, generally speaking, all is well.

I am a member (now, president) of the Edith Stein Society, an organization consisting entirely of Jews who have converted to Catholicism. It really happened by accident. I knew a woman who had converted to Catholicism. She was a Protestant. I had been an altar boy at a church where we met. She and I began to talk about the Church and the fact that I had been converted to Catholicism. Because she knew Father Ostereicher, who himself had been converted from Judaism to Catholicism, she asked me to come down to meet him. So I did. He told some of the people in the Edith Stein Society about me. I started receiving mail from them. Then they asked me to support the organization, so, I did. Well, as a consequence, I joined. I have been stimulated by my association with these Catholics who are of Jewish origin. I have found that Catholicism is really something to live by. I still do not consider myself a good enough Catholic. I would like to be. But I can't say that I am. Catholicism is an ideal. I try to live up to it to the best of my ability. I believe that the Church is the symbol of Truth. I have become a Catholic on an intellectual basis. Intellectually to believe that Christ is God and that He set up a Church and that He wants all men to be members of that Church means, to me, that I should be one of them. Each person is committed to serve God. The Church is there to serve God, and *that* is what I try to do.

If my children were to turn to another religion I would not be happy. I would, of course, think that my children are mistaken, if they turned to any other religion, including Judaism. However, if they thought that this were the right move to make, I would respect them just as my father did.

My sister has thought that I was "cuckoo." She thinks that I should have gone to a psychiatrist, but I feel that people tend to respond this way when anything unusual happens. I am happy with my wife and children. I am happy with the Church, and I believe that the Church is the symbol of the great truth that Jesus Christ is the Son of God who has come to atone for the sins of mankind.

Corinne and Frank MacIntyre

CORINNE: I'm from the Midwest, from Nebraska, to be exact. I lived there most of my life. My father and mother moved around considerably because he was in the construction business. My father was from Ohio originally. He was a Mennonite, and his father before him was a Presbyterian. My parents met and married in Ohio. My mother was a Lutheran. Their marriage proved unhappy, and they were divorced after about twelve years. My mother always thought that my father's religion was backward, and she let him know it. I didn't realize what was happening until, one day, my father left home—and that was it. The next thing I knew my mother told me that she had divorced my father.

My mother's parents had come from Norway. I understand that my grandmother, my mother's mother, had come over here in the 1870's. My mother's father too was a Norwegian. He came here at about the same time. For a while he lived in Chicago, but later he moved to Nebraska. They were strong Lutheran Church people. My mother was not really a very religious person, but I remember going to Sunday school in whatever church was closest to where we lived. This was really a rural area. Mother was better educated than my father. Her interest in books and reading was very marked. But her interest in religion was really not great. I was baptized as a Lutheran, I guess, because of her parents. I had gone to about nine different schools by the time I hit the eighth grade. My father's work kept us moving around from one place to another, wherever his kind of work was available. My mother's parents had died before she married and my father's family lived in Ohio, so there was really no big family to turn to. It was just my parents, and, when they were divorced, only my mother.

Even though I had been baptized a Lutheran, I didn't really think of myself as one. It was because I had attended so many different churches. But when I was about thirteen I finally settled on the Methodist Church. That was just before the divorce. My father didn't really care what church I belonged to. My mother came to feel a bit more religious, and felt that I had to be anchored some place so, when I expressed a preference for the Methodist Church, it was fine with her.

My religious experiences in that church were pleasant. I remember going to Bible school in the summertime. It was nothing I really took too seriously. It's just that I remember that it was pleasant going to that particular church. Later when I went on to college in Iowa, I took some courses in religion and enjoyed them very much.

When I was young we always observed Christmas and Easter at home. Mother tried to make these occasions meaningful religious experiences, but Dad was simply not interested. Mother had certain standards in religion as in everything else that made her want to impart her ideas as meaningfully as possible. I felt a strong tie to my mother. The relation with my father was really not good. He was a rather critical and dictatorial person. We found it hard to get along with him. There were always arguments and personal conflicts with him.

After graduation from college I taught English in a little town in southern Nebraska for four years, and then I got a job in Washington during the war years. Then, after that, I came back home and taught. I lived with my mother. She and I joined the choir in an Episcopal church, as professional singers. My mother loved to sing, and she was really very good. I still belonged to the Methodist Church and continued to attend on occasion. I think it was the social life, what little there was of it, that pleased me most.

During my college years, I dated out of my own religion, on occasion, but inasmuch as I wasn't too serious with anybody it wasn't very important. It was just a matter of going out. I had gone out with Catholic boys even while I was in high school, but I never took it seriously. My mother never spoke about my dating this way because she knew it was not serious. My mother was a

Lutheran all her life, and I think it bothered her probably in a way but she really didn't give much thought to my socializing. It really didn't upset her because she knew that I was just going out for the fun of it. When I was working in Washington I dated too, but there never was any problem about dating outside of Protestantism because it really didn't matter very much to me.

Those years in Washington were exciting ones for me. I was given a job in a social welfare program that took me into a great variety of communities throughout the country. I met many people and found the work during those war years very exciting and spiritually rewarding. On one of those trips, it was to Savannah, I attended chapel services with one of my girl friends. It was there that I met Frank.

FRANK: I was there in Uncle Sam's Army. I had been assigned to the dental unit in Savannah. I came from Medford, Massachusetts. I am a Catholic, born and bred. Since a friend of mine was going to the chapel I went along with him. We were both good Catholics, and we always attended church regularly. By the way, I have a brother who is a priest. I had been in Savannah for about six months when I met Corinne. The other doctor happened to know the girl Corinne was with. That's how we got acquainted.

My parents were both Irish Catholic. We had always lived in a predominately Catholic community and attended mass regularly. I have a sister too. She lives in Washington, D.C., now. My father died a few years ago, but my mother is still hale and hearty. She is a sweet little woman.

Well, since we were both stationed in Savannah, it was especially nice to meet up with someone who was attractive and fun to be with. We didn't date regularly, but, from time to time, I would see Corinne.

CORINNE: At first, of course, there was no question about our being of different religions. After all, there were just all kinds of people and religions represented in all these Army installations. But when we began seeing each other more frequently, religious difference seemed to become important to us both. The more we saw each other and the more serious we became, the more we realized that two different religions wouldn't work, and we would have to resolve the problem somehow.

FRANK: We were definitely in love, that we realized. I knew that I would never give up Catholicism. For me, it was a one-way street. If there was going to be any change it was going to have to be Corinne. This meant many serious discussions and arguments between us. I had always felt that I couldn't see how anybody could sign a paper saying that you would bring up children to be something you couldn't believe yourself. I always thought it was utterly ridiculous to agree that children would be brought up in a faith you, yourself, couldn't accept. What mother can really bring her child up as a Catholic who can't accept it herself? It doesn't make sense. That is why the idea of signing any statement about the rearing of children as Catholics didn't please me.

CORINNE: It took over a year before we came to some agreement. If we were going to marry I was going to have to be converted a Catholic.

Well, in the meantime, the war was over and I decided that inasmuch as Frank was going back home to resume his practice, I would go back to Nebraska, teach school, and be with my mother once again. I really wanted to have a chance to think the whole matter through, on my own. Actually it was two years later that Frank and I got married.

I told my mother all about Frank and particularly that he was a Catholic and that he wanted me to convert to Catholicism before we got married. I had, of course, written her about Frank, but I really hadn't said too much. It's so difficult to write all this out. Much to my surprise my mother really wasn't as upset as I had expected she would be. She wanted to be sure that Frank was the right person for me and that we really loved each other. By then she knew that I was very much on my own and the decision would have to be mine to make. I talked to various Catholic friends I had.

I discovered a lot of anti-Catholic sentiment from otherwise good people. I tried to raise all the questions I could. While I was doing graduate work at college I raised all kinds of questions with my instructors, most particularly with the instructor in the School of Religion who was giving the course on Catholicism. I read a lot of Catholic literature also and then I took a series of formal instructions.

Of course I had certain problems about Catholicism. The authority of the Catholic Church bothered me. It was far different in this respect from the Protestant churches. But really, there were no major theological differences of which I was aware. Jesus was the central figure here as He was in Protestantism. It wasn't as if I were converting from Protestantism to Judaism, which involves a completely different orientation. So with a few uncertainties (I would not call them reservations) I felt that I was ready to be converted.

During this time Frank came up to meet my mother, who liked him at once, and I went to Medford to meet Frank's mother and his family, including the brother who is a priest. But all this while I felt that something was wrong with my approach to the subject of conversion. I had, all this while, been thinking of conversion because I wanted to marry Frank. Important as this reason was, I felt that it just wasn't good enough. If I were to become a Catholic I should do so because I really wanted to, for its own sake! So there was more studying and more discussion with my professor of religion, who was himself a noted Catholic. After a while I really began to feel that I really believed in Catholicism and that I wanted the Church to have the authority to tell me how to live and what to do. When that decision was arrived at I really felt that I was ready to be converted. This time I told my mother that I had made a definite decision, and I remember her saying, "Well, it's your life. Do with it what you want." There was no anger or distress. It was all quite simple at that point.

The conversion actually took place in the Catholic church that was across the street from the Methodist church I had formerly attended. Although I had been baptized as a Lutheran, I was given what the Catholic Church calls a "conditional baptism." Frank and I were married in the Church about a week later. My mother attended the ceremony and so did Frank's mother. I don't think Frank's father liked the idea too much because he didn't come up. But Frank's brother, the priest, did attend and he gave the blessing. It was all very beautiful and very meaningful.

After our honeymoon, we came back to Medford where Frank had his practice, and we have lived here for these past twenty years. We are a unified Catholic family in every way. We attend church regularly as do our three children. They have, of course, been reared as Catholics. They went to parochial school and for a while our oldest went to a Catholic high school. Recently he transferred to the public high school because we thought he might get a better preparation there. Our younger children are attending Catholic schools. We are both active in parish work, and, as for me, I feel completely at home in the Church.

If our children were at some time to decide that they were in love and wanted to marry a non-Catholic I think that I would be a little disturbed. I don't know how much anybody, including parents, could do about it but I would do all that I could to discourage them.

FRANK: I would be upset too, of course. But this sister of mine about whom I spoke married a non-Catholic. I recall that I objected to this marriage, not because of religion but because I didn't like her marrying a man whom I didn't like.

CORINNE: I would prefer that the children should marry Catholics. But, if not, I would hope they would marry someone with a strong religious background. I would want them, however, to be sure that they married into families where they could keep harmony with their in-laws.

I think that ours is a good, happy Catholic marriage in every way. I'm not at all sorry for what I have done. The opposite is true. I'm really happy as a Catholic and as a wife and mother.

Stephanie Singer

I was born in New Hampshire in 1949. I have a brother and sister. They, too, were born in New Hampshire. My brother is five years younger than I. My sister is eight years younger. My parents are Jewish. Both were reared as Jews. My father was Bar Mitzvah. He regards himself as a good Jew. My mother, too, is a Jewess. She is the daughter of people who certainly regard themselves as good Jews. Both of these grandparents are active in the Jewish community. I imagine that it would come as a shock to them to think that I do not regard them as religious people.

Shortly after I was born, my mother and father moved to Rhode Island. My father was in business there. He had established a small business there and was doing quite well. They associated with Jews primarily but they were generally active participants in the larger community. I do not think that either of my parents was ghetto minded. Each wanted to be and, in fact, was active in the affairs of the larger community.

My father was born in Massachusetts, as was my mother.

My parents met for the first time at a birthday party that was taking place at my cousin's home.

I am not very close to my brother or sister. We just don't seem to get along very well. My parents feel close to all of us, and we feel close to them.

When I lived in Rhode Island I was reared as a Jewess. I attended the Sunday school regularly. I remember the rabbi as a fine man whom I enjoyed very much. He was a good and kind man. We have retained his friendship all through the years.

My parents would celebrate most of the Jewish Holy Days. They observed the Sabbath by lighting the candles on Friday evening, but my father did not recite the Kiddush even though he never worked on Friday Eve, the beginning of the Sabbath. He never made the blessing over the bread either. We always had two Seders on the Passover. We came from a large family so many members of the family were present at the Seders. My grandparents on my mother's side were part of a large family. There were usually from fifty to sixty people at these Seders. It was always nice to see the family in this way.

Later, when we moved to Las Vegas, we would observe the Passover too, but it was always with friends, not with the family.

My mother became ill when I was about nine years old. This meant that we had to move to the Western part of the United States if Mother was going to be at all comfortable. So we all moved to Las Vegas. My father sold his business in Rhode Island.

It was not an easy thing for my parents to make this move. After all, they had most of their family right here in the East. But it had to be done if my mother was to keep well. For us kids, it really didn't mean very much. Perhaps it was more of an adventure than anything else.

I really don't know whether most of my friends were Jewish when I lived in Rhode Island. We never really spoke about that. We were, I think, a rather cosmopolitan family.

The decision to move West was not an easy one. It meant that my father would have to sell his business and get started in something utterly new, but my mother's health was important so we decided to make this major change. That was in 1958. We have lived in Las Vegas ever since. I was eleven years old at that time. There was a lot of illness in our family. It was not only my mother but my sister too, and it was always something to think about. Then, for a while, my father had been sick too, so you can see, it wasn't a really happy household. We had our troubles, but I would say that our family spirit was good. I got along fine with my parents. But my sister and I didn't get along very well. I can't say why, but that was the way it was. Now that I am older, I do get along with her better but I try not to let her bother me.

When we got to Las Vegas, we bought a home, and, after looking around for a time, my father bought a retail business. He worked awfully hard, especially at the beginning, trying to make a "go" of it, and he succeeded. We made a number of friends in our new city. The folks belonged to the Jewish Community Center and to the temple (it was Reform), and they also joined a bridge club. They like to play cards, and, thereby, they met a lot of nice people.

During the past seven years my mother was in the hospital about six times. She would be well for a while and then get very sick and have to go to the hospital. She had different doctors taking care of her, but none of them really helped her very much. There were so many different things that would get her sick that I could hardly keep track. Of course we all worried about it, but Mother was always so cheerful that, really, we always felt that she was going to get really well, one of those days.

All this while my parents kept corresponding with my grandparents in the East. There were lots of letters and long distance phone calls. From time to time, my mother's parents would come out to visit us in Las Vegas. We never saw the other members of the family except two of my father's sisters. They visited us several times, and we all enjoyed them very much. My father's mother had passed away while we were living in Las Vegas, but we heard from his father fairly often. I think that I can say that I have always had a nice relationship with the family.

Las Vegas is a nice town. I like it there. I made friends, and especially when I went to high school I enjoyed it very much. There was always something doing at school and the kids were nice.

My parents had joined the temple and they enrolled my sister and me in the Sunday school, but I must say, I never enjoyed it. I never liked it. I always had the feeling it was useless because I always said I wasn't going to be Jewish anyway. Many years ago, when I realized what "conversion" was, I realized it was possible to change your religion. I didn't believe in the Jewish religion. That's the way I felt for many years. I didn't know how they—Jews—could possibly ignore the fact that the Messiah had come. Everyone was still waiting for something that had happened two thousand years ago. When I say "Messiah," I am referring to Jesus Christ. He is God Incarnate.

I can remember when I first found out about Judaism I just didn't believe it. I had always assumed that since Jesus was a Jew,

Jews accepted Him. I always believed that when people spoke about God they were referring to God the Father, God the Son, and God the Holy Ghost. I really don't know just where I got these ideas but they have been with me for a very long time. Come to think of it, I may have acquired these ideas at the private girls' school I attended when we lived back East. My mother had wanted me to start school, but they had a rule that if you are not six by January then you can't start. That meant that I wouldn't be going until about a year later. So Mother started me in a private school. It was Episcopalian, but we never had any lessons from the Bible or anything like that, there.

I went to that school for about three years; then my parents put me in another private school. Both of these schools were coeducational. They really didn't give us any religious background. Oh, yes, we'd say the Lord's Prayer when we got up in the morning and right after that we would say the pledge of allegiance and sing "America the Beautiful," but that was all.

Until you just asked me, it never entered my mind to wonder where I got this idea about Jesus Christ. I feel that I *always* had it. I can't remember ever anyone telling me about it or anything. I can remember we were all in Sunday school and we were all telling about who we thought was our favorite person in the Bible. That was in the Jewish Sunday school in Las Vegas. I remember that I said "Jesus." The teacher almost turned green, and he tried very hard to explain to me that Jews didn't believe in Jesus—and I was shattered. I never discussed this with either my father or my mother. I just didn't think there was anything to discuss. When they would tell me stories about Abraham or about Noah's Ark and all that, I thought, "Well, they'll get to Jesus later."

It wasn't until I was in the eighth grade that my parents got to know how I felt about Jesus, the Messiah. I remember telling my mother of my decision that, eventually, I would become a Christian. Of course, I wanted to wait until I knew more about it and to make sure I wasn't doing something I would later regret. I wanted to become a Christian because I *did* accept Christ as the Messiah. I knew it was Christianity that accepted Jesus. But before I became part of any denomination, I wanted to look into them all and find out which one. When you reach an age when you already have opinions of your own, it's hard to find a religion that coincides with your own opinions. I read many things, and, from time to time, I went with friends to their different churches and they explained things that were going on. I then made my choice. I remember going to a Baptist church, also to a revival meeting and to a Methodist church. Also, there were the Presbyterian and Roman Catholic churches. I read various books about these religions from time to time. I remember one book that had separate chapters about each religion, and each chapter was written by a representative of that faith. I studied all this very carefully. I would discuss it with my own friends who belonged to these churches.

I never really talked to the rabbi of the temple about my ideas because I didn't have the ideas solidly enough formulated to know what I was going to argue for. I had already spoken to an Episcopalian priest about my ideas. I asked questions about Episcopalianism and got his answers. I did talk to my parents about wanting to become some sort of a Christian. I remember that when I talked with my mother about it she wasn't shocked or anything. In fact, she said she could see it coming.

I dropped out of Sunday school when I was in the seventh grade because all that Sunday school teacher of mine seemed to be able to do was criticize the Christians. She was certainly bigoted. Her attitude bothered me, and I used to contradict her a lot. She finally got angry with me and told my parents about me. So they took me out of Sunday school because they could see this whole thing becoming so useless, and they knew I didn't like it. When I didn't like something I wouldn't work hard at it. No one from the Sunday school or the temple ever came around to find out why I dropped out. Of course, my parents continued to belong to the temple. My younger sister, the one I don't get along with, is a very religious Jew. I think she is the most religious in our family. She went to Sunday school and Hebrew school. My father can't figure out how I came to have my ideas about Christianity and always he keeps asking, "Where did I go wrong?" This has been his answer ever since he found out about it.

I spoke to my mother first about having made up my mind that I was going to be converted to Episcopalianism. I had made this decision after going to church there and after speaking to the priest. I went there one Sunday and decided that this is what I was interested in. It looked better to me than any other church had. Every other church except the Roman Catholic didn't have mass and I felt that it was important. The other churches were mostly family services. They just had a hymn and a sermon and the Lord's Prayer. This is all they ever consisted of. On the other hand, I don't like the Roman Catholic Church where the priest is up there and he has all the power and is the only one who understands all the words that he is saying. I have been to a Roman Catholic church since they changed part of the service to English. They still do most of it in Latin, but the responses are in English.

My mother really wasn't surprised when I told her how I felt. She was wondering, she said, how long it was going to be before I would say something to her. She never knew for sure whether I was going to convert. She said that she thought for a time that I simply was not going to be religious, and then I remember her saying, "I was wondering when you would have the courage to do something about it."

The Episcopalian priest had wanted to talk to my parents about me, after I met with him. He asked me if it would be possible for them to come to the rectory or would it be better if he came out to the house. I spoke to my mother, but, as I say, she wasn't feeling well so much of the time and, at that time, she was really not well at all. She said that as soon as she was feeling well she would like to talk to the priest, but she said not for him to come to the house as my father would not like it.

My father was very angry when he heard that I was planning to become a Christian. Shortly after I had spoken to my mother about it, Mother said to Dad, "There is something that I want to tell you about Stephanie. She and I have decided, and she is going to come in and tell you about it herself, tonight, but before she does I want to prepare you for it." That was the way she broke the news to him. So, when I came in to tell him, the first thing he said was, "Why do you want to become a Christian? Is it so that you can join some country club?" Well, I burst into tears. I said that however he wanted to react to what I had to say was up to him, but for him to judge my character like that when he knew me as well as he did— *this* hurt me. Well, afterward, he said he was sorry. He knew me better than that, spur of the moment.

My mother really had known about what I was doing long before my father. But she said, "Don't you tell your father about it until you have made a decision and you are ready to do something."

My mother responded as she did, I think, because she didn't feel close to any religion herself. At least that's what I think. She didn't have a very strong faith. She knew me a lot better than my father did. It was only later, when I started to develop into a woman, that my father and I really started to get along to the point where we were as close as my mother and I were. If I, at the age of twelve, had said to him, "Daddy, I'm going to be a Christian," it would have meant nothing to him. It would just be a silly child talking with a lot of crazy ideas in her head. But my mother knew how important this was to me. She could see I had some real ideas about religion.

While I was trying to decide *which* church to join (I had already decided to become a Christian) my school friends and their families would pick me up on Sunday mornings. I would go pretty often—as often as I could without getting into arguments at home. I figured that once I had chosen a church, I would go every week, regardless. I thought I would, at least, wait until I was old enough to get there by myself. After all I was just sixteen at the time.

How religious were my parents? Well, they attended the High Holy Day Services at the temple each year. They didn't go often on the Sabbath. Of late, they went more because my younger sister encouraged it by saying, "Can't we go to services this week?" My father reads Hebrew beautifully. He was trained up through his Bar Mitzvah, and he did everything right, but after his thirteenth birthday he really didn't study Judaism. I would say that my father never was religious. His faith is not that strong. He came from Orthodox parents. They kept a kosher home. My mother's family are good Jews. They have a long tradition about Orthodox Judaism. Both of my mother's parents are religious people, especially my grandmother.

When my father received the news that I was planning to convert to Christianity he began bringing books on Judaism, like Herman Wouk's *This Is My God*. This didn't particularly inspire me to go back to Judaism. I didn't think anything would because I didn't know that much about Judaism, but I know what I have to know about it. I was more interested in finding out about Christianity. I will never find a book that is backed by the rabbis that says that the Jewish religion believes in Christ. I believe in Christ. God promised that He would send us a Messiah that would bring us eternal salvation, and it seemed like everybody was waiting with open arms for Him. When He came He went for the people and the Jewish people went with Him, realizing who He was. But the others were still sitting and waiting. That is the way I always imagined it, and this is the way I still do. I believe that Jesus was born of a woman and that He was conceived by the Holy Ghost.

Up until I was in the eighth grade in public school, I did not realize that I could change my religion if I wanted to. It was *not* impossible. It wasn't something you were born with and therefore you could never change. Something like the matter of belief can be changed.

About my sixteenth birthday, I was baptized in the Church and became an Episcopalian. The priest is a wonderful man. I see him at evening prayer service every day. I go every day. I contribute to the Church whatever I can. I give every week. I contribute 50¢ a week, one-tenth of my allowance. I now teach a kindergarten class in the Sunday school. I feel thoroughly devoted to the church. I have an excellent relationship with the people. There is none of this—"Oh, she is not an Episcopalian. She is a Jew that converted." Of course, most everybody knows about me because, when they ask me, I say, "I just recently became an Episcopalian and my family all belong to Temple Isaiah."

My parents had lots of friends, and they didn't take to what I did. The months before I was baptized were especially hard because my mother became desperately ill, and she had to go to the hospital once again. The Episcopal church was next door to the hospital so I would go from the hospital to the church.

My parents reacted differently to my baptism. My father told my mother and my mother told me that it was all he could do to keep from going out and getting drunk that night. My mother went out and bought a dress for the occasion and then was too sick to go. I told her she ought not to go. I didn't want her to come. Nothing would have made me more happy than to have her and my father there but unless it was both of them I felt I didn't want either one alone. As for my father, it was probably one of the worst nights of his life, and I thought he needed her more than I did. Mother was very ill at the time of my baptism. I do not think that my mother's serious illness had anything to do with my conversion to Christianity. Her illness did not bring on my decision. I had, for years, already felt this way. Of course, for a while my father thought that all my talk about conversion was just a way of rebelling against him. But I think he is convinced now that this is really not so. The truth is I never found Judaism to be especially meaningful to me. We used to have Passover Seders at home. We had two. Friends would come to our home the first night and we would go to their home on the second night. Oh, yes, they were lots of fun. Purim too (the Feast of Lots) was a lot of fun. We always had a big Purim Carnival at the temple. I enjoyed Rosh Hashonoh (New Year) too, but they were *fun*. I never got any spiritual feeling from them. The dinners were delicious, but I never saw any religious background. I never saw these as anything that pertains to God. The only time I have the feeling that God is present is at the Holy Communion.

When my Jewish girl friends found out what I was planning to do, they just stopped associating with me. I had belonged to a club of Jewish girls but I noticed my Christian friends never dropped me before just because I wasn't a Christian.

I really never wanted to hurt my parents. That's why I waited as long as I did before converting. This isn't an easy thing to do. My mother was not hurt with me. *That,* I know. My father was, but I think he will change.

Mom died just about a week ago. My father said to me, just the other day, "I'll take Mother's place in church with you when you are to be confirmed in the church." *That's* how much he has changed already.

I'm young—just eighteen to be exact—and I don't date much, but I want to make it clear that I do not intend to marry a Jewish boy. It won't happen that I will fall in love with one because I simply will not date a Jew. I will not date out of my religion. I would not even want to marry someone who would convert for me. He would have to be someone who would convert *with* or *without* me, but it would have to be for its own sake.

If I marry and have children and they wanted to marry a Jew, I would tell them that it was entirely up to them. I would let them make their own decisions. I think there's too much of a tendency for everybody to try to run other people's lives. When I do what I feel I have to do, everybody in the family points at himself or herself and asks, "What have I done wrong?" They don't seem to realize that I did what I did because of God's guidance. It was God's Holy Spirit that did it—not them.

Sally and Art Bonder

SALLY: I was born into a Catholic family and, through all my years, until I married Art and converted to Judaism, I remained a good Catholic. Now, after twenty-five years of married life in which I have raised two sons and one daughter as Jews, I have gone back to the Catholic Church. Perhaps my story will explain all that happened during these years and why I have reverted to Catholicism.

My parents were both born in this country. My mother was a Lutheran, but she was converted to Catholicism when she married my father. Father was a widower when he married my mother. He had three small children. Family life was good for a time. My parents were good Catholics. We lived in a small community in Minnesota. My father had started life as a farmer, but, when conditions became economically very difficult, the family moved to this small town and my father opened a general store in town. He earned a fair living during those years. But, as the years went by, Mother became suspicious about my father's behavior with one of the women in that town. Before any of us children could begin to understand what had really happened, my father moved out of our home. In other words, they separated. There was no thought of divorce because the Church forbids divorce. I really did not get to know my father well until I was about fifteen years old. The separation was really so very gradual that none of us children really knew what was happening. My mother had never talked about it.

I was a junior at high school when we knew that Father was not coming back home. Up to that time he had gone away for a while and then come back home. But this time, he moved to St. Paul, Minnesota, and lived with one of my married stepsisters and her husband. Even then, neither he nor my mother had spoken about the definite break between them. It was really a very strange relationship that existed between my mother and father. Even when he left home, they seemed to be on very friendly terms. I never heard my mother utter an unkind word about my father. My father provided nothing for our support, so my mother took in boarders, a whole series of schoolteachers who were working in our town and in adjacent towns. It was really very rough on her. But it did provide enough income to help raise the rest of us. Despite the hard work, my mother was a cheerful person. She had always been that way. The children were all affectionate, good people. We got along very well during all those years. It isn't surprising that they leaned a little bit toward Mother because they could see what she was going through. We knew that my father, who had become quite ill, was living comfortably so we didn't worry about him much. From time to time we children would hear from him, but the ties between us were not very strong. Actually I visited there shortly after I graduated from high school. I wanted to get some kind of job and I thought that my chances would be better in St. Paul, so I wrote to my father, told him about my desire and he invited me to live with him and my oldest stepsister. And I accepted, with the approval of my mother. And, I must say, he treated me very well.

As for my religious life, I can say that I was a good Catholic. I was baptized in the Church. I attended mass regularly and went to a Catholic regional high school. All the other children were also good Catholics. We attended church every Sunday and otherwise followed the practices of the Church most faithfully.

During those years when I lived at home, things were not easy for my mother and us kids. We came close to losing our home on several occasions. We would move in for a time with one of the married children, but we somehow managed to stay pretty close to each other. As the kids grew up they moved out to larger cities. A couple of the children moved to Chicago, another moved to Kansas City. All got jobs of various kinds, but still we were a family. At least we had that feeling.

When I moved to St. Paul, I got a job in saleswork in one of the larger department stores. I worked there for a few years but I didn't enjoy the work. I worked in just about every kind of job, typing, cashiering, billing. I did a variety of jobs, none of them especially good and always making just enough to see me through financially.

One of my jobs was at one of the large hotels in St. Paul. It was there that I met Art.

Art was a musician. He had played with one or another band in and around the Twin Cities for many years. He really was (and still is) a gifted musician. Art's family lived in St. Paul. His parents were Orthodox Jews. Both his father and mother had been immigrants.

ART: My parents are good people. They raised us children—there were three sisters and one brother—to the very best of their ability. All the others, except me, were born in Europe, but they had come here as children and they were all real Americans. All of them are married now. I remember that my father used to go to synagogue services every day for morning prayers. When he couldn't go to the synagogue he "davened" (prayed) at home. My mother kept a kosher home. Sabbath was observed in the best traditional way. We all went to high school, and I got a year of college at St. Thomas, a Catholic college that was open to all. But because I had been playing the flute for a great many years—I started while I was in high school—I began to look around to see how I could make some money. I found a job with a band and soon became a regular member of the group. So that I had to make a choice between going to school and making some money. Remember, jobs were not so easy to find in those days. I loved my instrument, and I had always hoped that I would be good enough to play with a "name" band. When this opportunity came along, I felt that I simply had to take it. By the time I met Sally I was a regular member of that band. From time to time we would play "dates" all over the Midwest. I figured that this was what I was best fitted for. So there was no question about working regularly with this band.

My father was a tailor. He had a little tailoring shop—repairs, pressing, and cleaning—and did fairly well. That was all he really wanted. He was happy with the family. I can still remember how nice our Friday nights with all the family used to be. I'm afraid I wasn't as good a Jew as my parents. I only went to the synagogue on the High Holy Days, and I certainly didn't pray regularly each day. I was Bar Mitzvah and I attended Hebrew school up through Bar Mitzvah, but I didn't continue after that. We had many friends. All of them were Jewish. You see, we lived in the old Jewish neighborhood in St. Paul. All those years I lived at home, of course, I had peculiar working hours. We would rehearse in the late afternoons and play for dinner and dancing up to one o'clock in the morning. That meant that I didn't get to see much of the family, but I always felt close to them, especially to my mother, who was an especially wonderful person.

It was while I was working at the hotel that I met Sally. I saw her around, liked her looks, and got to talking to her so that, after a while, we became friends.

SALLY: We have been married now for twenty-five years. We have a family of three boys and one girl. The boys are pretty well grown up now. They have all been Bar Mitzvah and all went to Sunday school. The boys all went to high school, and two of them have already graduated from the university. My daughter is still in junior high school. One of the boys majored in physics, another majored in sociology, and the third is still in college and isn't quite certain about what he will major in. They have all been good students. Art and I are proud of them all. The boys were quite active on the college campus. They belong to fraternities and are highly regarded. They have many friends. I would say they are popular. One of the boys, the middle one, plays the amplified guitar. He is especially good in modern jazz music. He has played with his dad, in his band, many times.

ART: Sally and I knew each other for over five years before we decided to get married. I think we would have married long before if it hadn't been that I was very much concerned about what my folks, especially my mother, would say about my marrying a Catholic girl. In a family like ours, such a thing could be calamitous. Frankly, this worried me so I just wouldn't go ahead and say, "Let's get married," without thinking about how my family would take it. I talked to Sally many times about this. And she understood how I felt and why. All this while my folks were really not aware of Sally's existence. Now, of course, maybe I'm kidding myself when I say that no one knew. If a sister or brother knew, they certainly didn't take it seriously.

SALLY: Even though we talked about the problem of getting married we never even once, in those years, talked about the question of my conversion to Judaism. There just was no question about Art's being converted to Catholicism. Even though I think I was a better Catholic than Art was a Jew, I knew that he would NEVER consider such a move so I didn't ever bring it up.

ART: And I had too much respect for Sally to propose that she convert to Judaism and give up Catholicism.

SALLY: I think Art felt, too, that his family would not regard conversion as a satisfactory answer.

ART: What really brought the whole thing out in the open was World War II. I was drafted, and this brought the whole thing to a head. While I was in the Army in Texas, Sally met my folks. They knew I was going with someone then, but they had never met her.

SALLY: Art's mother had once before Art went into the Army, during a conversation with her daughter, remarked that it was too bad that Art hadn't gotten married. Then, maybe, he wouldn't be drafted. Then she said, if he was going with someone and she were sure that this was the girl for him, all Art had to do was tell her. Well, Art overheard his mother's comment. He had been in his room when she made that remark. So he stepped out and asked her to repeat the remark, which she did. That was when he told her about me. He also told her that I was not Jewish. Well, I guess that was really hard for her to take but, good sport that she was, she said that she would like to meet me.

ART: Next thing I knew my mother and sister came to me and said, "We would like to meet this girl." It was a Saturday afternoon (my mother rode on the Sabbath). I drove them downtown and introduced them both to Sally. My mother invited her to have tea with them at our home. That was the first meeting.

SALLY: And a stiff and almost embarrassing meeting it was. Art's mother and sister were in the back seat and I was in the front seat. I kept on turning around and we conversed a little, rather stiffly

I'll admit. I felt I was really on the spot. I had a difficult time of it, and I'm sure that his mother and sister felt the same way. I had gone with Art for so many years and I had never met any of his family before. Actually I didn't go to tea at their home that afternoon. I offered some excuse, but Art drove around for about an hour. Then we parted. I wasn't in their home, if memory serves me right, until Art was inducted into the Army. While he was at the induction center, I was invited over to Art's home by his sister, and this time I went.

I must say that I was received very well. But I must confess that I felt very much on the spot. I suppose any girl, under similar circumstances, would have felt the same way. Now, it really had nothing to do with religious differences. They were looking me over. Who was this girl Art liked? What did she look like? What kind of a person is she? I suppose I would have done the same thing had I been in that situation.

Now all this while I had kept in touch with my mother, mostly by letter. She was not one to interfere in my affairs, but she could have expressed opposition to my dating a non-Catholic because she was, herself, a good Catholic. But she never did that. In fact, whenever I would write to her about the boys I was dating (and I did a lot of dating) I often mentioned the church affiliation, but all she wrote, in reply was, "Say hello to John or Harry, or whichever one it is now." When I told her about Art and mentioned that he was a Jew, she replied, "If you like him very much, I don't object to him. The only thing I *do* object to is that you cannot see any of his family even though he has already met some of yours." She was referring to the fact that I had introduced Art to a few of my sisters. There was a difference in attitude, but I'm not sure whether it had to do with religion or rather because Art's family were closer to each other than my family was to me or to each other. My father had met Art on several occasions. He was very fond of him.

Well, even the "once over" of Art's family, I could take because we *were* in love with each other and that was all that mattered, even though I felt like an outsider.

ART: It's true that Sally's people responded well to me on the few occasions I met them. But, somehow, it was *I* who felt the religious difference. I sensed it. They were doing something more than just looking me over to see what kind of a fellow I was. Sometimes I felt that there was a bit of separation there due to the fact that I am Jewish. But maybe that was just a feeling and not actually so.

SALLY: It makes me feel badly because I know that Art has had that feeling all these years. I am certain that none of my family thinks any less of him because of his faith. They couldn't possibly because my children are raised in this faith and they certainly love my children. But I think he is the very perfect example of many Jews whom I know who approach non-Jews with the idea that they have a feeling of dislike for them. It's a feeling of oppression that, I think, is quite common with Jewish people, and, frankly, I have never seen anything where I could say that there are grounds for Art to believe that my people didn't like him or have any ill feelings toward him because he was a Jew. I have sensed Art's attitude for a long time. Often we will have a family get-together and they happened on Sundays. Now Art can't come. I mean, he'd rather not. He works late Saturday nights. Sometimes these things start at noon—sometimes it's a family picnic. Art doesn't want to go. He wants to stay home. Because he disassociates himself so many times from the family group, they think he doesn't want to be there—and Art thinks they couldn't care less. Actually it's a misunderstanding all the way round. But we were going to tell you how we got married.

Actually, we were married twice! Once, the first time, it was a Justice of the Peace near the Army camp in Texas where Art was stationed. I had wanted to be married by a Roman Catholic priest. I had told Art how I felt about that dozens of times. I haven't anything in black and white, but I was of the opinion that if and when we married, we would be married by a priest but without Art's mother's knowledge. Art wrote me from camp urging me to come down there and we would get married. I thought it meant that he would contact a priest. But when I arrived in Texas I found that he had not communicated with any priest. Before I left for Texas, I called Art's mother to tell her that Art had sent for me and that we were going to be married. She tried to be pleasant, but I knew how upset she was and I even understood why. When I got down there I found that she had already phoned Art and told him, "Don't do anything until I get there." That's what Art told me. She was definitely opposed to his marriage to someone out of her faith. That was very clear.

Art and I had never discussed being married by a rabbi, and I wasn't too fond of a Justice of the Peace marriage either. But then it became a question either of a civil ceremony then or to wait until Art's mother got there and have it performed in his faith. Rather than wait for his mother, we chose the civil ceremony, and it was all over by the time she arrived the following day.

When Art's mother heard about the civil ceremony she was very much upset. Her first suggestion was that the very next day we must go out to the post and find a Jewish chaplain and have this thing straightened out. The following day we did that. We left her at the service club and walked the road (it was a very hot day) to the chaplain's office. He was a young fellow. Anyhow, he asked me if I were willing to give up my faith and I said, "No," and then he asked Art if he were willing to give up his faith and he answered, "No." Then he said that we had done the only possible thing that could be done under the circumstances. So Art said, "Let's go back to the service club and convince my mother of this." The chaplain went back with us and talked to Art's mother, but he certainly didn't succeed in convincing her.

Art's mother stayed around the post for a week. She wanted us to go on with her to Fort Worth and see "a really BIG rabbi." Art simply couldn't do that because he had been on a three-day pass and could take no more time off. So she came back to her home. I can just imagine how the whole family responded to his mother's report on what had happened!

ART: Actually, I heard nothing from any of the members of my family. But we were married, and, insofar as I was concerned, that was all that mattered. Sally remained in the South with me for about two weeks and then, because the whole division was sent out to the West Coast, Sally went back to St. Paul.

SALLY: When I returned I lived with my sister. Neither she nor the others in my family seem to feel one way or another about my being married by a Justice of the Peace. They were just happy that I was married. One of my sisters had done pretty much the same thing some years earlier. But she got to feeling so badly about it that she separated from her husband, who was a Lutheran, until he was willing to have their marriage blessed by a priest. He never converted to Catholicism, but he agreed to have the marriage blessed and now they are living together again. They never did have children so it didn't affect her husband very much.

ART: Although I had thought that we were going to be shipped overseas it never happened, so for three years I was on the West Coast. When I saw how things were, I phoned Sally and asked her to come out there, which she did. During that time there were many discussions about religion and what we were going to do.

SALLY: We got along beautifully. Everything would be fine until he started talking about religion—something we had never done before we were married. It must have been his mother's influence (I'm not criticizing him or condemning him; I'm just explaining what happened), but Art started to talk about my converting to Judaism and then there would be a difference of opinion because I was not ready to convert. He would talk about our being married by a rabbi which, I concluded, meant conversion. Well, I was upset about it all. We had known each other for these many years, and I felt if this was the way it was going to end, I'd better get out. I'd leave, that's all. And so I recall vividly that I left at three o'clock one morning. I did it right on the spur of the moment, but I was fully aware of what I was doing and why I was doing it.

I went back to St. Paul and the first thing I did was get my old job back again. I don't remember writing to Art during the next three weeks. I had resumed working and had stayed away from Art's folks because I thought Art should be the one to explain things to his own family. It was shortly after I returned that I didn't feel as well as I thought I should, so I went to a doctor, who told me that I was going to have a child. Well, then I sent Art an airmail letter and told him the news. But I couldn't wait so I called him long distance and asked him if he had received my letter and he said, "Yes. I think it's simply wonderful; get out here as quickly as you can." I worked for another month until I had earned enough money to go out West. And Art was really happy to see me. When I began asking such questions as, "How will this child be raised? In what religion?" all Art would say was, "Let's wait and see. If it's a girl, there's no problem." But I asked, "What if it's a boy?" And again he said, "Wait and see." And this is the way I went through nine months of pregnancy.

It was awfully hard on me. I would have liked to have known what was what. During that time, when Art had a furlough we came back to St. Paul and Art and I stayed in my sister's apartment as opposed to his home. But I knew that it was because there really was no room there. Other members of the family were now living with his parents.

ART: We both wrote to my parents regularly. My mother really liked Sally. They got along well. Much better than I had expected. Of course, Mother and the others all kept talking about Sally converting to Judaism. They wrote to me too and always stressed the same thing. They said it was necessary. That is what they believed. Well, when John was born Sally was given good care in the hospital.

SALLY: At this point I must tell you my side of the story. I didn't know that, all the while, the family—including Art—were planning to have John circumcized like a Jew. They did all that without my knowledge. They had a regular religious service, gave John a Hebrew name, and by virtue of all that, he became a Jew. After it was all over they told me, and, of course, I cried bitterly. To do that to a child without my even being consulted! There was nothing for me to do. I was so upset that after Art had gone back out West and I got out of the hospital I went to live with my sister. I took the baby and went over there. I was very unhappy there. But Art's mother and his sisters came over to see me very often. They were lonesome for that baby. Well, their kindness sort of won me over, so, one day while she was visiting, I asked Art's mother if I could come to live in their home and they were overjoyed. Art's family were all very good to me.

ART: I was on the move again. They sent me from the West Coast back to the South. So when the baby was about five months old, I phoned Sally and asked her to come down there with the baby, which she did.

SALLY: Although I was happy with the baby and Art's folks had been so good to us, I felt that I was losing my own identification. Art had asked me, as long as I was living in his mother's home, to refrain from going to the Catholic church because he felt his mother wouldn't stand for that. So I didn't go inside a Catholic church as long as I lived with them. I was forbidden to go. But while I was in their home I really learned a lot about the Jewish religion, about their customs and practices. I didn't know why meat and milk couldn't be mixed but I found out. Like Art told you, she kept a very Orthodox home.

ART: I was discharged from the service shortly before the war ended. Sally, John, and I moved back with my folks because it was so difficult to find an apartment. We lived with them for about eight or nine months.

SALLY: We got along well. I won't say that conversion was a daily subject but it seemed to me that it crept in almost daily. His folks kept bringing it up. His mother especially. Art wanted more than anything else to fulfill his mother's wishes if it were at all possible.

ART: Well, they were my wishes, too. After the birth of my son it became important to me also.

SALLY: I guess there just was nothing else to do. I couldn't go on living like that. It was just too difficult. The pressures were too great. However much I felt that I was a Catholic, I really did appreciate these good Jewish people and their religion. I felt at home with them so, finally, one day, I decided to talk to a rabbi whose name I had heard. He was a very fine, gentle soul. He explained that I would have to take a series of lessons with him as my teacher. I agreed, provided that Art would also take these lessons with me, because I felt there was so much about his religion he couldn't answer and didn't know. The rabbi thought this was a great idea. So I told Art about what I had done and he agreed to take the instructions with me.

ART: You may wonder why, if my folks were so Orthodox, we went to a Reform rabbi for instruction. We both felt this would be better for both of us, especially for Sally.

SALLY: The Reform Church *was* better for us. And besides, Art's folks accepted this when I told them what I had done. They were just happy that it was going to be done. Art's folks respected that rabbi very much. I had heard his name mentioned in their house very often, and, always, with great respect.

ART: The rabbi met with us in the afternoons because I already had gone back to my music and was again playing in the hotel band.

SALLY: I was very sure by then that I was going to convert. I was sure that it would please my husband, and I wanted to please him. But I figured too, that it was better to have one religion in the house, especially since my son had already had the "Briss" (circumcision) performed which made him Jewish. I said to myself, "I'll try and do it." I was reasonably sure; let's put it that way. My conscience was bothering me, but it was bothering me, first, one way and then the other. It would bother me if I didn't do it and it would bother me if I did. I didn't have to worry about what my parents would have said because they both died shortly before I was married. I never discussed this matter of conversion with any other members of my family because I felt it was something between Art and me. If I had, I'm pretty sure I would never have gotten an affirmative answer from any of them—that, I know.

After six months of instruction, I was formally converted by the rabbi in his temple. It was very simple. It was a matter of signing a statement that I would regard myself as a Jewess and that I would rear my children as Jews. And shortly after that there was the Jewish marriage service. That was the *second* service for us. All of Art's family attended. It was beautiful.

Of course, Art and I became members of that Reform temple. The rabbi had asked us to, for reasons that are understandable. He felt that by belonging, we would come to the services and he could, the better, keep an eye on us. But we have really only come to the services on the High Holy Days and never to any of the Sabbath services except special occasions, like when my boys were Bar Mitzvah or friends' children were involved. But really, we have no friends there.

ART: But we really tried to keep a Jewish home. That is, Sally tried, but she stopped after a while.

SALLY: That's because it didn't seem to mean anything to Art or his family. The fact is, I went back to Judaism for thirteen years. I lit the candles on Friday night and I said the Kiddush (blessing over the wine) because Art worked every night and was seldom home. But none of Art's family outside of his mother did it. His sister and sisters-in-law not only didn't do it in their homes, they laughed about me doing these things. I just gave it all up. It wasn't my own family that influenced me to give these things up. When they all found out, about a year after the conversion, about what I had done they didn't speak or write to me for about a year. They felt I had made a very grave mistake. However, after a year's time, we all got together and wiped out the differences and went on from there. They took the attitude that "it's your bed, you lie in it; it's your baby, not mine."

At any rate, after thirteen years I was still trying to find something to cling to—something that would give as much meaning to my life as Catholicism had given me but, frankly, I couldn't find it. There was nothing in Judaism that I wasn't able to accept, but it wasn't enough. So often I have made the remark and I will make it again—I think Judaism is a beautiful religion. I think your holidays are magnificent. I think your rituals are all wonderful. But for me to revoke what I have been taught to believe is difficult. I don't know if it would have been easier if I had been given something more, added to my belief, rather than subtracting from it.

If my husband had himself been a more religious Jew (but knowing his work I can readily understand that this was not possible), perhaps my response would have been different. It's really hard to know. I do remember complaining that I attended the synagogue only once a year. To me that was not enough.

I needed something more. After having prayed to Jesus for so many years and now, to turn my back and say, "I don't believe any more that you are the Son of God"—I can't do that.

My sons were all Bar Mitzvah at the synagogue that Art's parents belong to. They did what we asked of them. My daughter is now attending Sunday school at the temple that we belong to.

When my father-in-law died, we dropped our membership in the temple and became members in his old synagogue. That seemed to us the decent thing to do. But after a few years we came back to the temple. I even joined the temple sisterhood thinking that maybe *that* way I would feel closer to Judaism, but I felt rather more like a hypocrite. I found myself hating myself. One day I told Art, "I can't live with myself this way at all. I *have* to go to church—I have to go back to the Catholic Church. I have to go to church once a week." I recall saying that if my going displeased him so and would not enable us to get along, I would let him keep the children and not mix them up any more and just go my own way.

ART: That was hard for me to take and I asked to think it over. I took a long time at it because I realized how serious this was, but, finally, I told Sally that I felt she was needed by us but I would not object to her going to church. But I also told her that I felt quite sure that this wasn't the answer.

SALLY: I have been going to church all these years since then. I have attended mass, but I did not go to confession. And I was still unhappy. That was because I couldn't accept communion unless my marriage was blessed by the church, and you know it was not.

Well, this has upset me all these years. I investigated the possibilities of that phase and, no matter what priest I talked to, I was told that my youngest child would have to be baptized. Finally, I talked the whole thing over with a priest in the town I had lived in as a child. He said he didn't believe that any of my children would have to be baptized, but any *future* children would have to be. He said he thought he could work this out fine.

What this meant was we would have to be married again, but this time by the priest and Art would have to promise that all future children would be reared as Catholics and, of course, baptized.

All this time I would tell Art what the various priests had said, and, of course, this was no simple matter for either of us.

ART: I thought about this a great deal. I figured we would have to take our chances as to whether or not there would be any more children. We weren't getting any younger, that's for sure. But the possibility of our having more children *did* exist. Because Sally was so unhappy I was willing to have the priest marry us once again if all the rest could be worked out and if Sally could stop being so upset. Still, Sally couldn't really get any commitment by the local priest to bless our marriage without baptizing the other children. That, I simply wouldn't permit.

SALLY: Believe me, I talked my heart out to that priest and, one day, he phoned me to tell me that he would do it. I guess the whole thing didn't take more than three weeks to get arranged. The priest performed the ceremony, and my sister and brother-in-law were present.

ART: My family didn't know any thing about this. I never told them a thing.

SALLY: There was no point to it. His sister might have guessed it, but his family feel that this is our business.

ART: And since my mother had died a few years earlier and she was really the only religious one in our family, I didn't feel that it was important for them to know. But our children know all about it.

SALLY: I was the one who told them. I made Art quite unhappy by telling them even after he had asked me not to, but I was very much afraid that if I didn't tell them (in the first place, I wasn't ashamed of it, and, in the second place, if ever anything happened to us both at the same time the children would be dreadfully confused if my family stepped in and said: "We're going to bury your mother as a Roman Catholic"), it would all be very unfair to them. They were old enough to understand. So I sat down one night and told it to the boys and their reaction was this:

"That's O.K., Mother, but don't ever change us. Leave us the same religion," and "I'm real happy for you, Mother, because I know how happy this must make you."

All the children know that I go to the Catholic Church. But I have tried very hard to impress them with the fact that what they believe in is just wonderful for them. I have said that it isn't the wrong church they belong to—it's right for them. And *mine* is right for me. My youngest son still asks me questions about Jesus and what kind of a Jew he was. I try to answer all questions so as not to confuse him or the others. Every once in a while they ask me to go to temple with them, and, because Art still works in the band at night, I go with them. I remember once, just after we had come home from a Temple service, that my younger boy said: "You know, Mother, isn't it too bad that everybody can't be the same thing?" I said, "Yes, it is. It's just too bad. Someday I hope they will incorporate Judaism and Christianity to make one religion out of them. I think that the Jewish Holy Days are beautiful. They were the Holy Days that Christ observed when He was on earth, and to me, it's just a continuation, really." That's the way I look at it.

ART: But all this really has created emotional problems for me. As far as the fact that she went back to her Church is concerned, if that's all she wanted to do and that's what made her happiest I couldn't deny that wish. But I certainly wish it had worked out the other way. I don't really know how it has affected the children because they discuss this more with her than with me. At night I'm gone and they are home with Sally. During the days, they are gone and I am home trying to catch some sleep.

There *is* a new problem, however, and whether it has come from all this, I don't know but it has to do with my oldest son.

SALLY: He is going to be married next month to a Gentile girl. He started going with her when he began living on the university campus. Things got pretty serious before I was really aware of it. The girl is a Methodist. My son is not converting to Christianity, but I'm not saying he never will because I don't know. At this point, he says he has no intention of giving up his religion.

I will say that when he came home and said to me, "Mother, how would you like some Methodist grandchildren?" and he sort of laughed, I replied, "This is not a funny question and you are not going to get a funny answer." I said I was going to give him a right-from-the-shoulder answer. I would not object to any kind of grandchildren providing he and the girl would make their decisions long before that ring was ever put on her finger and the answer would have to be agreeable to both of them. Further, they would have to follow through with what they had promised to do and not wait until children would come along and then decide. That was my advice.

ART: They are going to be married in the Methodist church by a Methodist minister. I was surprised that he would do it without my son being baptized, but he says he doesn't have to. As a matter of fact, the minister even offered to leave out the words of the blessed Trinity or whatever else there is in the service which he thought might offend my boy. But—and imagine *this*—my son said he replied, "No. Do it the way it's supposed to be done."

How did I react to all this? I wasn't even consulted. John is a very hardheaded boy. I kind of lost contact with him when I found I couldn't change him to think along my lines. I gave up trying to change any of his ideas. As a matter of fact, I'm very much upset over the whole thing! But how could I expect my son *not* to marry out of the Jewish faith when I did?

SALLY: It's hard to say exactly how I feel about John's marriage. I would be happy if all my children married Catholics. That's a perfectly honest answer because, if I said "No," then why am I a Catholic? If the other children marry persons other than Jews, I hope it will be to Catholics.

Paul Jordan

Q: As one of the most noted Unitarian-Universalist clergymen in the country, the story of your conversion from Roman Catholicism to your present religious philosophy has special interest for us. What

brought this change about? What about your parents and family?
What role, if any, did they play in your religious conversion? How
did it all come about?

P.J.: Well, as you have already suggested by the questions you ask,
my parents and, indeed, the community from which I came played
a considerable role in my religious evolution. It would be best if I
told you the pertinent facts about them.

My parents lived in the town of Collano, Kansas, when I was
born. They were both Roman Catholics. In addition to myself,
there were two half sisters and four other siblings. My father had
been married before and his first wife had died. By that marriage he
had two daughters, one of whom lived with us. In the second marriage, I was the oldest child.

My mother's parents had lived in Kansas and Missouri. Her
family had always been Roman Catholic. My father's family came
from Alsacia. They had always, insofar as I know, been Catholics. I
think that they were both good Catholics. My father, I suppose,
would be a typical male Catholic. He was not especially devout.
Practical matters were as significant to him as matters of ritual.
He practiced Catholicism, to be sure. He attended church regularly,
but he would not go to communion more than once or twice a year.
My mother was a truly devout Catholic as were the children. The
half sister, older than I, lived with us until she went off to a convent
and became a nun. Ours was a pious and devout Catholic home.
For a small town I would say that it had a rather devout Catholic
population, although the Catholics constituted only about ten percent of the total population. Protestants predominate.

In our home we recited morning and night prayers as well as
grace after meals. I attended the Roman Catholic grammar school
and the Roman Catholic high school in my home town. My brothers
and sisters also went to these schools. Attendance at these schools
was quite automatic. There was nothing philosophical about it. It
was too uncritical to have been thought about. We were Catholics
and that was the tradition. Being members of a minority group in
that Midwestern community might have been an added factor that

kept us especially close to this Catholic way of life, but it was primarily the result of our determination to be good Catholics that kept us on this path.

Q: Tell me more about your parents. What was their educational background? How did your father earn a livelihood? What were their interests?

P.J.: My father was a cabinetmaker. He could not tell, one week to another, whether he was to be employed or out of a job. I think that it is proper to describe our family as relatively impoverished. Father was relatively unschooled. He had had a little schooling in the Old Country but not much. He was about seven years old when he came to this country. He spoke English very well, as did my mother. But, of course, my mother's family had lived in this country for two or three generations. I do not know just how much schooling my mother had. My father was considerably older than my mother when they married. I think that Father was about thirty and Mother was around eighteen or nineteen years old.

I was the oldest child of this marriage. As I indicated, my father had been married before and his first wife had died. Of the two half sisters, both were good Catholics. I had a younger brother who was, I think, less dedicated to the Church than I was. (I became an altar boy, beginning with the first grade, and I kept that up until I was a senior in high school.) At least, my brother remained and is a good Catholic. He still lives out in Kansas. But a younger sister was married outside of the church. She too is a Unitarian. She married a Unitarian. All through our years, I think it proper to say that we were good Catholics—not only my parents but the children as well.

Q: What about your higher education?

P.J.: Well, I started at Creighton University, which is a private school in Omaha, Nebraska. I had the choice of two schools with the offer of a scholarship to either school. Both were Catholic schools. I chose the Jesuit school, which will tell you something about my own emotions. I made the choice myself. Both had made flattering scholarship offers and, naturally, I was pleased.

Q: Was it taken for granted that you would naturally go on to a Catholic school?

P.J.: Well, in my case it certainly was. You see, the Church was interested in pointing its good students in the direction of the Church. It hoped that such people would turn toward the priest-hood.

From the very earliest years, even when I was a young altar boy, I seemed to be heading in that direction. Being an altar boy brought me behind the communion railing, so to speak. It brought me into proximity with the priest. Psychologically it brought me into the celebration of the mass. It required unusual labors in behalf of the Church and brought me close to the central celebrating process of the Church.

By this means and, probably, by way of the recognition which is given the good students, all along the way, I moved closer to the hoped-for goal, ordination as a priest. The priest gave those of us who made a good school record recognition all along the way. For example, the priest might hand out the report cards in front of the class and he might say to this one or that one, "Keep that up and you will be good enough to become a priest one day." This kind of thing begins early and it gives you ideas about what to do with your life. The priest might express appreciation to an altar boy who had gotten a good grade. In front of the other kids he would say, "It's good to see you so frequently at mass," or "Here is a young man who gets up every morning at seven o'clock, comes in for mass at eight, and serves at the mass." Or "This is a really good indication. God may have something in mind for you."

Psychologically they were all pointing me in the direction of a priestly vocation. My parents, the priest, the Church, and the Catholic community—so it seems as I look back at it.

This was true, also, in the case of my half sister who became a nun. She was interested in education and everything pointed to her going into a teaching order. Today she is the Registrar of a major rural Catholic school in the West. Even though I have left the Catholic Church and, for these many years, am a Unitarian minister, we have continued our correspondence right straight through the years with only occasional lapses.

Q: You noted before that you chose to attend a Jesuit school. Was there some special reason for your choice?

P.J.: Well, the orders in Roman Catholicism are, each of them, in some sense representative of different personality types and approaches with the Church. The Jesuits were intent upon cultivating and developing the intellectual phases of the faith. They are among the foremost intellectual leaders, educational leaders. They are the defenders of the faith with Reason and the Mind as instruments. I deliberately chose Creighton University because I guess I rather admired this approach. I wouldn't say that I really did it on the basis of a well worked-out philosophy on my part. I did it unconsciously, I guess. But I only went to Creighton for two years.

Q: And then, things began "happening" to you?

P.J.: They sure did. This was "the beginning of the end." But really, in order to understand how the change in my religious life came about, I will have to go back to my high school days. When I was a sophomore in high school I started to work in a bookstore in my hometown. I would work at odd hours, after school, Saturdays, and during the summer. Well, a bookstore *is* books. The store sold textbooks, fiction, magazines, including the better magazines. Among them was H. L. Mencken's *American Mercury*. By the time I was a junior, I was regularly reading the *American Mercury*. This little bookstore was a kind of intellectual center for the town. As a consequence of all these contacts, through books and people, I found that I was crossing the line outside the fellowship of the Catholic faith into the Protestant community. In meeting persons who came into the store I was supposed to know something about the magazines or books and I got to know the people who were reading and who were thinking.

I carried on discussions with these people, about books, ideas, the contents of the magazines, particular articles, and so on. So far as I could see, there was no relationship between what I was doing then and what happened a couple of years later, but now, I am sure there was because Mencken had a way of fighting the tradition, fighting all orthodoxies. However, I didn't know that at that time. What was happening to my point of view, as I look back at it, was that I was crossing over from a Roman Catholic point of view of accepting authority from the Church. Unbeknown to myself, I was cultivating intellectual and critical attitudes in regard to everything. I was picking up ideas from books and magazines as well as associating with people in the local community who were doing the same thing. This shift in attitude to "now, let me see" and "what do I think?" was taking place culturally in this little community of intellectual life around the bookstore. My intellectual rebellion was beginning. It was something more than adolescent rebellion, I believe. This revolt is carried on pretty much quietly in relation to one's own family. In a sense, this was happening also, to one of my sisters. She sensed what was happening with me.

Q: How did you get along at Creighton?

P.J.: During the first year, I got along normally well, I guess. It was during that year that I had an experience with a priest who was, I think, an alcoholic. He was so lackadaisical about his celebration of the mass that I complained to him about his treating the mass lightly. There were other things too, that distressed me about him and the manner in which he conducted himself as a priest. You see, I had been taught the ideals of the Catholic Church as a youngster.

Intimate relation with the Church, as I experienced it insofar as this priest was concerned, helped me to see the prevalent practice. The gap between the ideal and the practice is noticed by a sensitive, dedicated youngster. On the basis of such things, the rebellious youngster, the adolescent youngster, automatically finds reasons for criticism.

I think that I was about twelve years old, when I found myself dedicating myself to the priesthood. In our town we had an Irish Catholic priest who was a very good preacher but not very interested in people. I can still recall him standing at the altar ready to sing, the altar boys seated on either side of him, looking toward the altar, not at the congregation. I can remember his criticizing the congregation sometime after Christmas in this poverty-stricken, lower-class, Roman congregation, because they hadn't given him as much in the Christmas collection as he had received the year before. And this collection went for his summer vacation in Ireland. I recall his giving them thunder. This sort of thing distressed me. As it happened that morning before I came to church things had not gone well at home. I had come to church expecting some peace when, instead, I was greeted by this petty display by the priest. I can remember sitting there with a growing anger at his yelling and screaming at us because we didn't contribute as much as we should have to his trip to Killarney planned for the next summer. I am sure that I was very profane in my thoughts. I couldn't help but think, "You ———, you don't know nor do you give a damn about the people in this parish. You are out to exploit, to get everything you can, and you call this religion. If I ever get a chance, I am going to KNOW people and where they live and what they do and in this intimate knowledge of them, I shall try to serve them in a way you apparently can't even imagine!" What I was thinking was, "You are such a bad priest I'm going to become a better one if I can." All this, mind you, at the age of twelve!

Q. You mentioned that "things had not gone well at home." Is there some situation of which you are specifically thinking?

P.J.: I guess that my father would not, by any stretch of the imagination, be regarded as a teetotaler. Every once in a while he went off on a bender. Well, this didn't "set well" with my mother and us kids. We would pray for him. We were on the side of my mother, who felt that he was breaking the Commandments. I identified my mother's view with the Church view. For me, they were one and the same. The Church view of life was the ideal. It was distressing, yes, disturbing to find such wide gaps between the ideal and the real practices of people. Some people become anticlerical as a consequence but they stay in the Church. Despite the growing number of critical attitudes I was taking, I had no idea about leaving the Church. I still intended to become a priest—but a good one, concerned with people, intimately, wholly. That is why I continued to take it for granted that I should go on to a Catholic university and continue to plan to be a priest.

When I left high school, I was possessed of what I still believe to be the most rounded religious faith in the supernaturalist tradition that has yet been evolved by the minds of hundreds of thousands of men and women working together over centuries. The Catholic faith into which I was born answered, for me, all the questions, not only of my life on this earth but it answered all questions concerning a future life which in this faith is as real as the present and more vital. It offered ways and means of avoiding eternal punishment in hell. It offered ways and means of achieving eternal life in heaven. My faith in Roman Catholicism was clear and strong and keen and, indeed, I was dedicated to it.

As I left high school, I knew what I wanted to do with my life. I was possessed of the best faith in the world and I wanted to help that faith to grow even stronger in the world than it was. I wanted to share the good views of this point of view with others in the world. I wanted to help people avoid the pitfalls of hell. I wanted to help them achieve an eternal life of happiness in heaven. I wanted to be a priest!

I wanted to tackle what by definition in that faith is the largest and most important and highest vocation to which a man may aspire, a vocation in which one communes with God, one in which in a miraculous way—one believes at least—one brings God to men and . . . as a human being with this goal before me and this faith to sustain me and to gird me, I had bright expectations, not only of a life hereafter, but of a life here and now.

Parents in a Roman Catholic society, as their highest aspiration, hope for a son who will be a priest, and mine were more than interested in my wish to enter the priesthood. And, of course, the school community in which I had grown up, in which I had gained some reputation for achievement, was one which was, in its entire body, happy to applaud this stated goal of the priesthood.

Leaving high school was, for me, a happy occasion of entering into the life of the religious institution of which I was a part, entering into it with zeal, dedication, entering into it with the hope of a creative good life in that faith, and after death, for all eternity.

But all this feeling did not push all the H. L. Mencken views and barbs out of my mind. At the university I asked questions, many questions, of my instructors. I didn't know at the time that I was really asking them of myself. I thought that I was asking them of my superiors. I thought when they told me, "This is a mystery which you cannot understand," and I'd ask them, "How could a human mind which cannot understand this mystery *possess* the mystery?" I thought they would give me some other answer besides the one I got. The one I got was, "It's a mystery and we don't understand it and the thing for you to do is to go out and pray about it." Well, there was a time during the latter part of my sojourn in that university when I was actually, literally, spending a larger part of my day on my knees in the chapel than I was seated either in the library or in the classroom. If praying was what it took to get over doubts, then pray I would do, and I did. And yet, I found more and more, as I prayed more and more, that my mind wouldn't stay on my prayers. It returned over and over again to those doubts, those discussions, those out-of-class arguments with other students and in-class arguments with professors. How frustrated can you get asking, "Why?" and "How?" and being told, "There is no answer" before something happens to you?

Increasingly, without my knowing it, I was becoming more and more angry at this frustrating faith which told me that it was the most reasonable faith existing. Asking may be a sin because asking may lead you to lose your most precious treasure—your faith. And yet, I had to ask, and asking was told over and over again, "There is no answer." Once—once, at last, when I was out of more classes than I was in and on my knees more than I was in the library or in class—once, I asked a question and got what seemed to me to be an answer that validated all of my right to doubt, an answer which, it seems to me, is a *Protestant* answer, an answer which gave me some little sense of self-respect in trying to "find out," using reasonable intelligence.

I asked a question in a consideration about war, the kind of war the Roman Catholic Church will sanction, and the kind of war which the Church will not sanction, and about the soldier who fights the war which is sanctioned or which is not sanctioned, and about the attitude of the soldier who may kill in a war which *is* sanctioned or *is not* sanctioned by the ecclesiastical institution. I was told that if a person went to war, in a war which the Church has sanctioned as a "good war" and went to war believing he was doing his patriotic duty by his nation and by his God, since the Church had sanctioned the war, that man, if killed in that war, could feel himself to be a hero and sinless. I was told that, in the same kind of war, if a different man went into it, though the Church had sanctioned it and said it was a holy cause, if that man went into that war believing that any person he killed was from his point of view a murder on his soul, *then,* if he killed, he *did* commit a mortal sin. Now, here was a place where, *not* the Church but the *individual attitude* toward the act of killing another human being would be determined as punishable by hellfire for all eternity. That is, a mortal sin (if the soldier believed it was murder) was the result in one case; whereas if he believed he was doing his patriotic duty he had the right to feel like a hero.

This was the beginning of the end of my Roman Catholic faith. For here, inside this "apologetics" class, I had found validity for my right to doubt. Here was an assertion inside the Church that an individual and what he thinks is going to determine whether he goes to hell or goes to heaven. It all depended upon what the individual thinks about it. And I am afraid that, with this fortification, they could no longer succeed in getting me on my knees to pray when they told me to stop doubting. From then on, I got "out of hand" as they said. It was only a matter of time until I got out of the theological school.

Those were difficult, trying days for me. Where does a fellow whose sister is a nun, who is well known in his home community, who is known to have gone off to college to be a priest—where does such a fellow go? What does he do? Should I go home and be an insult to my parents and to my nun sister? Well, I didn't go home. I felt I couldn't go home. I decided that I ought to travel around a little. "Bum" was the word we used. And "bum" it was. I needed time to test my ideas. One of the tests I used was to dare God. I remembered the saying, "If you curse God, God will strike you dead." And, I remember cursing God one bright, sunshiny day. "If you exist, God, damn you, God!" I said it just like that. Cold, "Come on, hit me!" I remember that the notion came to me to try it again, a few days later. I was "on the road" in a terrific thunderstorm down in the southwestern part of the United States. The clouds were black and the thunder was roaring and the lightning popping. And I got to thinking, "Now wait a minute. Could there be a relation between what I said a few weeks back and my being in this storm?" I thought about that for a while and I finally decided there might be some relation. If I really meant what I said, I had to do the same thing over again, right in the midst of this thunderstorm. So I walked out into that storm and walked out under a tree and I said, "All right, this is it," and I said my curse all over again. "And if he wants to strike me, let him strike!"

This is a kind of experiment that may seem ridiculous to you, but remember, I was nineteen years old, and bit by bit, the faith, the goal, and point of view were leaving me. It is not a pleasant thing, after one has gotten, in general, "the whole Truth" to find that one has nothing left except a fear of hell which, I reasoned, might really be there. For several months I did everything I could to push myself to test whether this hell would swallow me up, as they claimed it would. I felt I had to. In the doing, I did a thorough job of degrading myself and my old faith, committing most of the sins the church had told me were bad. I *had* to do it!

I remember one time, hiking up from Taos, New Mexico, up toward Colorado Springs in some rather bleak, semidesert, mountainous country. I was walking along a road which was probably a thousand feet higher than the valley floor below, and, as I walked around a corner of a hanging ledge, a cold blast of mountain air hit me and blew off my hat. It circled down the road and then blew off over a cliff. I watched it go and watched it fly down until it hit bottom and then I went over the side of the stone ledge, and, with my feet dangling over the cliff, I thought, "Why shouldn't I go after the hat—the short way—right down?" I had nothing to hold on to. I just didn't believe in anything, I mean I didn't. Not heaven, not hell, not God, not this earth, not life, not death—nothing. Nothing mattered for me. It was then that I really contemplated suicide. There seemed to be nothing left for me—no more goal, no expectations of doing anything but hurt those in the loving group in which I had been brought up. I knew enough then to know that a Roman Catholic could not understand the position I was getting into and certainly could not approve it. What was there to go home to? Not father, not mother, not brother or sister, not old friends, at high school and have them all say, "Hah—you started out to be the best and now—you're nothing!" There seemed no reason at all why I shouldn't commit suicide.

I was in kind of a vacuum, like the silence of a room, and then, vaguely, dimly, I heard a sound—just a sound. It was enough to distract me. It drew me out of myself. I looked to see where the sound came from and tried to identify it. It was a mockingbird in an old scrub pine tree, a hundred yards up the side of the hill, and it was singing. I looked at the bird for a while with a terrible concentration. And suddenly I was ashamed of myself. I don't suppose that the bird believed in heaven and hell, life eternal or punishment or reward. I was sure that bird wouldn't live the normal span of my life, probably only a year or two or three. No, it was just a piece of protoplasm flung up by the universe, mounted in that pine tree, singing in the sun of an afternoon, just singing and bursting its life with what seemed awfully and suspiciously like joy to me. I was suddenly ashamed of myself. Probably for the first time in months, I was ashamed of myself. For here was a blob of life, living the life it had to live—one day—one year—what matter? It was living. Sensitive to sunshine, enjoying apparently what it was living. Life might not be long or easy for that bird. But it was singing with what it had to sing with!

Well, I didn't commit suicide because even though the big goal and all I had been conditioned to believe in had somehow been taken away from me as the consequence of my own doubt, even though the important goal of the priesthood had vanished, and even though I could not go back home without some real sense of shame and torture to myself and others, I found that there was something left. And that "Something" was life itself!

I had been bumming about for around seven or eight months. I had, all that while, been reading and studying but, as the result of that experience on the cliff, I realized, "I'm alive! I've got to live!"

I came back to my hometown. It was a difficult time for me, especially with my parents. My mother was hysterical over the whole thing, as were the others. But my father was basically all right. His general view was, I think, "What you want, you've got to do. That's *your* business, not mine."

With a few dollars I had managed to earn, I opened a little bookshop in the town. Gradually some of the "intellectuals" in the community came in to look, to buy, and to talk.

Q: How did you discover Unitarianism?

P.J.: Well, one of the persons who came into the bookshop very regularly was the Unitarian minister. We always engaged in conversation. I found him most stimulating. After a couple of years, he said to me, "You ought to be a minister." His approach to religion was chiefly aesthetic, poetic, existential. I got to know him very well through our discussions in that bookstore. He came around there at night. He had lost his wife, so he naturally gravitated there in the evening. We carried on long discussions even before I found out who he was or what he was. Finally, after a couple of years, he asked me if I had ever thought of becoming a minister.

Once he asked me this question, I knew just as clearly as anything that I was sunk. The more I thought about it, the more certain I was that I should do just exactly that.

About six or eight months later, I had things organized so that I could go to the University of Chicago. I lost a lot of credits when I came to school but that didn't really matter. I was at school again, enjoying my courses in philosophy, sociology, history, education, and English but I got my degrees—a Bachelor of Science at Chicago and a Master of Divinity at Meadville Theological School.

Life opened out for me from then on. At the university I discovered what I would call an enlightened faith. I developed an appreciation of culture, Jewish, Christian, and so on. I became what I think may be termed "a religious person." In addition, I became a Judeo-Christian. I mean that that Christianity is very shallow which doesn't recognize itself as, in some sense, a heresy stemming from Judaism.

After my ordination, I went to a Unitarian church in Massachusetts, just outside of Boston. I spent a few happy years there and then went on to accept the pulpit I now occupy.

Q: How does one formally become a Unitarian?

P.J.: I suppose he becomes a Unitarian or Universalist when, by virtue of his attending a particular church, he feels he wants to join it. When he joins, he signs the church membership book. When churches bring a good many new people in every year, they will normally have a series of lectures for new members. I lecture on the history of the church as well as the history of the local church. I spend some time on the history of Unitarianism. I give from four to eight lectures.

Traditionally we like to say that the method of conversion is the slow, gradual change rather than the emotional, romantic change such as Billy Sunday would have recognized. But it can be accompanied by emotional experience. It can be a sudden transformation, but, usually, it isn't.

The Unitarian Universalist is a *free* church, by which we mean that in it individuals are free to be their own deciders in matters of faith, and each church and fellowship in the association is free to be itself, in its own way, as each person in them is free to be himself. "We have not only a right to think for ourselves in matters of religion but to act for ourselves also, nor has any man whatever, whether of a civil or Sacred character, any authority to control us, unless it be by gentle methods of argument and persuasion." That is the comment of Jonathan Mayhew, made in 1794, which exemplifies the spirit of the Unitarian Universalist movement. The emphasis is upon "gentle methods." The right of the individual to differ and the pluralistic nature of our churches and fellowships are respected; there is no bar to search for common faith in the free church.

Each person has a right and duty in the free church and each church and fellowship has a right and a duty in the free church to judge what is true and to do what is right as each believes it. As an article of faith then, all liberal truth seekers posit what, so far as we can know, is an infinite, eternally and essentially interrelated reality that is to be sought, to yield to us both map and motivation for our living.

I subscribe to this statement. I agree with it wholeheartedly.

The commitment aspect may be involved in an emotional experience in some depth, but basically we like to talk about it as the use of reason in religion, and this means the intellectual, critical approach. We talk about freedom in faith. We talk about freedom in fellowship. This means individual freedom. Of course, there is a good deal of anticlericalism among us.

I am happy about my change to Unitarianism. I simply could not have remained a Catholic. Today, the freedom of the individual mind, the use of reason, the living of one's life for the sake of living —these are the ideals that have special significance for me.

It was natural for me to come to Unitarianism. There was no other way for me.

Linda and Joe Buxbaum

LINDA: I am a Negro. About fifteen years ago I married a fine Jewish man. Our marriage has been a good one—a happy one. I think that since I converted to Judaism our marriage has been even better. Perhaps that is because there is a certain degree of unity that has been brought into our home as a consequence of the formal conversion. It may be, too, that our little daughter thinks of herself as a Jew. Because that gives her a religion, it also makes us both much happier.

My folks had lived in the South. My father had some land down there—not very much, to be sure—but he was better off than a lot of the Negroes down there. He had gone through the eighth grade in school. My mother had about the same amount of education. They were married in their little community and lived a good number of years down there. There were only three children—one boy and two girls. I would say that our relationship was good. We got along well. And all of us children got on very well with my parents.

My folks were Southern Baptists. They attended church services regularly. My mother was the more religious of the two. I guess my father, even though he attended church, was not really as religious as my mother. But the pattern of the family was definitely religious. The children attended church, of course. And I did too. I still remember the preacher's high emotional pitch. It was the kind of church that made clear that hellfire and damnation were the lot of anyone who failed to live the good life. It was really a very emotional church, and most of its philosophy was hell and damnation.

We moved up North, into the Midwest, because my parents realized that there would be greater opportunities for all of us, my father as well as the children, if we came up here. My father got himself a job and he held it for all the years he lived. Of course, we had our financial problems, but we managed somehow. All of us children went to school; first, the elementary school, and then on to high school. We all graduated from high school. I managed, somehow, to continue my schooling. I got jobs during the day and then took courses at a local college in the evenings. I'm happy to say that I got my A.B. degree. From my high school days, I became interested in science, and later, at college, I majored in it.

My sister also went on to college where she got her degree. But I went into teaching as a career. Since my graduation, I have been fortunate enough to get a really good teaching position (I'm in an elementary school), and things have gone rather well for me.

I never really had any major problems because I am a Negro. Certainly there have been no special problems in my teaching position. We always lived in an interracial area—there were Negroes and whites around all the time. In the school where I teach, I have whites as well as Negroes in my classes. Of course, I have had special problems because of my skin coloring. From my earliest years, in school and out, there were problems. Sometimes there were taunts from my playmates; sometimes, it was some remark made by strangers or by those to whom I applied for a job. But I cannot say that this was really a source of distress to me. It was just something you had to learn to live with and adjust to. Sometimes there were people who wanted me to identify myself, not as a Negro, but rather as a Mexican or as a Puerto Rican in order that I might be more acceptable to their families, who objected to Negro people. All in all, I would say that there wasn't really any open hostility.

My high school days were happiest for me because I did well in my schoolwork and also because I won some honors at school. I was elected to the National Honor Society and I was a member of the student council. I liked sports, too. So I participated in things and was, generally, well accepted by the other kids.

I got along particularly well with my mother and sisters and brother. My father was not an easy man to communicate with. I couldn't carry on much conversation with him. I guess it was his nature to be that way. There was nothing really wrong or unkind about him. It was just that we couldn't talk to each other. But, as I say, things went well between my mother and me. Both parents were proud of how well we kids did in school, and that was really enough.

It was about my senior year at college that I met Joe.

JOE: I am a teacher also. I had been working in Linda's hometown for about a year when one of my friends, an older man who worked at the same place I did, suggested that I meet Linda. I don't recall that Harry even knew whether I was Jewish. Certainly he didn't ask and I never told him. I didn't think that it was important, one way or the other. Harry was a broadminded guy, and he assumed that everybody else was as broadminded or liberal minded as he. He took it for granted that a liberal attitude toward people was right and proper. Just how he happened to know Linda I do not know. I don't recall ever asking him. I didn't talk too much, even in those days. I did my job as best I could and I let it go at that.

You see, I am rather dark complexioned. Some people have mistaken me for an East Indian, while others thought I was a Greek or a Mexican. But all that really didn't matter to me. If they knew that I was Jewish it was all right with me. If they didn't, it just didn't matter one way or the other. I do not believe that I was ever mistaken for a Negro. If I had it would have made no difference to me. I do not think that my skin coloring had any real effect on me and my attitude toward others, or, for that matter, to myself. Perhaps it did, perhaps it didn't.

I had only lived in the Midwest for a short time before I got the job at manual labor, as the result of which I met Linda. Originally I had come out of New York. In fact, I was born in New York. I spent all of my years, until my early 20's, in and around New York. I lived with my parents in a very Jewish neighborhood. It was really very Orthodox. Now, not everybody was really Orthodox, but it was certainly regarded as an area where there were pious Jews. My mother was certainly more Orthodox than my father. I don't have too many recollections of my father because my parents were separated about the time I was Bar Mitzvahed at age thirteen. I can't quite remember whether it was just before or just after the Bar Mitzvah. But I associate it with my Bar Mitzvah.

Both of my parents were born in New York. They were average people. My father was a laborer. He didn't have more than a grade school education. I don't think that my mother had more than that either.

I remember that I used to go to the Talmud Torah (Hebrew school) after public school hours. I went five afternoons a week. I had two brothers and two sisters. They were all very much younger than I. As I recall, I was about nine years older than the youngest. I went on to high school and then on to City College of New York, where I took a business course in the evening school because I had to work to help pay my tuition and help out the family as well. My brothers and sisters did not go on to college. I had to interrupt my education when I enlisted during World War II. I guess I wanted to get military service over with as quickly as possible. I served overseas. When I came back I went back to college, got my degree in business administration, worked at a variety of jobs, and then decided that I wanted to become a teacher.

During all those years I didn't go out very much. In fact, I would say that I seldom dated. I just wasn't interested. Even when I decided to come to the Midwest because jobs were so scarce in the East, I never really got around with other people very much. I happened to find a job as a manual laborer when I came to Linda's town. I was lucky to get a good paying job. I figured if I saved some money I could continue my education and become a teacher. That was my plan.

I really didn't have very close ties with my family. My brothers and sisters were around but we didn't talk much. I knew very little about them and they knew little about me. Although the relationship with my mother was good, I cannot say that it was excellent. My mother kept a kosher home, but I didn't care about that sort of thing. She was working most of the time to support herself and us kids. And she worked very hard! But there were no close ties between us. Even though my mother was religious, I certainly wasn't. My religious education had to come to a sharp ending when I was thirteen. I don't think I went into a synagogue again until just about the time Linda and I joined the temple following Linda's conversion to Judaism.

I cannot say what drew Linda and me to each other. Maybe it was because we were both interested in education. Maybe it was because we were both liberals. Whatever the reason or reasons (and there may have been many), we got along fine. I don't recall ever being concerned because of her skin coloring. Could it have been because my skin too was so dark? Honestly, I cannot answer that. I certainly don't think so. But we got along fine.

Linda and I never raised questions about her being Negro and me being white. I don't recall that it ever really concerned us. I did not hear anything about it from the few friends I had. Certainly Harry, who introduced us, never spoke about it. Of course, neither of us had many people we called "friends," and those we had were very much like us in their views. Differences in skin coloring would not really matter. We went together for about a year. We saw each other frequently and we decided to get married.

LINDA: Joe makes it sound very easy—as if it all happened without any stumbling blocks in our path. This is really not so. I remember that my parents and, in fact, all my family, were very much upset when I told them I was planning to marry Joe. It was a question of color, *not* religion. My immediate family wasn't very happy about it. They raised questions about the problems that might result from marrying a white man. My aunts and some of my uncles didn't like the idea either. They had a deep-seated resentment against white people. The whole idea as far as they were concerned was not a good idea. Even some of my friends who had gone to high school with me objected to it. They said that if I married Joe they wouldn't come to the wedding—and they didn't. Still I feel that the pressures were not more than usual for such a problem involving persons of different races. My parents, after all the discussions, simply said that, as far as any feelings against Joe were concerned, they had no objections but, insofar as the interracial marriage was concerned, this, they said, would have to be a decision of my own.

Now Joe and I had never really talked about religion. I knew that Joe was a Jew, but he didn't go to synagogue or observe anything that was distinctly Jewish. Yet, Joe knew that I was religious in some degree. I always went to church. I regarded myself as a Baptist, even though I certainly wasn't a very good Baptist, because I didn't really believe everything that was considered part of being a Baptist, or for that matter a good Christian. My intellectual outlook was different from that of my folks. I used to go to church because most of my friends were there, young people of my own age. There was always a highly emotional excitement in the church, and every time we went there they would tell us about hell and damnation and fire and all that. Well, that wasn't really my idea of religion. I don't know that I even accepted the idea of the divinity of Jesus. I went along with the idea but I don't think that I completely accepted it. In fact, I would say that I just can't accept it. I didn't accept the idea that Jesus rose from the dead or the idea of resurrection. Nor do I accept the idea of the Virgin birth. I didn't then, nor do I now, think that Jesus was more divine than any other human being. I guess that even though I somehow thought of myself as having religion, it wasn't the kind of religion I knew as a child in my parents' home or in the church. I knew that Joe didn't believe these ideas either. So you can see that talks about religious differences between us weren't very important. I knew that Joe was a Jew, but that only meant that his mother and father were Jews. It didn't affect us in one way or another.

JOE: Linda went to New York once, before we were married. I had asked her to visit with my mother and give her my greetings. I guess I wanted to see how my mother would "take" Linda. I wasn't sure that my mother knew anything about the fact that I was going with

Linda or that we planned to be married. Now, as I look back on it, I guess that she must have suspected it at that time but she didn't know for certain. I remember that she treated Linda very well and wrote that "Linda is a nice girl." When I finally came to New York myself to tell her that we were going to be married she took it hard. I would say that she became hysterical. There was much wailing, much crying. She asked such questions as "Why did you do this to me?" and "What are my sisters going to say?" It was a really difficult time for me, not because anything my mother said would have changed my mind but rather because my mother was carrying on so. It is strange that my mother, who always considered herself a liberal-minded person in such matters as race, suddenly stopped being a liberal when the issue got too close to home. It was distressing to realize this inconsistency. She had always said that she wanted her sons to marry Jewish girls and she was pretty positive about it. But why that was important she never explained. But really, it wasn't a matter of reason that was involved. That was the way she *felt*. It was a matter of emotional attachment, I guess. Anyhow, Linda and I decided to get married soon after that, and it was a clergyman who officiated.

LINDA: I cannot recall that we ever really talked about religion before we got married. But I knew that I wanted a religious ceremony, and when I mentioned this to Joe there was no objection. We were married by an Episcopalian priest in the chapel of his church. He was a great liberal priest. He was very well known for his civil rights activities. He was a white man. Inasmuch as we were both so very much concerned with civil rights, it seemed that he should be the man to officiate. We both respected him very much. We knew that he would understand us, and we hoped that he would officiate at our marriage. It was an Episcopalian service. But as part of the service there was mention of "the Father, the Son, and the Holy Ghost." Joe's mother, despite her feelings about our getting married (and it was a racial matter with her rather than a religions issue), had come to the Midwest in order to attend the wedding. Well, you can just about imagine what happened when Joe's mother heard these words. She just about fainted. She didn't say anything immediately following the ceremony, but later she said, "Everything would have been all right if that minister hadn't mentioned the Father, Son, and Holy Ghost." I guess it's one thing not to be a religious Jew, but it's quite another to hear a definitely and clearly Christian doctrine used as a part of a ceremony. Suddenly it is not just simply *non-Jewish*. It is actually Christian!

My parents came to the wedding, but my aunts and uncles who had objected to my going with Joe—all of whom had been invited— did not attend.

The relationship with these people in my family hasn't really improved very much since then. I speak to them when I see them, but nothing of any importance is ever said. We say "hello" and "good-bye" and little else. The relationship with my parents has been very good. Joe and I visit them all the time. Even though Joe's mother was so upset by the marriage ceremony, she was always friendly until her death just two years ago. Whenever Joe came up to New York, he would stay at his mother's home. We were never there together, so I do not know how she would have reacted if she had seen us both together in her home.

JOE: My brother intermarried with a Protestant girl, but I don't think that my mother ever really knew that the girl wasn't Jewish.

LINDA: But Susan was Jewish. Don't you remember that she was converted to Judaism by a rabbi? Surely that makes her Jewish.

JOE: Well, anyhow, I still think of her as *not* Jewish. Maybe it's because I question what this conversion really meant to her. Conversion is not easily undertaken. If it's done, it should be done right.

Since Linda and I were married we hadn't really talked about religion very often, and even when we did it wasn't really anything deep or weighty that we said. It was only after Joan was born that the conversation would get around to these subjects every once in a while. But, again, I say, there really wasn't anything very important about what we said. Linda went to church whenever she felt like it. I never went to church and I never went to synagogue.

I don't know just how it came about, but one day another teacher happened to remark about a certain rabbi in our town who was doing such wonderful work in the field of civil rights. I knew about his efforts of social justice, and, even though I had never met him, I had respected him as a truly great liberal. This fact became associated with conversations I had had with Linda about little Joan's upbringing. Somehow, even though I was not a religious Jew, I hoped that Joan would receive some kind of training that would make her aware of the fact that she was a Jew. Linda felt like that too. Well, one day, after school, I stopped by the synagogue and met the rabbi. As I told you before, I hadn't been inside a synagogue since I was Bar Mitzvah, and it was quite an experience for me.

I met the rabbi and had a good talk with him. I told him all about Linda and me. I told him about Joan and how we thought that she should begin to get some knowledge about the Jews and Judaism.

He heard all about my being a non-religious Jew and about Linda's feeling for religion even though she had outgrown her parents' religion and church. As for myself, I felt that I would like to join the synagogue, but I certainly couldn't speak about Linda's views or whether she was interested in converting to Judaism, because she hadn't come to any decision on this point. I was concerned about whether or not she could become a part of the congregation because she is a Negro. There really wouldn't have been a problem otherwise. Now there had never been any discussions between us before marriage about Linda's converting to Judaism. I never expected that of her. In fact, I could really see no good reason for it. I was not a religious Jew and there seemed no reason to enter into that kind of a situation. The rabbi was very considerate. He pointed out that if Linda wished to convert to Judaism he would help in every way, but that he knew that some people in the synagogue would not welcome Linda with open arms, even as he knew that there were many people—all whites—who, also, would not be welcomed. He expected that some people would be friendly and others would not. He felt that some folks would receive us as a couple, while others might not, but that this would be pretty much what we had discovered in all our relations with the society of which we were a part. When we walk down the street together, some people take a long second look at us—while others seem to take it all as perfectly natural.

LINDA: I suppose one might say that my decision to convert to Judaism came to a head with the birth of Joan. I regard myself as a religious person even though I do no longer accept the views of the Christian church with respect to the divinity of Jesus and other doctrinal matters. I believe that a child should receive religious training. I believe that it is the parents' duty to provide that kind of training. And I don't think that decisions with respect to such matters should be left up to the child. I think it is up to the parents. I think that once you have given children a strong religious background they have something to hold on to, and they can make better adjustments in the future. I feel that way. When Joan reaches adulthood and we have done the best for her that we can and we have given her the best background and religious training that we can as well as the best social outlook, we can then, and only then, let her be the one to make decisions. But at least we will have given her the best that we have to offer.

I think that I decided to convert to Judaism because, however my husband felt about religion, he is a Jew and his daughter should know her father's heritage. Inasmuch as I was so negative about the basic teachings of Christianity, I would not really be giving up anything I really treasured. I thought I might actually find myself much more at home with Judaism's views. Besides, it seemed to me that unity in the home was a desirable thing. I certainly wanted that in my home.

Joe certainly did not urge me to convert. It was my idea. The fact that he consulted with the rabbi before talking to me about it only means that we understand each other. I was not doing anybody any favors by converting. I wanted it for my daughter's sake and for my own sake.

I studied Judaism with the rabbi for over six months. The study sessions took place in the evening because, as you know, I teach school. Joe attended the first session with me and has not come to any class since. What impressed me with the Jewish religion was that you have more of a background of learning. You have ideas which are acceptable to people who themselves lack acceptance. You are allowed to reason and to think about whether you accept these ideas—and you don't have to accept them on face value. You can question and discuss them with a rabbi when you are confused. Besides, you really don't have to make a real "cut-and-dried" decision as to whether you are going to hell or whether you are going to heaven.

It took me about a year to make a decision about conversion. There was discussion between Joe and me. But he said that the final decision was up to me. If I wanted to convert, then I would have to get in touch with the rabbi. I did that on my own, independently of Joe.

JOE: I want to make it clear that even though I was a non-religious Jew, I always identified myself as a Jew even when making any contractual arrangements. I always wanted to be certain that people identified me as a Jew, that is, as a member of a specific ethnic group. I really do not have any special interests in nor do I have contact with the Jewish community although there is a large one where we live.

LINDA: The books I studied with the rabbi were very helpful. I think I gained an insight into Judaism and felt the close resemblance of Judaism to much that was happening and had happened in the Negro world. The story of the Jews' slavery in Egypt and the fight for freedom took on new meaning for me. When the formal conversion ceremony took place, I received the Hebrew name "Ruth" (because, in the Book of Ruth, we are told of Ruth's conversion to the faith and people of Naomi). My mother and father did not know that I was preparing for conversion. But after it occurred, I told them. I think that my mother was more or less satisfied that I had accepted some kind of faith because, for so long, she had seen me drifting. My mother told my father about my conversion. I did not discuss it with him. As I told you earlier, it has always been difficult for me to talk to my father.

I believe that my conversion has worked out rather well. I feel that much good has resulted from it. True, we seldom attend synagogue services, but that is primarily because of Joe's and my teaching hours. It is simply too diffcult for us, what with our school assignments, papers to grade, and our concern for Joan. We try to be with her as much as possible. Joan goes to Sunday school at the synagogue. She is happy there. At least I don't know that she has any problems other than the one of color. Inasmuch as the other children in her class are white and she is the only one who is brown, she wants to know why she is brown and why she isn't like the rest of the group. I tell her that everybody is made different and that it takes all kinds of people to make up the world and that everybody is not the same color.

JOE: I tell her that one color is not better than another color. They are just different.

LINDA: And Joan accepts this. But her friends away from the synagogue are Negro children. Joan goes to an integrated school and she plays with both whites and Negroes. It is her white friends who raise the question of why she is brown. I think that she is still debating this. We had an amusing situation one day when a neighbor's little boy who goes to the same Sunday school said to his mother: "Mommy, you know that the only Jewish friend I have is Joan." What will happen in later years, I, of course, do not know.

As far as the ritual of Jewish life is concerned, we do not observe very much. We know when it is Sabbath, of course, but we do not do very much about it. We do not observe the Passover Seder. Once we did when Joe's mother came to our home and made a Seder Passover meal. We light the candles on Hannukah, but we also have a Christmas tree in our home. We explain to Joan that we have a Christmas tree because of my parents. You see they visit us during this season, and we think we should satisfy them. If we tell them that we shouldn't have a Christmas tree they wouldn't understand. They think we would be depriving Joan of something because all the other children have one. So it's simple to have the Christmas tree.

Christmas is just a holiday that has no religious significance to her at all. Joan knows the story of Hannukah and all about the Maccabees. We do not observe Easter in any way. We go to services in the synagogue on the High Holy Days. On Sundays we bring Joan to Sunday school. We are not active in the synagogue because of our school work. That absorbs most of our time.

The attitude of the people in the synagogue toward us is, generally speaking, pretty good. But that is not true of all of them, of course.

We do not belong to any specifically Jewish organizations. About the only one I belong to is a national ladies' organization that is concerned with bettering human relations. We do not participate in Jewish philanthropies, nor are we interested in the State of Israel. Joan has a schoolmate who lived in Israel and she knows from him about Israel, but that is about all.

JOE: If we had more time and even if we had a choice of organizations, I might be more interested in professional teaching organizations; but that is about all excepting that we might take an interest in some civil rights organizations. We do not belong to the Urban League or the NAACP or CORE or SNICK.

LINDA: When Joan grows up and thinks of marriage, it would not be offensive to me if she decided to marry someone of another religion. I would be a hypocrite if I felt that way because I did the same thing myself. Both Joe and I feel that the religious problem is infinitesimal as compared with the racial problem. If Joan has a good religious education and is capable of making decisions at all, she will be able to take the religious problem in stride. Let her have something to hold on to and she can make adjustments in the future. The choice of religion is up to the individual. When she reaches adulthood, we can only let her be the one to decide.

As for us, we are both pleased that we joined this synagogue. It has done something important for us. What the future will bring, we cannot possibly even guess at.

5. *Types of Converts*

THREE DISTINCT KINDS of converts are to be noted among the forty-five whose life-stories are recorded here: (1) *Pro Forma converts,* (2) *Marginal converts,* and (3) *Authentic converts.* Each is distinguished from the others by certain noticeable characteristics.

The Pro Forma convert has no real interest in conversion as an end in itself. He has an ulterior motive that is most often associated with the desire to marry a person of another faith. He may be concerned with the establishment of some degree of religious "unity" within the family. He believes that a formal submission to conversion will, somehow, "satisfy" his partner in marriage and his spouse's family. In order to meet this requirement, he undertakes to convert and meets all the legalistic and ritual requirements that the church or synagogue, through its clergy, demands. He studies, he memorizes, and otherwise prepares himself so that he may achieve the ultimate goal he has set for himself. He is to be compared to the college student who has registered for a course in which he has not the slightest interest but which, once passed, will provide him with the college credits he needs for graduation. He may pass the course with a high mark and yet acquire absolutely nothing from all that he has studied simply because he has no real interest in or concern with it.

The Pro Forma convert observes all the rules; he follows the forms and meets all requirements except the basic qualification of sincerity of purpose. He is a nominal convert, a convert in name only.

I knew full well that Ann would not accept me unless I converted to Roman Catholicism. Frankly, I had no religion of my own. I had long ago ceased to be a Protestant. Whatever I knew or had read about Catholicism had not impressed me. Ann's family too made a point about my turning Catholic. It was clear to me that I could not hope to get Ann to marry me, so, without any religious convictions of my own and certainly with no particular concern for her religion, I volunteered to study for conversion to Ann's religion. I studied all the texts and lessons, I answered all the questions and joined in the discussions with the priest and others, always being very careful to answer in the approved way until I was informed that I would be officially converted. I went through the ceremony and all the ritual involved without thinking twice about it. All the instruction had really not changed my views. I still didn't really find anything in this religion or in any religion that made me want to make a real commitment. But frankly, I don't think it mattered much. I married Ann. Her parents accepted me. Our children are being reared as Catholics, and from time to time I attend church. It all means nothing to me.

* * *

It wasn't that I was a really good Protestant. In fact, I had not been inside a church in many years. My parents, themselves good Baptists, were very much upset with me because of my lack of concern or interest in their church or *any* church, for that matter. Ruth wasn't really any more religious than I. Her folks weren't what you would call devout Jews. They attended the synagogue only on the High Holy Days. Ruth's brother was Bar Mitzvah and Ruth had gone to Sunday school. But there just wasn't any religious spirit in her family or in Ruth. Yet, when it came to the matter of giving their approval to our marriage, I couldn't get them to agree unless I converted to Judaism. I was very much in love with Ruth and Ruth loved me. There was no question about that. So we talked it over and decided that, whatever the reason, we would have an unhappy time of it with Ruth's folks unless I converted to Judaism. That's why I went through with it. I found nothing offensive in Judaism; nothing that really disturbed or distressed me in anything I studied. But I knew that I wasn't really going to be much of a Jew. Certainly neither Ruth nor I had any idea about observing Jewish ritual and all the rest. We were content to "go through the motions," to accept what I had to, to do what I was supposed to until we could set up our own household and live exactly the way we wanted to.

Ruth's parents didn't probe for my motives. I guess they really understood that I was serious only about wanting to marry Ruth and nothing else.

I cannot, to this day, understand why her parents made such a fuss. Ruth thinks that it was because they wanted their friends to think well of them. Maybe that was the reason. But it might have been one of a dozen reasons.

My formal conversion satisfied them. Now I was a Jew in name. Our lives haven't been particularly Jewish since the conversion. We have Jewish friends but we have Christian friends also. Our children have gone to a Jewish Sunday school and we belong to a temple. But that is all surface stuff. I can tell you honestly, it really doesn't mean a thing.

*   *   *

Although I was born into a Catholic family and even attended a parochial school in my early years, I wasn't a very good Catholic. I did things to please my parents. As long as it made them happy, I was happy. When Doris, who is Protestant and whom I loved very much, told me that her parents would object to her marrying a Catholic, I told her the truth, that Catholicism meant nothing to me and that, if it would make her happy, I would convert to her faith. Doris told her parents what I had said and they, much to my surprise, readily agreed.

There really wasn't much to it. Doris took me over to meet her minister and we had a nice talk. I really didn't tell him how I felt about religion and I certainly didn't say anything that would really let him know how I felt about joining any church. Maybe he knew, maybe he didn't. He seemed so pleased to have me as a convert that he made it all very easy for me. So, in this way, I pleased Doris and her family.

I must say that my own parents were very unhappy about it all.

But they liked Doris so much that they let things go as they were going. I have joined the Baptist church. Our children are being reared as Baptists, and everyone seems pleased. But, I assure you, I am no different today than I was before I became a Protestant and a Baptist. Whatever change has taken place has, I think, occurred in the attitude of Doris' parents toward me—but in no other way.

* * *

My primary concern has always been "family unity." Even though my husband was not a religious Jew, I know that his family always identified with the Jewish people. I am still not certain that they had very much religious feeling but they certainly regarded themselves as Jews. Why my becoming a Jewess officially should have mattered to them, I really do not know. But it seemed important to them, that I be a Jewess officially. Because I value family and unity in the family and because, quite frankly, I had no religious moorings of my own, I decided that the proper course for me to take was to convert to Judaism. I did this not only for the sake of unity in the family but also because my daughter ought, so I thought, to know that she was a Jewess. It would then make things easier for her to identify herself. I am happy to say that things have worked out very well for us.

* * *

My husband simply had no religious feeling. He was a Jew but a very poor one, I think. When we were going together before our marriage, he told me how his parents felt about a mixed marriage. I was so in love with him that I offered to convert to Judaism if that would make his parents happy. I believe that is the only basis on which they would accept the marriage. I was pleased to do so particularly because my husband was working in his father's business. It would have been tough for him if his father decided to fire him out of the business. So I went through with it. But all the while I have been troubled because despite the conversion, I really still feel that I am a Catholic. And I have never gotten over the feeling that I am living in sin. Even though my children go to a Jewish Sunday school, I feel like an outsider, a traitor to my own church. The rabbi said that I was a fine student and, later, a good Jewess. But, believe me, I feel more like a hypocrite. I went through the forms but I still feel that I am a Catholic.

Should we change the names of the religions in the above excerpts we would discover the same attitude in 26 (57.7 percent) of the 45 converts studied here.

Although many converts begin marriage in this frame of mind, it should be noted that in some cases a gradual change of attitude occurs, and more positive degrees of acceptance of the new religious affiliation are manifested. In one case the joy expressed by the convert for her adopted religion is so genuine that there is the temptation to include her among the "authentic converts." With this one exception, however, all the others have used conversion as a means toward an end—a marriage that is psychologically strengthened by a nominal "unity of religion." It may very well be that if this purpose is well served as a consequence of conversion, there is good reason to believe that the formal conversion has justified itself. Religionists, however, dispute this line of reasoning. They point out that conversion should have, as its primary purpose, the full, wholehearted, and sincere acceptance of the adopted religion in terms of its ideals, values, attitudes, and religious practices. When these are wanting, there is little reason to be sanguine about the significance of the conversion.

The Marginal convert is distinguished by a desire to retain ties of some kind with the religion of his origin even though he has converted. He is represented here by 5 cases or 11.1 percent of our group. He lives in two worlds, with two religious philosophies whenever possible and is not completely "at home" in either. He celebrates Christmas *and* Hannukah; Easter *and* Passover. Such a convert often feels that his marriage has not been properly "blessed," if, having been born into a Catholic family, the marriage service was conducted by a minister or a rabbi. This type of convert, if a Jew who was originally a Christian, cannot understand why Jews will not accept Jesus as the Messiah. He is sorely troubled.

It was not an easy thing for me to make the decision to convert to Judaism. After all, I had lived all of my life as a Catholic. I had gone to Catholic schools and I had attended church regularly. Even though there were things in Catholicism that displeased me, such as the authority of the Church, I was nevertheless a Catholic. When I finally converted to Judaism, I really did so in order to please my husband's family more than for any other reason. I thought I was doing the right thing. What could be more important than to begin my married life in the spirit of unity? But when my first son was born, I remember how I cried when my husband and his family took it for granted that the child should be circumcized according to Jewish rites. This, I knew, was not the Catholic practice. . . . All through the years I was upset because my marriage had not been blessed by a priest. Of course I knew that a rabbi would officiate at my marriage, following my conversion. But it is one thing to know that this would happen and quite another thing to experience the sense of shock that it was a rabbi and not a priest who conducted the service. This bothered me so much that, after twenty or more years of marriage, I prevailed on my husband to be married once again in the Church where the priest could bless our marriage. It's a rather strange situation, I know, being converted to Judaism, belonging to a synagogue, and all that, and still feeling that I am really a Catholic.

In many cases, the clash between two divergent religious philosophies does not appear to be as sharp as the situation described above. Nevertheless, an undercurrent of uncertainty, of mixed emotions and equivocation, may readily be discovered.

I had always been a Protestant. In fact, there were many members of my family who were noted Protestant clergymen. When I converted in order to marry my husband, a Jew, you may be sure that I did so with every intent to live my life as a Jewess. God knows that I have tried to do exactly that. Yet, my children tell me that I am really not a good Jew; that I am mixed-up, and that often I waver between Judaism and Christianity. They insist that I often do and say things that make it clear to them that I am really standing outside Judaism, looking at Jews and at Judaism as if I were really not part of it. Can it be that they see things like that in me? But how can any person whose earlier years were spent in a good Christian home really act as if all that past could be erased from one's mind and assume new and different religious obligations without having problems and uncertainties?

Marginality, if these forty-five life-stories are taken as a sampling, appears most clearly when the marriage involves a Jew and Christian. It seems far less of a problem if a Protestant or Catholic intermarry or if a Roman Catholic and Greek Orthodox intermarry because Christianity is the common denominator of both.

By marrying my husband, who is Greek Orthodox, I found that I really didn't have to make any great changes in my thinking or in my way of life. I had been a Roman Catholic. We had always believed in Jesus as the Son of God. After all, I was still a Christian. What proved a little more difficult for me was getting used to the Greek people, learning their ways, enjoying their foods, learning a little bit of the Greek language. Conversion to Greek Orthodoxy really didn't bother me. In fact, I would say that was easy. It was the other, the differences between the Greek people and the Irish, that was hardest to adjust to. As time goes on I hope that this problem will be overcome.

Marginality, I think, is also evident in the several cases involving Jews who have converted to Roman Catholicism who speak of themselves as "Jews of Roman Catholic religion." That some such persons have found it necessary to organize themselves into a fellowship consisting solely of converted Jews seems to me to indicate a desire to be both Jews and Roman Catholics at one and the same time. There is no question in my mind concerning the wholehearted devotion and sincerity of these persons insofar as their religious affiliation is concerned. Nor are their motives for conversion to be questioned. I had, in fact, classified most of them as "authentic" converts from the point of view of their religious views, but, because of their acknowledged relationship to the Jewish people and its culture, I have now classified them as marginal. They are obviously sincere and authentic Catholic religionists who, at one and the same time, retain certain ties of identification with the Jewish people. They have no ulterior motive, to be sure; and yet, according to the tenets of Judaism, the act of their conversion to Roman Catholicism means that they have ceased to be Jews, both in terms of religion and in terms of Peoplehood. However much these persons may protest this point of view, it is nevertheless the view of Judaism, whose definition concerning its own nature must prevail. Under these circumstances, then, the marginality of these converts becomes evident.

The Authentic convert is a term I have borrowed from Hebraic sources. The Hebrew is "Ger Tzedeck" and it means the convert who, for reasons purely *intrinsic,* has converted to his new religion. Such a convert does not adopt his new faith for reasons either ulterior or negative. He does not convert in order to overcome a personal insecurity, nor does he accept a new and different faith because this may help to assure a happy marriage. This type of convert is concerned only with finding what, to him, is the "true" religion. He is determined to worship God and to serve Him with the fullness of his heart, mind, and soul. This concept, it seems to me, applies equally well to all converts whose motives are purely intrinsic, be they Protestant, Catholic, Jew, or any other religious philosophy. Authentic converts are to be found among all groups, but, as I see them, they are a minority.

Among the forty-five whose stories I have recorded, I have found fourteen persons (31.1 percent) whom I classify as "authentic converts." The test I have used in all instances is a simple one: Has this convert *any other* motive for conversion than the desire to find the true God and serve Him to the best of his ability? This concept will be best comprehended by excerpts from these case histories.

I was never happy with my religion. As an Anglican I was reared in a good religious home, but, almost from the time I became able to think for myself, I found great gaps in my feelings for the church or Christianity. I simply could not accept the theological suppositions and positions of the church. I read a tremendous amount of literature on Christianity in all of its branches and about Judaism and the religions of the East, as well. Although I found myself being drawn closer to Judaism than to any other religion, I was certainly not ready to make any decision that would officially take me from the Christian Church to any other. It was only because, at a much later time in my life, I happened to visit a synagogue on the High Holy Days that I became especially moved and impressed, not only with the beauty of the service but with the meaningfulness of the liturgy as well. I then began to read and study in earnest. It seemed to me that I was on the right road.

My studies resulted in my having many questions that, alone, could only be answered by a rabbi. So I summoned up enough courage to visit with the local rabbi, raise my questions, and listen to his answers. The more often we met, the more certain I was that, at last, I had found the religion that most clearly approximated truth to me. After a very long period of discussion, debate, argumentation, and study, I came to feel that Judaism was the answer that I really had been searching for all these years. My children were already grown and married. My wife and I were alone. We could do what we felt was right. When I talked over the possibility of conversion to Judaism with my wife, I found that she was not ready for this drastic move even though I was. She agreed that, whether or not she converted, I ought certainly to follow the dictates of my heart and mind, and I agreed. That was when I saw the rabbi once again and told him that I wanted to undertake an organized, carefully directed course of study that would, ultimately, lead me on to conversion. The rabbi was most helpful. He gave me all the time I required over a period of approximately one full year. You see, I wasn't in any hurry. It was most important to me to be absolutely sure of what I was doing. I studied hard and I read much. All the while the appeal of Judaism became stronger and more meaningful to me. I wanted to worship God, the Jewish God, the one God who was the source of all our ethics and morality. What is more I wanted to become a part of this people whose long and memorable history had moved me. There were no ulterior motives. I had nothing to gain materially, prestige-wise, or any other way. Simply put, my great, burning desire was to become a religious Jew. When I converted to Judaism in the presence of my rabbi, it was the greatest moment of my life. I worship God daily, I attend services regularly, and I have had the privilege and the honor of leading in the services as well. I have learned some Hebrew in order that I might the better know the language of the Prayer Book and the Bible. Since that moment of conversion I have, I feel, become a better man. I feel completely at home with Judaism and the Jewish people. I do everything I can to further my knowledge and understanding of Judaism. My wife did not convert to Judaism until two years after my conversion. She was not ready for it. But today she too is a Jewess and a good one. We are happy with what we have done. It was the turning point of our lives. Now I know the meaning of "spiritual enrichment," for those two words describe our experience.

Paul Jordan is another whom I would classify as an authentic convert. He began life as a Roman Catholic. Both he and his parents —indeed, all his family—believed that he would ultimately become a Roman Catholic priest. All of his education was directed toward that end. Yet, after years of preparation in Catholic schools and colleges, Paul finally became convinced that he could not, in all truth, accept Catholic doctrine. The months and years that elapsed between the time he made this discovery about himself and his ultimate decision to leave the Catholic Church and become a Protestant minister were trying ones for him. At one time, the intellectual and emotional burdens became so heavy that he thought of suicide as the only solution to his dilemma. But, fortunately, reason and common sense returned in time to get him to examine Protestantism and, at a still later date, Unitarianism. Paul is today one of the most noted Unitarian ministers. He has arrived at his religious philosophy slowly but primarily on the basis of reason and study.

Possessed of an exceedingly sharp and keen intelligence, thoughtful and learned, Paul is, in my view, an authentic convert to an unorthodox religion. He preaches to and serves his fellowman with dignity and honor. He is, I think, as much an authentic convert as is the most orthodox and traditional of converts.

Benjamin Chasin's life-story also supports the definition that I have given of an authentic convert.

> I came from a good Jewish home. My parents were Orthodox and I received a fair Hebrew background. I was Bar Mitzvah like other Jewish boys. In my early years, I really didn't think much about religion, but, as I grew older, I began to read and study not only Judaism but other religions as well. I was particularly moved by what I read of the early history of Christianity. The life of Jesus and His disciples entranced me. I began to ask myself questions about what connection, if any, there were between Judaism, the history of the Jewish people, and Christianity. It seemed to me that God had ceased to communicate with the Jewish people at that point in history where Jesus came upon the scene. I came to believe that God's voice was heard once again through Jesus and that God continued to speak to Mankind through Christianity of which Jesus was the founder and through His Church, the Roman Catholic Church. The more I read and studied the more convinced I became of the truth of this observation. I then began to study Catholicism in earnest. I was not impressed with Protestantism because it was not the first Christian Church. I was always looking for the connecting link between Judaism and Christianity. All of my studies have convinced me that I have found the true Church, through which God speaks to this day. So it was natural for me to turn to that Church and to Jesus. I converted to Catholicism because I want to find God and to serve Him.

Each of these three types of converts has been defined with full awareness that all converts have other characteristics as well. The motivation of the convert must remain the primary factor upon which our attention must be fixed. Whatever causes the individual to consider and ultimately to accept formal conversion must serve as the primary factor that distinguishes one type of convert from another.

There is the likelihood that the forty-five cases of conversion may be regarded as too few in number on which to base this typology. I do no more than suggest that I have attempted to distinguish "ideal types" of converts, a methodological contribution that has significance regardless of the number of cases.

6. *Success or Failure?*

CAN THE SUCCESS OR FAILURE of a conversion be determined with
any degree of accuracy? "Success" and "failure" are, in this instance,
subjective terms and such measurements as we may use in our
assessment must spring from the objectives, goals, and purposes of
(a) the convert, (b) the families related to the convert, (c) the
minister, priest, or rabbi who has prepared the candidate for conversion, (d) the standards and objectives of the church or synagogue
into which the convert has formally entered, and (4) the often confused and confusing views of the friends with whom the convert
come into contact. Each, in his own way, defines "success" and
"failure."

Yet the success or failure of an ecclesiastical conversion can
hardly be judged by these standards alone for they depend, in large
measure, upon how the convert responds *not* up to, or even at the
moment of, conversion but rather over a period of months and
years that follow the act of conversion. The response of the convert
to a given situation or series of situations over the years may prove
much more meaningful than any pledge given at the moment of the
formal conversion ceremony. For example, success or failure may
be judged in part on how the convert actually rears his (or her)
children or what, if any, religious values are emphasized by the convert in his personal and communal life. It may also depend on the
degree of identification the convert develops with the religious community into which he has entered and how these values are trans-
lated in action in the larger community. The values that the convert
incorporates into his home and life are also valid tests of success or
failure.

In the case of Sally and Art Bonder, (see pp. 171–189) for example, Sally formally converted to Judaism, in accordance with the wishes of her husband and his family. She reared her sons as Jews; each was Bar Mitzvah in the synagogue. She and her spouse became members of a synagogue, and, on occasion, she attended the worship service on the Sabbath. Yet throughout the twenty-five years of her marriage she was deeply distressed because she had left the Roman Catholic Church. What is more, through all that period of time, she believed that she was "living in sin" because her marriage had not been blessed by a priest, who represented for her the true religion. After almost a quarter of a century of marriage, during which her husband, children, her husband's family, and the rabbi had regarded her as an authentic convert, she returned to Catholicism and even prevailed on her spouse to remarry in the Church, thereby securing the blessing she so much wanted. It was only after this long period of time that the failure of this conversion became evident.

In the case of Helga and Joe (see pp. 316–318) there was little reason at the time of the formal conversion to believe that Helga would, over the years, become an authentic convert. Yet her sense of indentification with her new faith became stronger and more firmly fixed as time went on. At the time of the interview, two decades after the conversion, it is evident that she is today indeed an authentic convert.

As we have noted, the standards and objectives of church and synagogue with respect to conversion are not uniform. Since creed and dogma are most prominent in the matter of conversion to Christianity, converts are frequently judged on the basis of their affirmation of the creed. Judaism's emphasis is, however, considerably different.

The Book of Ruth contains what is regarded as the classical example of what is to be expected of such a convert. We are told that Naomi, the mother-in-law of Orphah and Ruth, daughters of Moab, pleaded with her daughters-in-law, following the death of their husbands, to "go, return each to her mother's house; the Lord deal kindly with you, as ye have dealt with the dead; and with me. The

Lord grant you that ye may find rest, each of you in the house of her husband." Orphah and Ruth "lifted up their voice, and wept. And they said unto her, 'surely we will return with thee unto thy people.' " But Naomi, with all the eloquence and persuasiveness at her command, urged her daughters-in-law to return to Moab and their own people because she had no other sons whom these two could marry. The Bible tells us that Orphah "kissed her mother-in-law and departed." But Ruth refused to leave Naomi. At that climactic moment, Ruth turned to Naomi and said: "Entreat me not to leave thee, or to return from following after thee; for whither thou goest, I will go; and where thou lodgest, I will lodge: *thy people shall be my people, and thy God my God*" (Ruth 1:1–17). In addition to the pledge of love and loyalty to Naomi, a purely personal declaration, Ruth not only declared her acceptance of the Jewish idea of God but her desire to identify with the Jewish people as well. These two, *total commitment to and complete identification with* (1) the God of Israel as well as with (2) the Jewish people, go hand in hand. They are, according to Judaism, of *equal* importance. One cannot be separated from the other nor can one be accorded greater significance than the other. It is generally believed that Ruth's classic statement is, in fact, an ancient Hebrew formula.

Christianity's emphasis upon formal acceptance of a particular creed, with variations of that creed related to a particular denomination, is equally clear. The divinity of Jesus, the idea of immaculate conception, that He rose from the dead, His role as the Messiah, as well as the belief in His Second Coming are, among others, creedal requirements. It is simply not possible to be a Christian without a particular set of beliefs, all of which are directly related to the central belief in Christ, the Messiah.

However, the use of these criteria alone for the measurement of success or failure of conversion cannot, in itself, assure us of the objective, dispassionate evaluation that is so desirable.

The priests, ministers, and rabbis whose cooperation made possible the recording of the life-stories of these forty-five converts make it clear that even they, the teachers of these converts, could hardly be objective in their ratings of the success or failure of their pupils.

These clergymen, despite their regular, intimate, face-to-face contact with these candidates for conversion over periods of time ranging from one month to a year, were often at a loss to evaluate fully either success or failure. They had prepared them, carefully and conscientiously, for the ceremony of conversion. They were devoted to and serious about their responsibilities, but, often, they indicated that they could, at best, only listen to the formal replies given by these candidates for conversion and judge them not solely on the basis of their formal responses but, even more, on such factors as "sincerity of purpose," "goodness of heart," and other equally intangible factors. Following the formal conversion, the clergy most frequently tended to judge success or failure in terms of attendance at church or synagogue services and participation in church or synagogue auxiliary organizations such as brotherhoods, sisterhoods, Holy Name Societies, and other church-serving circles.

Interviews as well with members of families into which many of these proselytes had married lead to the conclusion that, with but rare exceptions, these converts are almost solely judged by families on the basis of (1) ritual observance and (2) church or synagogue attendance. All too often, families who pass judgment upon the convert are really inadequately prepared to do so inasmuch as they themselves have few positive religious standards or values to guide them.

Conversion should mean that, in addition to the change in ritual practices, certain other changes have taken place in the convert with respect to (1) his beliefs, (2) the values he lives by, (3) the attitudes he espouses, and (4) the degree of identification he has with the people whose ranks he has now entered.

Clearly it is not sufficient to suggest that when the candidate for conversion has ceased to be a "believing" Christian he has become a Jew. Nor does inability to accept the doctrine of the infallibility of the Pope, of itself, make one a Protestant. "Fallen away" Catholics, Protestants, or Jews do not automatically become good or acceptable converts to another organized religion. Persons who are indifferent to the teachings of the church or synagogue of their origin are no more likely, I think, to prove successful converts than are those who, hitherto, have had their own positive religious views. "Ecclesiastical converts," those persons who change their affiliation from one organized church to another, with whom we are presently concerned, differ from the "inner converted" or "twice-born" in that they are seldom positive believers in or active supporters of the faith of the family in which they have been reared. Indeed, in the cases of these forty-five persons, all, with no single exception, had, at some time or other and for a variety of reasons, fallen away from their original church or synagogue. Thirty-five persons had, over a considerable period of time, gradually become indifferent to all religion including their own, while ten, believing that the theological ideas of their original church or synagogue were inadequate, actively sought a new affiliation whose views would be in consonance with their own. In all cases, the process that led to ecclesiastical conversion of the forty-five was gradual. In twenty-six persons it was the direct consequence of a desire to marry a person of a different faith.

Among these forty-five converts, I have not noted any sudden or marked changes in ideas, values, and attitudes from those previously held. When specifically asked, the converts were generally at a loss to point to any real changes that had occurred with respect to their views concerning the nature of God. Converts to Roman Catholicism and Greek Orthodoxy from any other form of Christianity would, of course, not be expected to change their belief in this respect because, generally speaking, this belief is one that all authentic Christians hold in common. In the case of those Jews who turned to some form of Christianity, there had been a falling away from Jewish belief at a considerable time *prior* to the formal act of conversion to the new faith. In the case of those persons who came from Christian homes and whose early religious training was Christian, the failure to accept Jesus as divine or as the Christ is noted long before the thought of conversion to another faith has become evident.

The beliefs of these converts even after periods of time ranging from one to twenty-five years have, in the main, not changed markedly from those they held *immediately* prior to their conversion. Actually, these persons may be regarded as having, long before their conversion, fallen away from theological views generally associated with their former religion. Conversion, in some instances, helps them to acquire some positive beliefs as contrasted with the negations that characterized them at an earlier stage. Now, instead of *not* believing in the divinity of Jesus, they accept the positive view that there is a God and that He is One. Representative beliefs of the converts to Judaism include the following:

If you have been reared in a Christian home and all through your years have come to think of Jesus as the Son of God and, even more, as God Himself, as I did all through my early life, it isn't easy to accept any other idea about God. But, as I grew older, I began to feel that God couldn't really have ever been a person like Jesus was. I began to think of Jesus as having real parents, Joseph and Mary, and I simply could no longer accept the idea that Jesus was immaculately conceived through Mary. I guess as I grew older and learned the "facts of life," I simply could not accept the other explanation. The miracle of birth was wonderful enough without my having to add to it the idea that one woman, somehow, was different from all other women in the way she became pregnant. Added to that I came to feel that it was simpler and even more reasonable to think of God as One, completely One. When I began giving some thought to the matter, I found that I was turning more and more to the Jewish concept of God and, frankly, I began to feel better about it. I felt that I was no longer hypocritical when I accepted this, to me, new idea. Of course I didn't talk about this with my family. They would have been disturbed if not really angry with me for not accepting Jesus as God. But as long as I could hold onto my new belief without upsetting my parents, I was very happy.

When I fell in love with a Jewish boy who had the same idea about God and who called this the basic idea in Judaism, I felt that somehow this was almost foreordained, that I should marry him.

* * *

I had become a disbeliever in Christianity long before I married my Jewish wife. Actually, although others thought of me as a Christian, I wasn't really a Christian at all. I did not believe that Jesus was the Son of God, different from all other human beings. I did not accept the idea that He was born of a virgin or that God had somehow impregnated his mother, Mary. I did not believe that Jesus was other than a human being in every way, a good man in every way, but only a human being like the rest of us. I had long ago ceased to believe in the idea that he had risen from the dead and all the other fanciful ideas that Christianity teaches. So, when I met a Jewish girl whose ideas were so very much like mine, I felt that I had more in common with her than I did with other Christians. Long before I formally converted I think that, in terms of ideas, I was more of a Jew than I realized.

*   *   *

It isn't only that I didn't believe in Jesus as the Savior that made me turn from Christianity to Judaism. Actually, I came, over a period of time, to feel that there must be one God who had a unique Being, quite different from anything that I had learned from Christianity. When I got to know the man who later became my husband, I began to think much more about the nature of Judaism. It dawned on me one day that the Jewish idea of God was really the one I had been groping for—that God was One and indivisible in any way. He had no corporeal form. That pleased me so very much. The more I thought about it, the more convinced I became that, really, this was the idea of God I had been searching for all these years. I began to feel good when I could accept this idea completely by declaring my loyalty to Judaism. Suddenly I felt like an honest person once again.

Examples of the beliefs of converts to Christianity follow:

My beliefs as a Jew had never really been strong. I didn't know very much about Judaism other than what I learned in my own home. We all "believed in God" and we simply let the matter rest at that. But my husband was a good Christian. He believed in Jesus as the incarnation of God, as the Son of God.

The more I got to know him, the more this idea appealed to me. Maybe I was the kind of person who required that ideas be concretized in some way. When I used to think of God, I used to think of Jesus. These two became one to me. Jesus was very real. I knew that he was not God, but He represented all the Godlike qualities to me. It became easy for me to think of Jesus as God. I found no problem at all when I converted to Christianity. Jesus was very real to me.

*   *   *

It had seemed to me that there must have been something wrong with the Jews because God obviously turned His back on them. How could it be otherwise if He allowed Christianity to become a major religion? I reasoned that God was unhappy with this people whom He had originally chosen and that He had turned to Jesus to continue the ideas and values that were important to Him. If God could turn to Jesus then Christianity must be the true faith, the one God really wants us to follow and live by. So, you see, it was by reasoning that I came to the belief that Christianity at one point in human history became the religion God wanted us to follow. It was Roman Catholicism that expressed God's ideas because it was the first church to follow after Judaism. Jesus had founded this religion; at least it was the religion that was based on Jesus and His way of life. So, naturally, I turned to this church.

Careful reading of the personal stories of these converts suggests that long before conversion and the thought of conversion their beliefs have changed to a marked degree, but usually, however, only in a negative sense. As a consequence, in terms of belief alone, conversion for these persons is very easy to accept. In most cases the convert officially affirms a belief or series of beliefs that, for a long period of time, in a nebulous sort of way have approximated his very own.

The falling away from belief in the original faith, the acceptance of the belief in a personal God, the failure to accept Jesus as the Son of God, or the Messiah, the belief that man is *not* born in sin or that he is not inevitably destined to remain a sinner, characterizes the views of most converts from Christianity to Judaism. In the case of Jews who have converted to Christianity, too, the falling away from Jewish beliefs and practices appears to be characteristic. Still, within this latter group, rejection of identification with the Jewish people, in some way, does not seem to occur. The process of conversion for these converts generally begins with denials and negations rather than with affirmations.

"Values"—the second of our criteria—have been defined as "broad categories of desiderata." Allport[1] says that "it is our sense of what is good and right." Whatever we esteem, prize, or approve above other things is a value. Each of us lives by a set of values. Society's values become evident by what it permits and forbids, by what it regards as good and what it thinks of as evil.

I have found no evidence that the values of these forty-five converts have changed in any significant degree, as a consequence of their conversion. Just as they prized "the family," "family unity," "love of spouse and children," before their conversion, the same values are evident after their conversion. Those who have given evidence of their enjoyment of their family prior to the formal act of conversion seem to hold to the same standard thereafter. A series of personal questions directed toward these converts, centering on their values in life, elicited answers that with but two exceptions lead me to the conviction that their values, the goals to which they aspire, the hopes they have for themselves, their families, and society are little different in quality from those which they have held before their conversion. The values or desiderata that people prize in life seem to depend in large measure upon the nature of the parents, the family, and the cultural and intellectual milieu in which these converts have been reared. Conversion appears to have sharpened an appreciation of family life in two cases, beyond what it was prior to the formal act of conversion. In these cases, both persons had experienced an unhappy home and family life. Marriage, following conversion, proved to be very happy. There was an excellent relationship between husband, wife, and children. In both instances the marriages involved erstwhile Protestant women who married Jewish men.

I have never really been interested in "causes" or organizations. My folks never were involved with anything like that and we kids never felt that this kind of thing was particularly important. All we wanted to do was live and let live. Of course, we never harmed anybody. We were all peaceful people. We just weren't concerned with such things as social justice or civil rights or things like that. It was enough for us to try to live good, honest lives and mind our own affairs.

* * *

Well, it depends upon what you call "values." We all had our values such as honesty, truth, and being hard workers. We thought that these were the values by which people should live. Even though we never had very much, we always lived good, honest lives. That's the way my parents had taught us and that's the way we lived. We would never harm anybody but I don't think we would have gone out of our way to help make these ideas a reality for more people.

Now, after my marriage, I am still the same way. I think that, in this sense, no change has really taken place in my life. I don't see anything in my new religion that demands that I should really be different from the way I have always been.

* * *

The things I value most in life are love and honesty. I remember that when I was a child I was always unhappy because my mother and father didn't get along. They were always quarreling or actually fighting. This always upset me so much that I remember saying to myself, "All I really want is love instead of all the fighting and hatred." So when I found the man who really loved me as I loved him, I felt that I had the best thing that life could offer me. I remember too that one of the reasons for the fights between my parents was that my mother would accuse my father of "cheating" on her. We were very much upset when people used to say that my father was "running around" with some other woman. That's what made me come to the conclusion that honesty between husband and wife was so very important. As I grew older, I began to expand on my concept of honesty and realized that it included so much of life that it was really most important. All through my years, I have felt the importance of these two ideas—I value them highly.

I still hold to these values and I think I always will. I am pleased that my religion emphasizes them, as it does. Where can you find any other religion that says that love is the most important value in the whole world?

*   *   *

I have studied Roman Catholicism very carefully and I find that its values are really the same that I had been taught by my Jewish mother and father. Forms may differ but the values remain the same. I have not changed my values in any degree.

*   *   *

I don't recall a single instance when I was studying for conversion to Greek Orthodoxy that I was ever told that my values, the things I prized most or wanted most in life, would have to change if I was to become a good Greek Orthodox. Father Sylvester, who knew me over a long period of time, always told me that he wouldn't consider me as a convert if I were not a good person of high moral standard. All he was trying to do, he said, was to make me familiar with the ways, ritually and otherwise, that the Orthodox followed. He was concerned with the ritual of the church and the home. I've changed these, of course, but not my values.

*   *   *

You may question the values by which I have lived—actually bearing and rearing three children without being married to my husband. I took all the heartache that was involved because it seemed to me that this was better than having my husband be unable to tell the truth to his mother when she would ask him if he was married. Some people say that I have a wrong sense of values, but that's the way it is. We did not marry and I was not converted until my husband's mother died.

Maybe, according to their standards, I was all wrong. But, if I had to do the whole thing over again, I'm sure I would do it again. Each person has his own standards and values. I tried to live by mine. Even though I have converted to the religion of my husband, Judaism, and I know, according to my rabbi, that Judaism is strongly opposed to what I did, I still think that my way was right. It saved my husband grief and, because I have always loved him and still do, that was reason enough for me.

* * *

I don't see any major differences in the values of Judaism and those of Christianity. After all, they can hardly differ so very much if you realize that Christianity is the daughter of Judaism; that it came out of Judaism.

Both want a good world, a peaceful world where people can live together in harmony. Both think of people as the children of God. Both think of God as the Father of all humans. Both emphasize goodness and truth. Both urge us to imitate the qualities of God. The Christian sees the qualities concretized in the person of Jesus. So there is no real difference there as far as I can see.

* * *

The values of Judaism and Christianity are, as I view them, really not different from each other. Each stresses the value of the individual person. In fact, as I came to study the two religions I began to feel that Christianity placed even more stress upon the importance of the individual than does Judaism. In Christianity, each person must accept his faith *as an individual.* You cannot claim adherence just because you are born into a particular family. You cannot say "my mother and father who are Christian automatically make me a Christian." Each individual has to account for himself. And that is what pleases me about Christianity. I am an individual. Whatever choices I make are made by me alone.

* * *

Judaism is an optimistic religion. It reminds me that I must never get discouraged, that the future is going to be brighter than the past. If I am a child of God and His co-worker, I must help to make it so. I am always moved by this idea. It gives me a definite, important place in the world. However much people talk about how unimportant a role humans really play in the world, that we are like little ants and nothing more, I think that Judaism is always saying, "You, man, have a very important role. You can change the world if you want to because your effort, your work really counts. God is counting on you to do His work for Him. He needs you. You mustn't fail Him." I derive great comfort and support from that idea. It helps me to be a better person.

*   *   *

I don't need the idea of a God to help me to live the good life. I feel that man has the human intelligence to do remarkable things with his own life and with the world. If he uses his intelligence wisely, this world cannot help but become better. I think that it is my task to bolster the morale of my fellowman, to help him to realize his own intelligence and his own capacity. Once men become aware of that, they proceed to do a far better job with their lives. They begin to fulfill themselves.

Values, "the desirable end states which act as a guide to human endeavor,"[2] the goals toward which we aspire, the aspirations we have concerning "what ought to be" change so little that we must negate them as a means of measuring change in these converts.

The third criterion by which degrees of change within a convert may be judged should be found in his or her new attitudes toward life.

An "attitude" may be defined as "a mental disposition to act for or against a definite object."[3] Attitudes result "not from one specific act or response but to an abstraction from a large number of related acts or responses."[4] There is a certain consistency or predictability of responses.[5] They dispose us to act or respond in certain ways.

The attitudes of the "pro forma" converts, eighty-five percent of our sample, do not appear to have changed as a consequence of conversion. Every effort was expended through extensive conversation with these interviewees in an effort to discover changes in this area of concern. I can report only that these converts were primarily concerned with making a success of their marriage by consciously avoiding any situation or attitude that would antagonize a spouse or members of the spouse's family. To be sure, the success of the marriage was thereby assured, but the success of the conversion, per se, was not evidenced in any way.

Changes in attitude are clearly evident among those whom I have classified as "marginal" converts. The "marginals" appear to be ready to enter into a wholehearted acceptance of their new religion in a frame of mind that can best be described as positive. They, at the outset, give every evidence of wanting to be wholly integrated into their new religion, but, for reasons that may be nostalgic, with memories of their past relationship to another faith or, perhaps, out of fond memories of the home from which they came and values and attitudes of parents and families, they find it difficult if not impossible to feel "at home" in their new religion. Januslike they turn in two directions, toward the old and toward the new, and are at home in neither. Their attitudes toward the new religion are generally positive but their past intrudes itself to the point where they, like an auto driven with its brakes on, are impeded and even stopped before they can make any real progress.

The "authentic" converts in our sample give positive evidence of change in all respects. The beliefs, values, and attitudes toward the adopted religion are such as to leave no doubt that theirs is an intrinsic change in all respects. Examples of such change are indicated by (1) a convert to Judaism, (2) a convert to the Greek Orthodox Church, and (3) a convert to Roman Catholicism. A convert to Judaism states:

> My attitude toward life has changed as a consequence of my conversion to Judaism. I was formerly a Catholic. Everything I did was, in a sense, regulated and controlled by Catholicism. I would always ask myself, "Is this in accordance with the Church

and its ideas?" But even if I answered my own question posi-
tively I had a feeling of resentment against the Church for trying to control me so completely. Now, as a Jew, I feel that the
Jewish idea of the responsibility of the individual for his own
acts, that he does have free will and free choice, permits me a
certain freedom I never before enjoyed. What's more I no
longer feel like a sinner. This has affected my whole attitude
toward life. I feel as if my choices are my own, but I try to make
them in accordance with what I think is God's will. I'm sure
that my choices are not always right but they are *my* choices,
made honestly and free from the kind of pressure I knew before.
That's why Judaism has an especially strong appeal.

A convert to Greek Orthodoxy declares:

My life as a member of the Greek Orthodox community is a
happy one. But it was happy before, when I was a Catholic.
Now my attitudes are based on "what is good for my family."
If I think that I am doing that, then I do not worry. My husband
and I talk things over. Our attitudes are built around our children and the family. To us that is the main thing. I used to be
upset because I violated the Catholic doctrine with respect to
birth control, but now I feel much different. My husband and I
make the decisions without regard to the Church. Maybe that is
still wrong, even according to the Greek Orthodox religion. I
do not know; but what I *do* know is that the family is so important that my husband and I should be responsible for what
we do. This is a change in attitude which has resulted from my
acceptance of the Greek Orthodox religion.

A convert to Roman Catholicism says:

I never knew what it was to feel that I loved something as I
now love the Church. It has made the great difference in my life.
The Church for me is not just the one in my neighborhood. It is
everywhere. I have the feeling that wherever I go the Church
has already been there, that it will, through its doctrines, guard
me and protect me. I have a new and better attitude toward all
people because of the Church. I now see all people as God's
children under His care and loved by Him.

The greatest of changes that occurs in the ecclesiastical convert, as may be expected, is that which takes place in ritual practice. Ritual observance is so much an integral part of organized religion that it may well serve as an index of change. Such practices as (1) attendance at religious service and the degree of regularity of attendance, (2) observance of the dietary laws (in the case of Jews), or dietary prohibitions of the Roman Catholic Church, (3) observance of the Sabbath, the kindling of the Sabbath candles and the chanting of the Kiddush, (4) observance of Holy Days and Festivals such as Rosh Hashonoh, Yom Kippur, Passover, the Feast of Pentacost and the Feast of Tabernacles, by Jews, and the observance of Christmas, Easter, All Saints' Day, and other Holy Days by many Christians, may provide some indication of the overt changes that should be expected to take place in the ritual practice of converts. Examined in context with changes in beliefs, values, and attitudes, ritual practices may help us to shed additional light upon this phase of the converts' religious life.

Examination of the ritual practices of thirty persons who were converted to Judaism reveals the following:

Converts to Judaism

(1) Of the nineteen Protestants who were converted to Judaism (5 men and 14 women) none attends daily services in a synagogue or temple and none offers daily prayers in their home. (Traditional Judaism does not require that such prayers be recited *only* within the synagogue.) Four of these persons attend Sabbath services in the synagogue regularly (of these, three are women and one is a man). Three of these converts (two women and one man) worship in a synagogue, either at the Friday evening service or on Sabbath morning about twice a month. In only one instance (a woman) are the dietary laws observed both within the home and outside of the home. In three cases, dietary prohibitions with respect to the use of pork products are observed within the home. In all instances these women maintain this standard because "my

husband likes it that way." Yet, outside of the home, these traditional dietary requirements are, with but two exceptions, not observed. It should be noted, however, that of these nineteen, eleven
were formally converted to Judaism by Reform rabbis who, themselves, do not observe the dietary requirements of traditional
Judaism. Five persons (all women) were converted to Judaism by
Conservative rabbis, each of whom stressed the significance of
these dietary requirements. Yet, of these, only one woman abides
by these regulations. Three persons were converted by Orthodox
rabbis. Of these, two observe the dietary laws in part (the use of
kosher meat in their home) while the third fails to observe this
requirement in any degree both within and outside of the home.

Seven of these women regularly kindle the Sabbath candles at
the outset of the Sabbath. Of these, three had been converted by
Conservative rabbis, while three were formally converted by Reform
rabbis, and one was converted by an Orthodox rabbi. Of the five
married male converts, three chant the traditional Kiddush (blessing over the wine) at the Sabbath Eve table. Two of these men
were converted by Reform rabbis and one was converted by a Conservative rabbi.

The significance of the High Holy Days to these converts becomes obvious when we note that all nineteen of these converts attend a synagogue or temple service on Rosh Hashonoh and Yom
Kippur. The emphasis placed upon these days both by the rabbis who
have served as instructors of these converts and by the families into
which they have married is readily apparent.

Passover, the Festival of Freedom, commemorating the Exodus
of the Hebrews from Egyptian bondage, is observed in the homes of
seven converts with an appropriate "Seder" when the "Haggadah"
(the narration of the story of the Exodus) is recited. In only four
cases, however, is the injunction to eat only "Matzot" (unleavened
bread) during the eight days of the Festival observed. The other
Pilgrimage Festivals, Shavuot (the Feast of Pentacost) and Succot
(the Feast of Tabernacles) are, with but two exceptions, disre-
garded by all the converts. Hannukah appears to be observed in

greater degree than any other Festival or Holy Day other than the High Holy Days. Ten of the converts declare that they kindle the Hannukah candles, decorate their homes, and provide gifts for children or grandchildren at this season of the year. In only two cases have any of these converts placed a Mezzuzah upon the doorpost of their home. Traditionally, this practice is intended to indicate that the residents identify themselves with the Jewish faith.

The Jewish ritual is really very wonderful, and fulfilling as well. If I observe it I always find that I gain something for myself and my family. Maybe all these rituals and things that are put in the name of God as His Commandments are not really His orders. Maybe it was the rabbis of old who ordered us to observe them. For me it doesn't really matter, for two reasons. First, I think of the rabbis as men who tried to know God's will and if they decreed that we should observe certain ceremonies or do certain things, I think they were reporting what was God's will. In the second place, I find that, by observing the practices they urged, I feel like a better person. I am happier. I feel at one with God and His purpose."

* * *

When I kindle the Sabbath candles and recite the blessings as my children stand near me, I think that that ritual makes me a better person. I really *feel* the holiness of the Sabbath and my role as Jewish mother in making the Sabbath holy. It may not be important to some people to prepare for the Sabbath as I do, by preparing a special meal, or by setting the table with a white cloth, putting my finest dishes on the table, or listening to my husband chant the Kiddush (the blessing over the wine) but believe me, it means something to me and my family. The Sabbath and its ritual adds an important dimension to my life.

* * *

Ritual is important to me. It really helps me to understand my religion and, I think, that is good enough reason for observing much, not all, of it.

(2) Eleven of these converts to Judaism were formerly Roman Catholics. Of these, none attends daily services in a synagogue nor do they pray in the privacy of their homes. Four persons (two couples) regularly attend Friday evening services in the synagogue and, on occasion, worship with the congregation at Sabbath morning services. (In the case of one couple, the conversion was undertaken by a Conservative rabbi while, in the other, a Reform rabbi served as the instructor.)

I was taught the Jewish ritual about the dietary laws and they seemed important to me when I was studying with the rabbi. But, after my marriage, I found that my husband's folks didn't really observe any of this. In fact, they used to laugh at me when I first spoke about observing it. Even my husband, who wanted me to know all about this and even insisted that he was Orthodox, never really observed the dietary laws. When I said I was going to make our home kosher he objected, so I do not observe very much of the Jewish ritual. I think it would be nice to do but my husband and his folks are the ones who have really prevented it.

*   *   *

We really don't need ritual in our home. Neither my husband nor I are inclined toward ritual and ceremony. In fact, that is one of the things I like about Judaism. You can do what you want. It's voluntary. No one tells you that you won't get to heaven if you don't observe something. Well, that's for me. I believe in God. I am an ethical and moral person. That is the view my husband and I have of Judaism.

*   *   *

To me, going to the Temple on the Sabbath Eve is the most beautiful and meaningful of all rituals. I like to pray with the others in the congregation. I like to read these ancient prayers and find that so much of it has relevance for me. I like to read the Psalms especially. It is so nice to know that so much of the Hebrew Prayer Book is made up of the Psalms of David. That is the kind of ritual I like.

*   *   *

We don't observe the dietary laws. I don't see why they should be regarded as important. Maybe to other Jews, but not to me.

*   *   *

Ritual doesn't mean a single thing to me. I did not observe any Christian ritual and I do not now observe any Jewish ritual. I'm fortunate in having married a Jewish girl who feels pretty much like I do about it.

*   *   *

I certainly don't intend to become a ritualist at any time. I was converted by a Reform rabbi who himself doesn't observe much ritual. So I feel that it certainly isn't required of me.

*   *   *

One of the first things I did after my husband and I decided that I would convert to Judaism was to go to my future mother-in-law and tell her that I wanted her to help me to establish a good Jewish home. I did it not just because this would please her but because I felt if I'm going to be a Jewess I should be a good one. I knew that ritual was very much a part of the traditional Jewish family life, so I tried to observe it correctly. I'm really happy I did because I think not only that it made for greater happiness in our home but made me happier, personally.

None of these eleven converts observes the traditional Jewish dietary proscriptions either within the home or outside of it. All, in fact, eat biblically prohibited foods. Four of the female converts out of a total of eight kindle the Sabbath candles while none of the male converts (there are three) recites the "Kiddush" at the Sabbath table. In all cases, the High Holy Days are observed by attendance at synagogue or temple services.

Passover is observed by five of these converts with a "Seder" service either in their own homes or with other members of the family. In only four cases is the prohibition against the eating of other than unleavened bread (Matzo) observed. In no case are the other pilgrimage festivals (the Feast of Tabernacles and the Feast of Pentacost) observed in any degree. Hannukah is observed by the kindling of the candles for a period of eight nights by six of these converts. In only one instance has a convert reported that a Mezzuzah has been affixed to the outer doorpost of the home.

Attention should be called to the fact that, of the nineteen former Protestants, fifteen are married and all eleven former Catholics are also married. The lack of interest, the indifference or apathy of their spouses, it should be noted, may play a significant role in the choice of Jewish rituals these persons fail to observe.

The majority of the converts to Judaism (70 percent) with whom we are presently concerned, were converted by Reform rabbis. Their practices appear to be in conformance with the general practices of Reform Judaism, as are those (23 percent) who were converted by Conservative rabbis. It is interesting to note that, of the three persons (7 percent) who were converted to Judaism by Orthodox rabbis, all observe the dietary laws *within* their homes but *none* observes it outside of their homes. None of this latter group attends synagogue services regularly or at all, because the rabbi has advised them that riding to the synagogue on the Sabbath constitutes a violation of traditional Jewish law. Because of the distance of their homes from the synagogue they are thereby precluded from worshipping with the congregation. Yet, although these converts may recite their prayers within their own homes, none of them does so.

Converts to Roman Catholicism

The nine converts to Roman Catholicism are uniformly observant of the practices and ritual of the Church.

Each attends church services regularly, observes the dietary restrictions of their church, and of those who are married and have children of school age, all but one send their children to a parochial school. In the case of the one exception, his conversion took place long after his children had passed the high school age.

Theologically, however, their views are not always in consonance with those of the Roman Catholic Church. In the two cases where this view was expressed, both persons (men) indicated that discussion with the priest convinced them that absolute conformity of belief was not required of them. Whether or not this is a true representation of the priest's views, it is worthy of note that, in each case, baptism and confirmation in the new faith was accepted by these converts without qualification.

Of the four converts to Roman Catholicism who were formerly Jews, three are men and one is a woman. Each of these persons has, I believe, converted to Catholicism out of honest conviction. I regard each of them as an "authentic convert."

Each appears to have had no ulterior motive for conversion. In each case, conversion was the result of conclusions arrived at, free from emotion or stress. Each believes wholly in Roman Catholicism as the true religion; that somehow, God was disappointed with the Jews to whom He had earlier revealed Himself, and, as a consequence, that God turned to His Son Jesus and bade him to take over the responsibility of serving as the medium through whom God's will for humankind would ultimately be fulfilled.

Each of these three men is a highly intellectual person. Two are college professors; the other possesses an M.A. degree and is professionally engaged in a community service.

The one woman in our sample very early in life concluded that Jesus is the personification of God. All through her years she held to this view and she had been tempted to convert to Roman Catholicism many times. Her failure to convert to Roman Catholicism at a much earlier point in her life resulted from two factors: (1) hesitancy to discuss religious problems with her parents out of fear that she would be repulsed, and (2) the likelihood that she might some day meet an eligible Jewish man who might propose marriage.

In her late thirties, she is now convinced that, if she should eventually marry, it can, just as easily, be to a Roman Catholic as to a Jew. Despite these practical considerations, she has clearly demonstrated her affinity for Roman Catholicism. She is ritually observant even though she does not accept all the ramifications of Roman Catholic theology. She thinks of Jesus as God, and yet she does not believe that He was immaculately conceived. She believes that Jesus was the greatest *human* who ever lived, and yet she says that he is, somehow, *God*. Confused as her theological concepts may be she, nevertheless, regards herself as a devout Catholic and is wholly observant of Catholic ritual.

Of the five persons (three men and two women) who have converted to the Roman Catholic Church from some form of Protestantism, conversion has affected their attitude toward ritual in considerable degree.

Two of these male converts were, until their teens, members of religious Protestant families where regular church attendance was expected. Each believed in the divinity of Jesus and thought of Him as the Son of God. In the case of one of these converts, the turn to the Roman Catholic Church resulted in large measure from the belief that the regimen of the Roman Catholic Church was far stronger and more desirable than the volunteerism that had, so he believed, characterized his former church. Hence, attendance at church service on a regular weekly basis, as a religious requirement, is greatly admired. All feast and fast days are meticulously observed. Friday, the day on which, to this point, dietary prohibitions with respect to the eating of meat were prescribed by the Church, were also rigorously adhered to. This convert makes it rule to attend a church service each week. He also attends whatever lectures the church has listed on its calendar. He is also generally an active participant in the organizational life of the church, including its Holy Name Society. Whatever the church requires of him, religiously and organizationally, he fulfills to the best of his ability. He believes in discipline and regards the Roman Catholic Church as the disciplinarian par excellence.

The second of these two male converts is far less concerned with Church discipline, although he, too, attends weekly church services regularly. His ritual practices are performed willingly and without reservations of any kind. He and his wife, a born Catholic, do not practice birth control in any form, believing that such a practice is contrary to the edicts of the Church. Catholicism's primary appeal to this convert lies along lines of social action. He is a strong believer in the need for a strong policy of social concern and action by the church and believes that, in addition to the fulfillment of Church requirements with respect to communion, the mass, and dietary proscriptions, the Catholic has a duty to help establish a more equitable social order. For years he has actively participated in tangential Roman Catholic movements that are intended to improve the human condition.

The third of the male converts to Roman Catholicism has married a Catholic girl and is definitely an "authentic convert" in his own right. He observes the prescribed ritual of the Church. He prays daily and almost invariably attends a mass daily. He looks upon this as a religious duty and would regard himself as a sinner if he failed to do so. He is meticulous in the observance of any and all ritual requirements. Less an "intellectual" than are the previously mentioned converts, he is nevertheless a truly devout Roman Catholic.

Of the two Protestant female converts to Roman Catholicism, both are clearly devout in terms of their observance of ritual. The first of these women has (primarily, I think, in the interest of family unity) become an observant Catholic, fulfilling the Church's standards and requirements. Her husband has himself always been a "good" Catholic. The wife is a regular weekly attendant at church services and is an active member of the church auxiliary organization for women. Her children have attended parochial school. She takes pride in her Roman Catholicism and regards herself as a Roman Catholic without reservation.

The second female convert to Catholicism appears to be a rather unstable person. Until the conversion she identified herself as a Protestant. However, her early years were, in fact, little related to or associated with the church of her parents. She had few ties to the Protestant church, although, on rare occasions, she attended services. From her earlier life, little attention was given to her religious life. Because she had always needed parental guidance and discipline, which was lacking, it was natural for her, as she relates her story, to turn ultimately to the Roman Catholic Church.

Her son, the product of her marriage to a Roman Catholic and the "apple of her eye," received a parochial school education. Because he had found such great personal happiness as a Catholic, the mother ultimately turned to the Roman Catholic Church. She has, at one and the same time, found a means of intensifying the loyalty and the love of her son for her by her conversion to Catholicism as well as a means of reducing, or at least alleviating, her own frustrations. The discipline of the Church has been "good" for her. The Church has substituted for the parents whom she never really knew. She is, as a consequence, a devoted Roman Catholic. She attends church services on each Sunday and observes as carefully as possible the ritual requirements of the Church. Her theological views are simple: Jesus is the Son of God. He is the personification of God. He was immaculately conceived. He rose from the dead, and He will come once again. Hers is a simple faith, free from any complexities. She too may today be regarded as an "authentic convert."

Reactions of some of these converts to ritual and church observance are varied:

> The very first time I walked into a church service and saw its ritual, I was really moved. I guess not all people respond the same way but, to me, there is nothing more beautiful than church ritual and pageantry. It doesn't have to have meaning to satisfy me. If it is beautiful, then that is enough. I love it.

*   *   *

> I would never have converted to Roman Catholicism on the basis of its ritual alone. It was the logic of Roman Catholicism that impressed me. It had answers for everything and, in the vast majority of cases, they were reasonable answers.

*   *   *

> I am fascinated by the ritual of the Catholic Church. It is all so very beautiful that it doesn't matter to me whether or not I understand it all. It's the beauty of the thing that impresses me.

*   *   *

Personally I don't care for ritual. I do what I have to do, that is kneel and bow, etc., because the Church says "this is the way." But I'm really not a ritualist. Because I believe in the greater Truths of the Church, I simply do what is expected of me with regard to ritual. I don't feel that I am being hypocritical. I feel, rather, that there is nothing in this world that is going to satisfy every person completely. Observing the ritual of the Church is, I think, a small price to pay for the comfort and blessing which I feel because I am a Roman Catholic. How can I accept the privileges without also accepting what the Church tells me are my responsibilities?

Converts to Greek Orthodoxy

In the case of the three female converts to the Greek Orthodox Church, acceptance of the obligation to attend church regularly and to participate in its religious and social life was agreed to without qualification.

Of all the persons included in this sample, there appears to be none who has adjusted more readily than these Greek Orthodox converts.

The ritual of the Greek Orthodox Church is very rich in meaning. In fact, it isn't too much different from that of the Roman Catholic Church insofar as I can see. I like it primarily because of its beauty. I don't look for hidden meaning in it. Its beauty is quite enough for me. I observe it because I find it so lovely and, too, because my husband's family observe it. This ties me closer to them. They are happy and proud of me when I follow the same ritual that they do.

* * *

I have found the Greek family to be more important than the Greek Orthodox religion. At least I have found that if you want to really be a part of the Greek family then you had better also accept the Greek Orthodox religion, because family life is so important in our church. You just can't really separate them. I love my husband very much. The church is important to him and to his parents. If I want to be sure of their love then it is important for me to become a part of the church to which they belong. Inasmuch as religion didn't really matter very much to me as a child, I felt that I could accept his church without any trouble to my conscience. I do all that the church and my family expect of me. It really isn't difficult at all. They believe in Jesus and so do I. What matters most is that we be a unified family and, through conversion, I have attained that.

After all, I'm a Christian and I always was. By joining the Greek Orthodox Church I am still a Christian, but now I'm the kind that my husband and his parents like most. So that is reason enough for conversion.

In each case, according to their testimony, their religious beliefs, values, and attitudes have not changed in any degree as a consequence of conversion. Insofar as religious practices and ritual are concerned each found it easy to adjust to the new church. For each, it meant the use of a new prayer book, becoming familiar with the Greek language as a means of identifying themselves not only with the church but with husband, parents-in-law, and newly acquired friends. Each of these converts is now a regular attendant at church services to which she comes on each Sunday and on Feast days, as well, with husband and children. These converts insist that whatever practices have changed, in any degree, are associated less with the church and its requirements than with the distinctive patterns and standards of the Greek family, which they declare to be unified in love and loyalty in greater degree than they experienced within their own families. Recognition and appreciation of this factor has led them to accept the ritual of the Greek home readily and willingly. It should be noted that the proselytes were Christians prior to conversion and that they remained Christians thereafter. Inasmuch as the ritual practices of the Greek Orthodox Church largely center around the church, this has posed no major problem for any of these converts. The changes that presented problems are centered about the home and the extended family. Here the distinctive ethnic factors that differentiate the

Greek family from others come to the fore. Greek cooking, for example, was pointed out as of far greater concern to these converts than church ritual. The close personal ties between members of the family and the Greek community presented a challenge to the proselytes, who had never before experienced such a relationship with their own immediate families. Such matters affected the lives of these people far more than did the required changes in religious rites.

Converts to Protestantism

The two converts to Protestantism are both women and former Jewesses. The older of the two is a mother, and her conversion to the Congregational church occurred after the death of her husband. The younger is in her teens and was converted to the Episcopalian church. It is my belief that her insecurity, loneliness, and anxieties resulting from her mother's grave illness contributed to her ultimate decision to convert. Each has adjusted easily and quickly to her new faith. In neither case did Judaism as a religious way of life prove meaningful. The emotional differences between these two converts become readily apparent when, in the case of the older, a dislike of ritual was expressed while, in the case of the convert to Episcopalianism, the intricacies and formalism of the church ritual were greatly admired and loved.

*   *   *

The lone Unitarian Universalist in our sample was formerly a Roman Catholic. In consonance with Unitarianism, he is not a ritualist in any sense, unless the church service itself at which he officiates be regarded as a form of ritual. But even then, ritual plays no important role, for it is neither prescribed nor required.

*   *   *

Although the performance of prescribed ritual acts aids the convert by assuring a degree of acceptance and identification within the new religious community and is often consciously used for that purpose, full identification is more likely to result from full emotional involvement in the new community.

Conversion should result in something more than a church-approved outward behavior or ritual observance. It ought also to bring about a feeling of religious "belonging," of feeling that one is an integral part of the particular religious community into which one has formally entered. Although this "we" feeling is readily noticed in some converts almost from the moment of conversion, this feeling is not always apparent. However, it ought not to be expected as a natural consequence of formal conversion alone. The sense of belonging is generally a gradual process, the result of continuous, ongoing contact over a protracted period of time. On occasion, it may never take place. On others, it may occur at a much later period. This depends not solely upon the nature of the convert but upon the responses of members of the new religious community as well.

Judaism places great emphasis upon identification with the Jewish people, whereas Christianity stresses personal acceptance and commitment to a creed. A "Christian" who does not believe in Jesus as the Savior is an anomaly. Yet there may be Jews whose only identification is with the Jewish people and the community of Jews. Such Jews may be actively concerned with the future of the Jewish people, actively supporting philanthropic, cultural, and social causes involving Jews while showing little or no concern for creedal matters. Identification with the Jewish people is, as we have already noted, traditionally expected and is especially looked for, in the case of converts to Judaism.

In the case of most of these converts, Jewish and Christian, such involvement is generally not apparent. Few of these proselytes participate in the total religious community. Catholic converts generally participate in those activities that are parish sponsored. Jewish converts, if women, usually become members of temple or synagogue sisterhoods but do not generally become members of overall Jewish organizations such as Hadassah, the Women's Zionist Organization, Council of Jewish Women, American Jewish

Congress, or American Jewish Committee. None of these persons has identified with fund-raising community organizations such as Jewish Federations or Jewish Philanthropies. Most claim to have many Jewish friends with whom they meet socially. In the main, identification with the Jewish community is not clearly evident. Usually Jewish friends are cultivated because of the desire of the Jewish spouse to maintain such friendships. Relations with the immediate family of the spouse are, however, even sought after.

As for the male Jewish convert, the degree of identification with the Jewish community is generally not high. Temple and synagogue relationships are maintained. Affiliation with temple men's clubs or brotherhoods and membership in the temple is generally undertaken in order to assure some form of identification, but organizational ties or active participation in the larger Jewish community appear neither to be desired nor sought after. For the convert, it is basically religious ties that are regarded by him as most important. Inasmuch as conversion to Judaism traditionally has involved ties to the Jewish community as well, these converts generally fail to meet this test.

Converts to Roman Catholicism, as recorded in our case histories, indicate that their interests are directly associated with the Church and its auxiliary organizations. Of the converts to Roman Catholicism whose life-stories we have recorded, there is little evidence to indicate that their associations go beyond the boundaries of the particular church which they attend. In the case of those converts whom we have discussed, they find few if any ties with Roman Catholics who happen to be members of other ethnic groups. Three of these six converts to Roman Catholicism are members of the "Edith Stein Society," an organization consisting almost entirely of Jews who have converted to Roman Catholicism. They seem to find outlets for their social interests in the company of other Jews who have converted to Roman Catholicism.

Of the three converts to Greek Orthodoxy, none is actively involved in anything other than the program of the local Greek Orthodox church. Inasmuch as the total life of the community appears to be centered in the Greek Orthodox church, there is no way of ascertaining with certainty exactly how they view Greek Orthodoxy.

Converts to various kinds of Protestantism, too, build their lives around their church and its programed activities, while greater participation in the larger Protestant community is also evident. But, inasmuch as the Protestant community is the largest of the three groups, it is to be expected that such a situation would prevail.

An overall view of these ecclesiastical converts with respect to (1) beliefs, (2) values, (3) attitudes, (4) ritual practices, and (5) identification leads me to believe that the changes that have occurred in these converts are relatively few and comparatively minor in each of these categories. No new "all-pervading world-view or changes from one . . . perspective to another"[6] is noticeable, primarily, I suggest because most of these persons are pro forma converts.

If religious experience is, as Glock and Stark[7] define it, "a very deep sense of peace and well-being, a kind of warm support of assurance that all is well within and without," then formal conversion, in all but eight instances, has failed to produce such an experience, except that in all but one case where the convert is married, the formal act of conversion appears to have provided the marriage with a greater stability and assurance of success than might otherwise have been true.

Forty-two of these converts were converted to their new faiths for periods ranging from five years to over twenty-five years. Of the total, I have found that while "practices" generally change in considerable degree, "values" and "attitudes" change least. "Belief," in the cases of those persons who have converted to Judaism, have usually been arrived at long before the formal conversion has taken place. In the case of converts to Roman Catholicism, beliefs appear to be most important. Great stress is laid upon them by the Church. As for the converts to the Greek Orthodox faith, creedal matters do not appear to be of major importance. Identification with the Jewish people, in the case of the converts to Judaism, is, with but minor exception (six out of thirty converts), slight and hardly significant. Identification with other Catholics insofar as the Roman Catholic converts are concerned is also generally marginal, as is the case too of the converts to any of the forms of Protestantism. In the three cases of converts to the Greek Orthodox religion, identification is clearly evident. Relations to the Greek family into which the convert has married, as well as to the church, which clearly represents the total community, are maintained on a high level of interest and concern.

In ritual matters, converts to Roman Catholicism rate high, as do the Greek Orthodox converts. Protestant proselytes, with far fewer rituals to observe, do not appear to regard them with any degree of special interest or concern. Converts to Judaism are, in the main, not ritually observant, whether measured by traditional or Reform standards. The vast majority limit ritual observance to attendance at worship services on the High Holy Days.

An over-all evaluation of the success or failure of these forty-five conversions cannot be made easily. The authentic converts should, of course, be recorded as successful inasmuch as the motives that impelled them to seek conversion are purely intrinsic. But what conclusions are to be drawn from the pro forma and marginal converts? If the formal and informal requirements of Church and Synagogue are the basic criteria, then, I think that these converts leave much to be desired. If, as a consequence of conversion, beliefs, values, attitudes, practices, and sense of identification have changed only in minor degree, if at all, there is reason to suggest that the conversion effort has, in fact, failed insofar as the Church and Synagogue are concerned.

7. *Observations and Conclusions*

THERE ARE STUDENTS of the subject of intermarriage who believe that mixed marriages, i.e., those in which each of the parties to the marriage retains his original religious affiliation, are as likely to prove successful as the average. The majority, however, believes that the marriage that has the added strength derived from unity along religious lines is far more likely to assure its success. If the marriage of two persons of different religions appears certain, then formal conversion of one of the persons to the religion of the other is often urged as the only realistic and logical step, and an increasing number of persons seems to agree with this point of view. The formal conversion of one party to the religion of the other tends to assuage the anguish and torment of parents and relatives. Eighty percent of all conversions in the three major faiths are said to result from the desire to marry someone of another faith. Authentic conversions as I have described them constitute a very small number (certainly, no more than ten percent) of the total number of conversions in the United States.

Whatever the motivation for conversion, it is important to take a searching look at the *process* of conversion as it is generally practiced by clergymen of the major faiths, as reported by our interviewees.

As I see it, five distinct groups of people are directly or indirectly involved in each case of ecclesiastical conversion. They are (1) the clergy, (2) the husband or wife of the convert, (3) the parents and family of the convert, (4) the parents and family of the convert's spouse, and (5) the group or society in which the convert is to live. How each responds to the convert both prior to and following the formal act of conversion may spell the difference between the success or failure of conversion. It may, further, assist the convert to move from the pro forma or nominal category to that of an authentic convert. With each of these categories in mind, I offer certain observations that may prove helpful to all who wish to make ecclesiastical conversion a richer and more meaningful experience.

1. The Clergy

It is highly important that we bear in mind the fact that the rabbi, priest, or minister bears the major if not the sole responsibility for the conversion. It is he who must make the decision that will ultimately either accept or reject the candidate. He acts not as an individual but as the representative of church or synagogue. He is the sole authority upon whose judgment the religious institution he represents must depend. It is he who must be convinced of the sincerity of the applicant, and he must be able to look into the future and offer, at the very least, a glorified guess that the candidate for conversion can be trusted to respect and honor his religious tradition. Being human, he does not always guess correctly or wisely.

Much time and conscientious effort is presently being expended by clergymen to assist the candidate for conversion to comprehend the ideas and ways of the "new" religion. The privileges and responsibilities that are associated with a new and different church or synagogue identification should, of course, be fully understood by the candidate. Dedicated religious leaders often spend untold hours, days, and months in a determined effort to assure the success of a conversion. Experience over these many years with such candidates makes it clear that, with but minor exceptions, the average clergyman often goes well beyond the call of duty when the conversion situation presents itself. And yet, a careful examination of the forty-five conversions recorded in this study leads to the conclusion that, but for minor exceptions, these conversions were not generally accompanied by changes in either the ideas, values, attitudes, or practices that should naturally be expected in the convert. If conversion means anything, it ought certainly to imply that at some time in the future noticeable changes in these areas should have occurred. The fault, it is often assumed, lies with the convert inasmuch as evidence, in the case of our forty-five converts, appears to point in that direction. Although serious doubts may be raised about the success of these conversions, it is not altogether clear that the convert is, in all cases, necessarily at fault. A review of these life-stories and an examination of the process of conversion as it is generally practiced by church and synagogue leads me to other conclusions. I offer certain suggestions that may help to improve the present vexing situation.

Ministers, priests, and rabbis generally tend to turn such candidates over to a formal class for converts. These classes, generally conducted by competent clerical instructors, often fail to provide the opportunity for direct, personal, face-to-face contact and discussion with the initiating clergyman that should, I believe, play an important role in the conversion process. In large cities, where the likelihood of numerous candidates for conversion is usually present, after the formal course of study has been completed, the candidate is referred back to the cleric with whom the candidate first met. Assured by the class instructor that the candidate has "passed" his examinations, there is generally little further direct, intimate relationship between the candidate and the clergyman. What usually transpires at that point, the formality of the conversion ceremony itself, is seldom sufficiently personal and meaningful. A strong bond and tie between the clergyman and the convert that will prove helpful if and when problems present themselves is seldom established. As a consequence, the newly accepted convert seldom has any person to whom to turn with the problems, questions, anxieties, or doubts that arise in the months and years that follow formal conversion.

There is seldom, if ever, a "follow-up" of the convert by the clergyman. I believe that, for a period of one or two years following the conversion, regularly designated personal meetings between the convert (and spouse) and the clergyman ought to take place. This is, I believe, the most practical way in which to assist both husband and wife to meet the problems that result from the religious differences that either or both encounter. In almost all of the cases I have studied I have noted this glaring omission which appears to apply with equal force to the clergy of the three major religions. Clergymen are, to be sure, generally already heavily burdened with numerous responsibilities within their congregation, parish, and community. However, the assumption of the initial responsibility for the religious welfare of the candidate for conversion must, of necessity, imply the added acceptance of the responsibility to assure, wherever possible, the success of the conversion process. No one, to my knowledge, in all of my thirty-eight years in the rabbinate has become a "good" Catholic, Protestant, or Jew in six easy lessons. It can hardly be accomplished if the direct responsibility that the clergyman must feel for each candidate for conversion is avoided. If it is true that "a chain is as strong as its weakest link," then that weakest link in any religious tradition can prove to be the convert who, though formally prepared to meet all technical and legal requirements expected of him by his new faith, has no direct personal and ongoing relationship with his clergyman.

Discussions with these converts led me to believe further that a greater purpose could be served if all candidates for conversion would be required to attend the classes for conversions in the company of the intended spouse. At least eighty percent of all conversions that presently take place are undertaken for the purpose of meeting the formal requirement that *both* husband and wife be of the same faith. There is no guarantee that the most orthodox and beautiful of religious ceremonies performed by a clergyman will in itself assure the success of such a marriage.

Most converts with whom I have discussed the matter indicate that "unity of the family in all matters, including religion," is their desired goal. They indicate their intense belief in the need for religious unity and singleness of purpose within the home. I have found that, all too often, the so-called "religious" spouse, for whose sake the other partner to the marriage is willing to convert, has little more than a passing interest in the religion of his ancestors; that, in fact, passivity or indifference to religion often characterizes him. This is often true of the other members of his family as well. For reasons best known to them, they may cry out for conversion as the only way that will soften family resentment, and yet they, themselves, may be completely indifferent or dormant religionists. They may care little about the specific way of life that is associated with their religion and often fail to practice its ritual, observances, and ceremonies. The circumstances just described are much more general than is usually believed.

How then can such situations be met?

Whenever marriage is known to be the ultimate objective of the convert, the intended spouse should, under all circumstances, be required to attend all classes, discussions, and informal sessions together with the candidate for conversion. If unity of the family is the major objective of the conversion, then surely every possible means that may lead to that result may prove helpful. The very fact of being together, learning together, discussing theological and other matters together, in the presence of the clergyman or even privately, may help to create another bond that may serve to tie two lives together more effectively. Greater understanding of the viewpoint of each of the parties is spiritually increased. The newly established family is thereby strengthened and its common religious orientation is thereby improved. Such a couple stands a better chance of establishing the kind of home that can redound to its credit. The new convert ceases, then, to be the weak link in a weak chain.

There is so much to teach the candidate for conversion about the "new" faith that instructors—be they ministers, priests, or rabbis—can hardly do more than present a cursory view of their religion's philosophy and attitudes within the generally accepted three- or four-month course of study. Wherever possible, it seems to me, a far longer period of formal study, ranging from six months to a full year, should be required. Given the very best of such formal instruction, the candidate may still be insufficiently prepared to be expected to commit himself fully to the new faith. But, at the very least, a greater effort will have been made than is presently the case.

All classes for candidates for conversion in the three major religions presently include lessons of theological, historical, and ceremonial significance. The material covered in these classes is—according to the lessons and textbooks I have examined, which constitute the norm for such classes—far too limited. Little, if any, time is devoted to the idea of ecumenicity that in this day should assume greater significance. It is, of course, the duty and responsibility of church and synagogue and its clergy to point out the significant differences that exist between church and synagogue. The candidate for conversion to Judaism, for example, must know and understand that the Jewish view of Jesus differs radically from the Christian view. The convert to Christianity must know and understand the distinctively Christian view of original sin among other doctrinal and creedal matters. There are, indeed, significant differences and contrasts far too numerous to be cited here. Yet, with all these distinctions and differences, there is also an urgent need to impress ideas and values of the common origin of Man, the Fatherhood of God, the Brotherhood of Man, and the need for all men to work together for the ultimate improvement of human society upon all men, without regard to the particular church or synagogue and their denominations, to which we may be committed.

The right of men to differ in their religious beliefs, and, as a consequence, to act on the basis of their convictions is, of course, neither to be questioned or debated. What is distressing to this observer, however, is the overweaning zeal that causes so many otherwise good religious souls to believe that by digging even wider and deeper chasms between other religious groups and their own some higher purpose is served. Belief in the truth and logic of our particular religious philosophy does not imply the necessity of tearing down or looking negatively upon the views of others.

The tasks we have in common in these days, the need for building a society in which differences, while acknowledged and accepted, will not stand in the way of the assumption of our common responsibility to establish higher standards in our society, a greater sense of the dignity and worth of each human being regardless of race, creed, national origin, or class, deserve our immediate concern. Teachers of religion ought certainly to be among those to make this possible. It is the privilege and duty of the clergyman to introduce the candidate for conversion to this concept. He must stress *not* the superiority of his religion and the inferiority of others, but the highly significant truth that whatever religious faith we possess must be utilized not only for the preservation of our own faith but for the betterment of humankind.

I offer this added word to rabbis who are concerned with the conversion process. The varied requirements for formal conversion to Judaism as prescribed by Orthodox, Conservative, Reform, and Reconstructionist rabbis and their respective rabbinical organizations tend, I believe, to create a chaotic condition within the Jewish community. There is at present the tendency on the part of the interested parties to "shop around" in order to find an acceptable form of conversion. The end result is that a far greater divisiveness is created within Judaism than any minority people can afford. Further, it points up the great need on the part of Jewish religious leaders to define, with greater clarity, who is a Jew, and what form allegiance to Judaism should take. As presently practiced, conversion often raises more questions than it resolves, for there are numerous indications that Orthodox rabbinical authorities do not accept the practices of Conservative and Reform rabbis—in this as well as in other areas—as legally correct and binding, even as non-Orthodox religious leaders question the views and practices of Orthodox rabbis as being valid or meaningful in this day. The present practice can only lead to utter chaos.

The attitude that is generally held with respect to ecclesiastical converts whose conversion results from a desire to marry a person whose faith is other than his own, should, I think, be reconsidered. Marriage may not be the very best reason for accepting converts to any of the three major faiths; but if it assists, in whatever degree, in providing greater stability and a sense of unity to the partners to the marriage, the conversion may be justified. Further, if by conversion, the indignation and hurt of parents and families are alleviated, there is, I think, further reason to recognize its therapeutic value. The devout religionist, while noting that each of the three major religions provides a method for conversion, tends to regard conversion for the sake of marriage as a "second best" procedure. The primary objective is clearly stated by all organized religious bodies, as the preservation of a faith *for its own sake.* When conversion takes place for reasons that are other than purely intrinsic, the preservation and perpetuation of a faith is definitely not assured. For this reason, argues the religionist, such conversions must be discouraged.

While the logic of the position appears to be unassailable, it must once again be noted that all theory to the contrary, most conversions take place *because* of marriage. The assumption that all such marriages will fail or that such converts will not, in time, commit themselves wholeheartedly to the newly acquired faith is not borne out by the facts. Of the forty-five converts whose life-stories are herein recorded, thirty-six became ecclesiastical converts for reason of marriage. Although few if any marked changes in basic ideals, values, and attitudes have been noted among the majority of the "converts for marriage's sake," we must also record the fact that in ten of these cases certain changes have occurred that suggest the likelihood of full commitment to the new faith at some later date. It is certainly not beyond the realm of possibility that the children of these converts may become fully committed to the newly adopted religion.

Given this new factor, the preponderance of "conversions for marriage's sake," in our day, shall we then write these people off and arbitrarily refuse them admission as converts? While we may remain apprehensive (with some justification) about converts and conversion for the sake of marriage only, we should accept the challenge which this study presents. These people are obviously serious about wanting religious unity in their home and family. They should, I believe, be accorded every opportunity to prove themselves worthy candidates for conversion and ultimately worthy of trust and confidence by the church or synagogue with which they have chosen to affiliate. Every serious effort must, of course, be made to eliminate the obviously undesirable, the insincere, and the opportunists from among the would-be converts. However, those persons who, insofar as we can judge, are serious about wanting religious unity in their homes and who are sincere seekers after truth as it is represented by the sought-after church or synagogue, ought, I believe, to be regarded as worthy candidates for conversion.

If the convert is not contemplating marriage at the time when the formal conversion takes place, the part that the clergyman must play in order to encourage and strengthen the convert increases in importance. His readiness to continue the role of confidant, teacher, and friend must be clearly evident and unequivocal. To this point, the convert has, in the main, acquired the theories and philosophy of the new religion. He has yet to apply that which he has learned in the classroom to his personal life as well as to his milieu. The sincere convert is often confronted with grave questions that need to be answered and problems that need to be resolved. The clergyman who "follows through" from this moment on, renders the greatest of all services to the convert and, as a consequence, to his church or synagogue.

2. The Convert's Spouse

The spouse whose religion the convert has formally adopted can by his or her own attitude toward the religion affect the convert's religious philosophy and action more than any other person. Indifference or apathy at this point is responsible for the failures of more converts than any other single factor. If religion means little or nothing to the spouse it will, in all likelihood, mean little or nothing to the convert. If the conversion has been undertaken for extrinsic reasons, such as "to make for unity in the home" or with a minimum of concern or regard for the nature and quality of the newly acquired religion, there is no reason to expect that the convert will ever ultimately become an authentic convert. The incentive that could be provided by the spouse is lacking. Conversion under such circumstances, however rigidly the rules of church or synagogue may have been followed in the preparation for and completion of the formal conversion ceremony, will more than likely be rather meaningless. That is why the role of the spouse of the convert must be stressed. It is within his or her power to effectuate the change that may ultimately result in an authentic conversion.

The spouse who fails to recognize the responsibility that rests upon him when, because of him and for love of him, a conversion has taken place, is, I believe, guilty of two offenses. The convert has not only been uprooted from a religious tradition while family and other associational ties have been disrupted or broken, but no spiritually enriching tradition has been substituted therefor. A spiritual vacuum is created that remains to be filled.

The convert who has conscientiously undertaken to prepare adequately for conversion has, almost invariably, acquired a knowledge and understanding of the symbolic meaning of the ritual of his newly acquired faith. Promises and pledges have been formally made, in the presence of the clergyman, to live up to certain religious requirements. At that climactic moment converts generally appear ready to assume the duties and obligations prescribed by church or synagogue. But something happens within a few short months following the conversion that cause promises and pledges to be forgotten. When there is no reenforcement and strengthening of one's views by husband or wife, the convert tends to be discouraged and undecided.

The case of Sally Bonder (see pp. 171–189) may provide an

example of the failure of a husband to provide the spiritual resources that would spell the difference between success and failure in conversion. Sally Bonder, a devout Roman Catholic, was formally converted to Judaism because her Jewish husband and his parents desired it. But Sally's husband had little concern for Judaism. After more than twenty-five years of marriage and despite every effort on Sally's part to enrich her spiritual life through Judaism, she reverted to Catholicism, the consequence, I believe, of her husband's failure to indicate that his religion had any real significance for him.

The positive role that a devoted and devout spouse can play in the spiritual life of her marriage partner is further illustrated by Nancy and Arthur Stout (see pp. 320–321). Nancy, a devout Catholic, set so high a standard that Arthur, her husband, moved from the category of the marginal to the authentic convert, thereby enriching both lives.

Yet another convert asks:

> If my husband doesn't care about going to church and if his mother and father actually mock me because I try to go every Sunday, why should I put myself out to do so? If that's the way they want it, then it is O.K. with me.

Such a comment made time and time again during the course of these interviews by converts to all three major religions constitutes a severe indictment that ought not to be ignored.

3. The Convert's Family

We can hardly expect that the parents and family of a candidate for conversion will be pleased or even that they will passively accept the idea of conversion of a son or daughter to a different faith. Whether or not they are themselves churchgoers or otherwise comport themselves as religious people, there is enough evidence in the life-stories of our forty-five converts to make the general resentment and opposition of parents clear and unequivocal. In many of our "cases," parents refuse to attend the marriage ceremony. In all but a few instances parents seek to persuade their son or daughter to give up the idea of conversion. In only a few instances does a mother or father readily accept the view of the potential convert. The influence of parents is, however, obvious in all instances.

Converts who come from unhappy or broken homes appear to be more inclined to act independently of the wishes of their parents. There are indications that such parents, perhaps because of their own unhappy experiences, are less likely to thwart the desires and wishes of a child who intends to be converted to a new religion. In most cases, however, parents look upon the conversion of a child as a traitorous act inasmuch as it appears to question their values and the values of the religious institution to which they belong. As a consequence tensions between parents and conversion candidate are frequently noted.

In only a few instances have we noted that the convert is not adversely affected by the parental attitude. Most people have no conscious desire to hurt or offend their parents, however much they may wish to do so subconsciously. The tensions that often result when a child moves in a direction that he knows is contrary to the wishes of the parent tend to make the conversion even less effective and meaningful than it might otherwise have been. Many such converts become marginal converts; Januslike, they look in two directions, that of their parents and that of the new religion, at one and the same time.

I do not believe that the parents of a convert can be expected to provide moral support to the convert prior to and including the time of conversion. There is, however, reason to suggest that, once the conversion has taken place, parents, once their hurt, resentment, or anger has abated, should try to face the new situation with honesty and courage. It is, I believe, wiser for such parents to seek to understand the reasons that have brought the conversion about. If at least eighty percent of all conversions take place out of a desire to marry a person of another faith, then the happiness of the convert in marriage must become the ultimate concern of parents.

If happiness has resulted from the marriage, parents ought, I think, to reconsider their position and as quickly as possible re-establish as warm a relationship with the convert and spouse as is possible.

Even if the conversion has taken place without the incentive of marriage, the test here too is the sense of inner security and peace of mind of the convert. Continuing harassment of the convert will serve no good purpose. I would urge such parents to "cease and desist." The mental health of the convert is too important to be disturbed by even the most well-intentioned of parents. Let the convert "find" himself. I offer this counsel not only on the basis of my study of these forty-five converts but also as a consequence of well-nigh four decades in the active rabbinate as well as the response of experienced and dedicated Protestant and Catholic clergymen whom I have consulted.

4. The Convert's In-laws

Although the responsibilities of the clergy are so very numerous, those of the family into which the convert enters are even greater. The family and its response to the convert more often makes the difference between the success or failure of conversion.

Parents, for reasons best known to themselves (I shall not here question their motives), often insist upon formal conversion as the price that must be paid if they are to "accept" an interfaith marriage. But following the period of instruction in which the candidate for conversion has been taught not only the theological beliefs and values of the new faith but its ceremonial practices as well, the impression is often gained that the family into which the convert has entered is little if at all concerned with such matters. In fact, there is frequently a deep resentment because the convert has taken seriously what the family itself cares nothing about. The convert who senses this lack of concern, indifference, or even resentment is hardly likely to move from the nominal or pro forma stage of conversion to the highest and most meaningful stage of authenticity. Parents who respond in such a manner do a disservice not only to the newly converted but to their own son or daughter as well. As long as the convert senses suspicion, stand-offishness, or rejection by newly acquired family there is little reason to believe that the nominal convert will ever become an authentic convert. Instead of providing every assistance to the new convert, explaining the practical aspects of the new religion in all its details, and indicating the relevance and meaningfulness of the practices and observances of the religion, the opposite tendency is more frequently noted. The difficulty, of course, arises from the fact that, in reality, the religious life often has little meaning and significance for the family. The convert may very quickly sense this negative attitude and, as a consequence, will cease to make any positive effort to become an authentic convert. The purpose of the formal conversion is thereby defeated and must be categorized as a failure. The responsibility for these failures must rest with those well-intentioned but ill-advised parents who, at the very moment when understanding and even love are often so anxiously sought, fail their children.

The role that a family may play in changing a convert from a negative type to another and more positive role is further illustrated by the story of Laurel Backman (see pp. 299–301). Even though her husband was a rather negative kind of Jew, Laurel, impressed with the sincerity and devotion of her husband's parents, sought zealously to maintain the high Jewish standards of her husband's parents. Her husband's failure in this area was completely overcome by her respect for the sincerity and devotion of her in-laws.

The three persons who converted to the Greek Orthodox religion were all influenced by the religious attitude of the husbands' families (see pp. 44–49, 107–115, 314–316). This was true also of Fred Davis (see pp. 301–302) and Helga Silverman (see pp. 316–318).

In all cases the parents and family of the spouse into which the convert moved effected a greater degree of positive relationship with the new faith than would otherwise have been possible. The cooperation of parents to whose faith the candidate is turning is also needed in order that religious practices, ritual, and standards may be witnessed by the convert in the home and correctly explained and interpreted. With the parents as instructors, a rapport is established that goes quite beyond formal instruction. Parents are likely to be drawn closer to the candidate for conversion even as he in turn becomes more intimately associated with and understanding of the family.

If, with the cooperation of the clergy, families, particularly parents, assisted the candidate to understand and appreciate the new faith long before the formal conversion and marriage ceremony, the present stand-offish attitude that characterizes so many parents may, in all likelihood, be overcome.

Although the number of pro forma converts is, I believe, far greater than that of authentic converts, personal experience with such converts over a period of years has convinced me that, given the proper care and attention following the formal act of conversion, a convert of the former type may ultimately become an authentic convert. The basic ingredient that so often tends to effect this change is tender loving care offered by the parents and family whose religion has been formally adopted. The qualities of personal warmth and friendliness may produce a positive response to the newly adopted religion that far surpasses anything that the clergyman and his instruction may be able to achieve. It is particularly in this area that so many parents and families fail. However much objection there may have been to the interfaith marriage and to the subsequent conversion, when the latter has been decided upon and agreed to, parents have the duty and responsibility to assist their convert to make the most of his or her new religious status. To do otherwise is to provide a serious handicap both to the success of the marriage as well as to the meaningfulness of the new religion.

5. *The Convert's New Community*

The society in which the convert is expected to live following the formal conversion often tends to remain suspicious of and aloof from the new convert. Often, and not without foundation, there is reason to question the sincerity of certain of the converts. They, as well as others, can "live a lie" and remain basically untrue to all that they have pledged to be or do. The society of which we are a part senses this fact even though it may not always be articulated. Still, as I see it, the convert, by virtue of the very acts of preparation and formal conversion, deserves the opportunity to be provided with every reasonable assurance that social acceptance will not automatically be withheld without due cause. I have noted this tendency in twenty-seven (60 percent) of the cases reported to me by the forty-five converts. It is particularly emphasized within two of the minority religions—Judaism and Roman Catholicism. Social acceptance of the convert should, at the very least, consist of providing an opportunity for the convert to indicate the qualities of character, mind, and cultural and spiritual interests and concerns that give his or her life meaning. Failure to do so is frequently discouraging if not ultimately defeating to the convert.

The story of Linda Buxbaum (see pp. 204–217), a Negro, offers positive evidence of the role that society, in this case a Jewish congregation, can play in helping a convert to accept her newly adopted faith. Both rabbi and congregation provided every opportunity for the convert to feel at home with the people whom she identified as Jews. Whether or not this conversion would have gone beyond the pro forma stage is debatable had it not been for the warm, positive response of this particular congregation.

The social controls exercised by the religious society of which we are a part play an important role in the conservation of our values, to be sure. Often, as in the case of conversion, the society is even more conservative than the officially prescribed rules require. Inasmuch as each of the three major religions has designated rules for the admission of converts and has set procedures by which its clergymen can operate, it seems harsh and even utterly unrealistic for individuals and groups within these societies to react to converts and conversion as uncharitably as they sometimes do. There is need for a reexamination of these attitudes in our day.

However zealous we may be for the preservation of the distinctive religious beliefs, values, and practices we associate with our respective religions, we have the duty and obligation to give to the convert every opportunity to become authentic. But to make this possible requires not only time but compassion and understanding by the clergy, the spouse, the parents, and family of the convert as well as those of the spouse and by the religious community and society into which the convert enters. Even then, not all converts will rise to the authentic stage. My observations of these forty-five converts lead me to conclude that the number of such converts can be increased and their quality improved if given the opportunity. The task is of course not simple, but the rewards are great.

Appendix

SYNOPSES OF TWENTY-FOUR INTERVIEWS

Dorothy Crane

Dorothy Crane is an only child. She was reared in New York City by parents who are Jewish. Her home, as she remembers it, was quite Orthodox. Ritual was observed particularly because her devout grandmother desired it. Dorothy's early life with her family was most pleasant and satisfying.

When she was very young, only three years old, Dorothy recalls that her parents once visited with Protestant Christian neighbors. Dorothy was brought along. The discussion on that night related to the coming of the Messiah. The neighbors spoke of Jesus as the Messiah, and Dorothy's parents demurred. But Dorothy seemed very much moved by the idea and seems never to have forgotten that evening. She says, "I carried the idea that Jesus was the Messiah all through my life. I was intrigued by the idea." That idea was never further discussed in her home either with parents or grandmother.

Following the grandmother's death, the various Jewish rituals that had formerly been observed were given up by her parents. Although Dorothy began to read Jewish history from time to time, she never attended a Sunday or Hebrew school nor did she observe any distinctively Jewish ceremonies or rituals.

Her only contact with Jewish religious life came through a summer camp experience. There, in a Jewish camp, she was reintroduced in degree to Jewish ritual. Dorothy enjoyed the experience. She then asked for permission to attend a Sunday school, but then, after a brief period, she simply stopped going without any objection by her parents.

Possessing a good singing voice, Dorothy was provided by her parents with a voice teacher with whom she studied for many years. As a consequence, she secured employment as a member of various church choirs, all in Protestant churches. Although this experience helped her to appreciate Christianity in greater degree than ever before, she was still not moved to consider conversion. At that point such a thought had not even crossed her mind. Dorothy continued her education in one of the local New York City universities. She intensified her music education as well and continued to sing in various church choirs.

Despite seemingly fine relations with her parents, Dorothy felt a great loneliness. She seldom dated and even then, dated non-Jewish boys, much to the hurt of her mother (her father had passed away while Dorothy was in college).

Dorothy gradually discovered that she could not hope to have a great career as a singer, and gradually she accepted other kinds of employment, as a clerk in department stores. Growing older, she found that she was dating very little. One of Dorothy's friends, a Catholic, was very devout. Often when the two were together, the conversation veered toward Catholicism and the comfort and satisfaction the friend found in the church. Often these two attended church together.

Gradually, as a consequence, Dorothy began to consider conversion to Roman Catholicism. She had no real interest in Judaism nor was she "going with" any Jewish boy. She had, for some years, lived alone, away from her mother. Whenever she found herself to be especially lonely she walked over to the neighborhood Catholic church and sat quietly in meditation. As a consequence of this experience over a period of three years, Dorothy finally summoned up enough courage to speak to the priest about the possibility of conversion. She was encouraged to take a series of lessons and finally, formally converted. Dorothy's mother is extremely distressed, but Dorothy is happy with her church affiliation. For the past three years, Dorothy claims she has found security and a happiness she never knew before.

Ed and Polly McClintock Weiss

Ed Weiss has always regarded himself as an Orthodox Jew. His parents, brothers, and sisters have, through the years, been devoted members of the synagogue. Further, the traditional Jewish practices have always been observed in his parents' home, and Ed, like others in the family, has been observant of the Jewish ritual.

Ed was so preoccupied with his business interests that he, although thirty-one years of age, seldom went out socially. What little time he had away from business was spent with parents, brothers, and sisters. Had anyone even suggested that Ed would ultimately marry a non-Jewish girl, he would have been laughed at. It all sounded so utterly preposterous. Yet that is precisely what happened!

Ed cannot say exactly how it occurred, but he does remember "noticing" Polly McClintock, who was a secretary in his business, and speaking to her from time to time.

Polly, born of Irish Catholic parents, was a devoted daughter, the only child of these two devout people. Unlike them, Polly had begun, as early as her high school years, to question the tenets of the church. She had even become skeptical of the divinity of Jesus. Even though she attended church regularly she did so out of consideration for her parents and a concern that her friends should not think ill of her. When her father died and, shortly thereafter, her mother was taken ill, Polly devoted almost all of her time to her mother. She went out very little and then, only to the movies with friends of the family. Polly had taken a secretarial course following her high school graduation and almost immediately thereafter found employment in Ed Weiss' retail store. Her days were totally uneventful. Her life revolved around her mother and her job.

Polly cannot say just how it happened but she found Ed coming over to talk to her, inviting her, on occasion, to have lunch with him, and, on rare occasions, to have dinner together. After well over a year of these sporadic meetings, luncheons, and dinners, Polly and Ed found themselves going together rather regularly. One evening Ed told Polly that he was in love with her and wanted to marry her, but, out of regard for his parents as well as his own personal convictions, he could not feel free to do so unless Polly would consent to be formally converted to Judaism.

Polly, too, was torn between her loyalties to mother and to the church. It was not that she regarded herself as a good Catholic. It was rather that she identified herself with a Catholic family. Unable to decide what to do, she finally confessed her dilemma to her mother, and much to her surprise, she heard her mother urge her to convert to Judaism in order that she might marry Ed. Fortified by her mother's words, she, independently of Ed, visited with the Orthodox rabbi and told him her story, asking among other things, whether her marriage to Ed as a convert might not affect his standing and reputation within the Jewish community. When she was assured that it would not, Polly agreed to convert to Judaism and then to marry Ed.

Polly devoted over a year to an intensive study of Judaism, guided by the rabbi. She was formally converted to Judaism and then in the traditional Jewish manner married Ed.

These two have been married for over fifteen years. They maintain a "Jewish" home, observing the Sabbath, festivals, and Holy Days, and are exceedingly careful about the proper observance of the dietary laws both within and outside of the home. They have two children, a boy and a girl. Both children have received a Jewish parochial school education and are generally regarded as "religious." Both Polly and Ed are respected members of the Jewish community. Ed's parents are proud of both Polly and Ed. Polly's mother has since passed away, but she too favored the marriage.

Polly says: "Ours is a good marriage, but it could never have been had I not converted to Judaism."

Lucille Hanrahan Goldberg

Lucille lived most of her early years in the southern part of Minnesota. Her parents, devout Catholics, had three other children, all younger than Lucille. Neither parent had received any schooling beyond the elementary grades. Her father was a carpenter; her mother, a housewife. Both were respected members of the community. They were active members of the church and were regarded as devout people.

Lucille had attended the parochial school in the region, was a regular attendant at church and an active participant in its many youth programs. She was a popular youngster, with many girl as well as boy friends. There had been only one Jewish family in town that Lucille remembers. People liked them but wondered about them because they were obviously not religious.

Lucille's school and home life was pleasant but uneventful. It was only when she was about to graduate from high school that she gave some thought to her future. The advice of both parents and friends was that she ought to become a nurse. There seemed to be no good reason for not doing so; whereupon, following graduation, and with the blessing and financial support of her parents, Lucille enrolled for a nurses' training program at one of the major hospitals in Minneapolis.

The new life that opened up to her in this metropolis proved to be quite a revelation to her. There were so many different kinds of people. She met more Protestants than she had ever known before, and there were Jewish internes on the hospital staff too. At first, hesitant about about dating persons of other religions, Lucille found that other girls in nurses' training were dating outside of their religion, and, following the course of least resistance, she did likewise. She was careful, however, to keep this information from her parents, fearing what they might say or do.

It was at a party that Lucille met Dan Goldberg, a Jewish youth who was just starting his business career as a salesman. Almost from the very beginning they responded well to each other. Each knew the religious affiliation of the other, but neither seemed to mind. Lucille's one worry was that her parents might, somehow, hear that she was dating persons of other religions.

Dan had little feeling about his Jewishness. He was a Jew, but neither he nor his parents were religious or observant. He had dated non-Jews almost from the beginning of his social life. His parents had urged him to marry a Jewish girl, but he couldn't understand why it mattered to them. He felt himself to be quite independent of them. Within a six-month period Dan had proposed marriage to Lucille, and she had, with but a moment's thought, accepted. There was, however, one important consideration. It was to be understood that she was to remain a Catholic even though her children would be reared as Jews. Dan agreed. There was no trouble about Dan's parents. They liked Lucille very much. But it was not easy to secure the approval of Lucille's parents. They regarded her action as treasonous. Lucille, very much in love, agreed to be married by a justice of the peace.

The marriage took place fifteen years ago. Although Lucille had not converted while her two daughters were growing up, she never informed her children that she was, in fact, a Roman Catholic. When the children were old enough to attend a religious school, Lucille, although never asked to do so, enrolled her daughters in a Jewish religious school and began to observe certain Jewish practices within the home, such as kindling the Sabbath candles. Never did Dan request this of her. On the other hand, he never protested her new practices. Inasmuch as Lucille's parents broke all contact with her at the time of the marriage and Dan's parents never discussed religion or Lucille's practices, the two daughters were never aware that their mother was anything other than a Jewess.

When the oldest daughter was about to reach the Bat Mitzvah (confirmation) age of thirteen, Lucille visited with the rabbi of the congregation and divulged her great secret. But Lucille informed the rabbi that she "could no longer live a lie" and asked to be converted to Judaism before the Bat Mitzvah. The rabbi agreed to assist provided that Lucille undertake an intensive course of study preceding the formal conversion and further, that, following the ceremony, she and Dan would be remarried in accordance with the Jewish tradition.

Lucille and Dan agreed to follow the rabbi's advice and, after a six-month course of study the formal conversion and the remarriage took place. One month thereafter, the Bat Mitzvah of the daughter occurred at the Sabbath Eve service. That evening, Lucille whispered to the rabbi: "Now I feel that I am really a Jewess and my family is a religious unit at last." No one, other than Lucille and Dan, is aware of all that has occurred.

Mrs. Edna Pressman

Edna Pressman has lived all of her life in a small town in Pennsylvania. She is the daughter of parents who live in the same community. Edna's father was a Protestant and her mother a Catholic. However, they were married in the Catholic church, and Edna and her younger sister were reared as Catholics. She attended a Catholic parochial school through the elementary grades and, for a period of two years, attended a Catholic girls' school.

Edna describes her parents' marriage as "unhappy." Her parents separated when she was five years old. The children never saw their father again until Edna was about eighteen years old. The sole responsibility for the rearing of the two girls rested on Edna's mother. When her mother finally legally divorced her father, Edna's mother felt that in the eyes of the Church she was no longer a "good" Catholic, and this distressed her greatly. A year thereafter, Edna's mother remarried, this time to an Italian Catholic. The mother has a younger sister who married a Jew. Each has retained his own religion. Edna thinks of her Jewish uncle with great affection and believes that this family experience prepared her to accept the marriage proposal from Nathan Pressman. She feels, too, that the Church's attitude toward her mother, because of her divorce, was unjust. "I don't believe that God or Jesus would deprive her of attaining Paradise just because she divorced my father."

Edna never went beyond the second year in high school due to the economic pressures in her mother's home. She worked at a variety of jobs, finally deciding to go to a "beautician school," from which she graduated a year later. It was during this period that she met Nathan, who was then teaching high school. Edna knew that Nathan was Jewish and Nathan knew that Edna was a Catholic. Nathan had dated other non-Jewish girls frequently. Nathan's parents were Orthodox Jews. They observed the dietary laws and other rituals, strictly. Nathan did not regard himself as Orthodox. He was, however, very much identified with the Jewish people.

Edna's mother liked Nathan but made it clear to Edna that she would prefer that she marry a Catholic. Very much in love and aware that Nathan would never convert to Catholicism, Edna, realizing that Nathan's religion was important to him, decided to convert to Judaism. Both discussed the matter with the local Reform rabbi. When Edna informed her mother, there was a "scene," with emphasis on the idea that "it would never work out." Members of her family tried to dissuade Edna, but to no avail. Edna wavered but, finally, after a little over a year, decided to go ahead with plans for the conversion. Following six months of study with the rabbi, the marriage took place.

Nathan's family, too, had been upset but, when conversion was agreed upon, their unhappiness subsided. The conversion ceremony included the traditional immersion and the acquisition of a Hebrew name. None of Edna's family attended the marriage service.

The marriage has been a happy one. Nathan attended night school and earned a law degree. Edna continued to work until she became pregnant. These two now have three children, two boys and a girl. Each has attended Hebrew school. The Pressmans have, for years, been affiliated with a synagogue. They attend High Holy Days services and, on occasion, attend the weekly Sabbath service. They do not observe the traditional dietary laws. The Pressmans have been married for thirty years.

The oldest son is now married to a Jewish girl, which pleases

Edna and Nathan. "But," says Edna, "if any of the children married a non-Jew, I wouldn't feel badly because I would never want to dictate to them. My own experience makes me feel it would be wrong. I try to have the children feel that they are Jewish but whatever their choice, I would be satisfied. Their father would not be happy about it but he would have to get used to the idea."

Edna admits to having been uncertain about being a Jew, for many years following her marriage. But Nathan has been such a good husband that all doubts have disappeared. She believes that the unity of the family must be preserved and that conversion was "right" for her because it has made a good marriage possible.

Louise Carle

Louise was born and reared in Southern California, the daughter of middle-class Methodist parents who "sent their children to Sunday school but, themselves, only went to church on Easter and Christmas." The Sunday school was changed whenever the family moved as a matter of convenience. At times, it was a Christian Science Sunday school, at other times it was a Unitarian school. There was no consistent pattern.

Louise had always wanted to be a doctor, but her grades were such that this became unthinkable. Following graduation from high school, Louise decided to become a nurse. After completion of the nurses' training course, she fell madly in love with an Italian Catholic and married him, over the objections of her parents. Their objection was based on the fact that he was of Italian origin. The religious element mattered little to them. But Louise was informed by the priest that he could only officiate if she promised to rear their children as Catholics. Both she and her "intended" objected. Hence, their marriage was solemnized by a Justice of the Peace. For two years, Louise and Mike were very happy. Then Mike became ill and, following an operation, he died, leaving Louise with a six-month-old child.

Mike had had many friends, among the closest of whom was

Larry Isaacs, a Jew who was regarded by Louise, too, as a dear friend. Larry was married, but it was an unhappy marriage that suddenly ended in divorce.

Following Mike's death and Larry's divorce Larry would come over to visit with Louise. Within a year, the friendship ripened into love, and Larry asked Louise to marry him.

During the period following Mike's death, life was exceedingly difficult for Louise. Mike's parents had not been helpful. They had, in fact, always resented Louise, believing that she had taken their son away from his parents and the Catholic religion. Louise continued her nursing career in order to support herself and her baby. For a time, the baby resided with Louise's parents while Louise worked at various hospitals.

Larry's parents had come to know Louise while Mike was still alive, and they attempted to help Louise in every way possible, unaware that their son Larry was thinking seriously about asking Louise to marry him.

For about a year Larry kept proposing marriage to Louise only to have Louise postpone her answer. "Frankly, I was worried about being married to a Jew. He was a grand person, but he was a Jew and his parents, I knew, hoped that he would, someday, marry a Jewish girl." Louise also felt that Larry proposed marriage because he was "sorry for her, what with the baby and all." After much discussion with her girl friends, Louise decided that if she was going to marry Larry, she would first convert to Judaism. When she made this proposal, Larry objected because he believed her to be insincere. Louise, however, finally convinced him and, subsequently, Larry's family that "this was the right thing to do."

Louise and Larry visited a Reform rabbi and arranged for Louise to study with the rabbi in preparation for the formal conversion. About six months later, the conversion ceremony took place and was immediately followed by the marriage service. Neither of Louise's parents attended the ceremony nor did any members of her family. Her parents still feel that she has done the "wrong thing" even though the marriage has been a happy one for the past twelve years. The daughter, legally adopted by Larry, is attending the temple Sunday school. She has never been formally converted to Judaism but thinks of herself as a Jewess. Most of the friends of Louise and Larry are Jewish. Their home is free from any Jewish ritual but they are affiliated with a temple.

Oswald Williams

Oswald, a Negro, just twenty-two years old, was born in a small city in Alabama. He has two brothers and three sisters, all younger than he. His parents, natives of the area, both work. The crowded condition of their small home made it necessary for Oswald to live for a brief period at his grandmother's home, just a short distance away. While Oswald was three years old, his mother took him on a visit to an aunt (the mother's sister) in Illinois and left him there. He lived happily with his aunt and uncle until he was twelve years old. Gradually he began to yearn for his parents so, at age twelve, he was sent back to Alabama. Both uncle and aunt were "very good" to him. Oswald's parents are Baptists. His aunt and uncle are Quakers. He has always had a warm and close relationship with his male cousin with whom he was reared. Uncle and aunt are very active in their devotion to the religious life as represented by the Quakers. His parents too were highly religious Baptists. Every summer Oswald would return South to visit his parents. While the parents lived in a segregated neighborhood, Oswald's uncle and aunt lived in an integrated northern area. There is a close bond between all the members of the family which Oswald obviously shares and enjoys. When he returned to live with his parents once again, he enrolled in an all-Negro school and with equal ease, began attending the Baptist church of his parents. Despite the vast difference between the Baptist and Quaker services, Oswald did not feel disturbed or upset. "I preferred the Quaker atmosphere over the Baptist but since I was there, I knew I had to adapt." But actually, Oswald admits to being displeased with his church and its ways. Each summer he returned to his former home in Illinois. Throughout the years, increasing dissatisfaction with the church of his parents is noted. By his senior year in high school, Oswald openly rebelled, because "he didn't like the services or the minister." Too much "hellfire and damnation" preaching. As a consequence, Oswald, much to the consternation of parents and grandmother, tried to find a new and better religion for himself. Christianity itself proved to be distressing, for Oswald could no longer believe in the divinity of Jesus. Another branch of the family, living in Florida, were Roman Catholics.

Oswald went on to a small Southern college at the partial expense of his parents. He has won several scholarships also, thereby reducing his over-all college costs. College is a real source of pleasure to Oswald. Although his cousin is now attending law school at a Northern state university, the two boys are still the closest of friends. Two years ago, Oswald decided to take summer school courses in a Northern university. Here, he met a number of Jewish students. Impressed with them, he became curious about their religion and began to read avidly about Judaism. He has read and studied Judaism in considerable depth. He enjoys reading "just about everything." The more he read, the more convinced he became that he should be converted to Judaism. He spoke with his parents about his intentions and they, deeply distressed, tried to discourage him. In addition to being a Negro, he would now have problems associated with being a Jew. "I have asked myself, 'Am I ready for this? I believe I am.'" Oswald is "going with 'a Negro girl' whom [I hope] to marry but [I hope] too that she will convert to Judaism." Oswald has just completed his formal conversion to Judaism after studying with a rabbi for the past several years. He is convinced that Judaism will prove completely satisfying to him.

Sarah and John Kragg

Sarah is the daughter of a scholarly East-European Jew who, in order to earn a livelihood, has become a tailor. Sarah's mother, a Russian Jewess, an unlearned woman, had a serious mental breakdown from which she never recovered. In and out of institutions for many years, she tried to take the lives of her children. Both Sarah and her brother suffered greatly during those years. Her life as a child and adolescent was wretched, resulting in an extremely unhappy and lonely life. Dirty and unkempt, with no one to care for her, Sarah herself became ill and suffered numerous "breakdowns." The only person who really cared for her during those years was a Polish Roman Catholic lady and her young son, who lived next door. Whenever pressed by these conditions, Sarah would run to the apartment of the neighbor. Sarah's father, badly beaten by the mother's illness, was simply unable to assist Sarah in any way.

Mrs. Kragg, the neighbor, was a devout woman. But her son John turned from the church when, so he claims, he was refused a seat in the church because he did not have a nickel to "put in the box." A few years later, Mrs. Kragg became a member of "Jehovah's Witnesses." Other members of the family were distressed with her.

John's father was a drunkard. He used to beat his wife regularly, to the disgust of John, his brother, and sister. John remembers his mother with love. He hates his father. John never went to grade school beyond the seventh grade. Then, he took off "from home," trying his hand at many odd jobs in various parts of the country, including service in the Navy as an able-bodied seaman.

John met Sarah when Mrs. Kragg tried to help Sarah during her mother's breakdown. Living in the next building, she did whatever she could to assist her. Sarah's highly emotional nature got her into trouble with many people, including her schoolteachers. Both John and Sarah were such lonely, unhappy people that they found in each other something that made for warmth and understanding. While Mrs. Kragg would feed, comb, and clean Sarah, John looked sympathetically and understandingly on Sarah. As a consequence, they started to go "steady."

Sarah's father discovered that she and John were seeing each other regularly. For the first and only time in his life, he struck

Sarah. "The idea of a Jewish girl going with a Christian boy!" John's mother said only, "Whoever you want to marry, I will accept." Sarah remembers her as the only source of love and warmth she had in her early years.

Sarah and John were married by a Justice of the Peace when she was eighteen years old and John, twenty-five. However much Sarah's father had opposed the marriage, he nevertheless attended the marriage service. Sarah's mother was in an institution at that time.

John had refused to convert to Judaism at the time of the marriage, even though he knew that it would please Sarah's father. "If I don't believe, I don't convert." Sarah had agreed to raise their children as Catholics. Two daughters were, in fact, christened in the Church. Over long stretches of time, Sarah would become ill, on the verge of a breakdown, but, somehow, with the aid of physicians and psychiatrists, managed to recede from the brink. Sarah somehow became interested in nursery training work and, despite her inadequate schooling, passed all courses with honors. She has demonstrated talent not only as a teacher but as a painter and sculptor as well.

John's economic position improved so that these two and their children were able to purchase a small home in a suburb just outside of Boston. Suddenly, Sarah felt that the children should be reared as Jews, and, with John's consent, they began to attend a congregational Hebrew school.

One day, John's oldest daughter said to him, "Dad, look at those lucky kids. They're going to temple with their fathers. Other kids are going to church with their fathers. Why don't *we* go?" John set to thinking about his daughter's comment and decided that he ought to become a Jew and "make ourselves a family unit."

Sarah says that on the day her daughter was christened, she determined that, some day, she would return to Judaism with her children.

John says that the five years that have passed since he formally converted to Judaism have been the happiest years of his life.

Evelyn Webber

Evelyn was born in a small town in the northern part of Massachusetts. She regarded herself and her parents as Christian even though her father, himself reared as a Baptist, had no real church affiliation, while her mother was a Unitarian. Evelyn had attended Methodist, Congregational, and Christian Science churches at various times. Although church formalities were not emphasized, both parents stressed ethical and moral conduct. Both parents were college graduates.

Evelyn was graduated from high school with no particular distinction. During her senior year, she started going steady with a classmate, and, immediately following graduation, she married him.

Evelyn explains her hasty marriage by pointing out that, despite what appeared to be a good family life, her parents did not get along; her father was an alcoholic and her mother was "high strung." Evelyn says: "I thought I could run away from it that way."

Evelyn and Dave were married about two and one-half years. Dave began to drink and "proved he wasn't any good." The marriage ended in divorce, but only after the birth of two children. Then, Evelyn and the children moved back into her parents' home.

Evelyn got a job in Boston and decided to bring the children with her. She found it too difficult so she boarded the children out when she worked. Later, she placed the children in a Catholic day school. She drifted from one position to another, but always supported her children. During these years, there were incipient romances that lasted for very short periods of time.

Evelyn enrolled the children in a Congregational Sunday school, and she herself attended regularly. She felt that the early Catholic day school training given her children needed to be counteracted because, to her, it was so bigoted. It was during this period that Evelyn began to read about many different religions, including Judaism. A friend living in the same building introduced her to Jewish ideas and values and seemed so pleased by her experiences with Jews and Judaism that Evelyn continued to read more and more about Judaism, finding herself more pleased and satisfied as time went on. In the matter of her personal life, however, Evelyn was unhappy. There were many broken romances. Psychologists and a psychiatrist gave Evelyn counsel. Still Evelyn could not "find herself." Religiously, Evelyn had long since ceased to believe in Jesus as the Christ. But Evelyn was not pleased with this negation. She sought for something positive in which she could believe. She continued reading and visiting various churches as well, but nowhere did she feel at home. Reading Herman Wouk's *This Is My God* proved to be the most exciting experience in Evelyn's religious rebirth. This she followed up with a course at one of the Jewish temples, generally taken by candidates for conversion. Evelyn had no such intention when she began the course, but as the class continued, she became certain that she should be converted to Judaism. Following a year's study, the formal conversion took place.

Evelyn, still caring for her children, who are both adolescents, is a regular attendant at Sabbath worship services. She has also been invited to teach Sunday school. She dates on occasion but has no plans for marriage. Her children are not Jews. The son regards himself as a Catholic, while her daughter says she is a Protestant.

Cora Haines Schwartz

Cora is a New Englander, born and bred. Her parents, both Episcopalians, were also born in New England—and *their* parents (on both sides of the family) before them. Cora is the oldest of three children. She has a brother and a sister. The small seacoast town in Maine from which Cora came was, with but few exceptions, a Protestant religious community. Only three Jewish families resided there with a rather small Catholic population.

Cora describes her early years as "uneventful." She attended the elementary and high school and graduated from the latter with no special achievement record or failures, either. It was only at high school that she realized that there were such people as Jews who lived in her town. That was when she started going with a boy who, she later was informed, was Jewish. The small number of Catholics and Jews got along well in the community. There was little trace of any overt prejudice. Cora claims that she never heard a derogatory word about either Catholic or Jew from her parents or other members of her family.

Following graduation from high school, Cora worked in a factory and then served as a clerk in a retail store on the main street.

During her high school days, Cora had been dating a boy (Protestant) whom she knew all her life. The family believed that she would eventually marry this boy but when she dated her Jewish classmate she found herself very much in love with him and actually thought of converting to Judaism for his sake. But the "romance" ended two years after Cora's graduation from high school. She says: "On the rebound, I married the other boy I had been seeing off and on."

Cora first became interested in Judaism as a consequence of her dates with the Jewish boy. She, voluntarily, with no "pressures" from him, began to read about Judaism. It was at that time that she began to question the divinity of Jesus.

The marriage to Jim, the Protestant, continued for twenty-five years and produced two children, both of whom were reared as Methodists, the church affiliation of their father. Both of these children are now attending high school.

Cora's marriage to Jim ended in divorce. Jim was a "heavy drinker and highly unstable." The home was an unhappy place both for Cora and the children. When Cora could not tolerate the situation any longer and the children were grown to adolescence, Cora finally sought and was granted a divorce. Jim has left the area. Only twice in the past five years has he seen his children and then, only for a few brief moments. Cora got a job as a clerk and supported her family as best she could.

Jacob, a Jewish merchant in the town, had been married to his Jewish wife for twenty-four years. They had two children. But, says Jacob, "the marriage was really an unhappy one for most of those years." Finally, by mutual agreement, a divorce was agreed upon. Jacob enjoys a fine reputation as a businessman and as an active member of both the Jewish and general community. He regards himself as an Orthodox Jew. His home has always been "strictly kosher," his children have received the most intensive Hebrew education available in the community. He has been the president of the synagogue.

Jacob met Cora shortly after his divorce—and enjoyed her company. Cora's son and daughter liked Jacob from the start. Jacob states that even though he wanted to marry Cora, he realized that this could not be unless she would convert to Judaism as an Orthodox Jewess because he really felt strongly about Judaism and, further, because he wanted to continue to be part of the Jewish community.

Cora agreed to convert and, after several visits with the local Orthodox rabbi, decided to prepare for the conversion by undertaking to study Judaism, aided by the rabbi. She states that her children, while remaining loyal to Christianity, raised no objections to her conversion, principally because they liked Jacob and his children.

The formal conversion, traditional in form, occurred five years ago. The four children live together with their parents and all appear to be happy. The Jewish community, shocked at first that Jacob married a non-Jewess, have come to accept Cora as a Jewess. She maintains the dietary laws, observes the Sabbath, and comports herself as a devout Jewess. Cora says, "I not only *am* a Jewess, but I *feel* that I am a Jewess. I'm completely at home."

Cora's parents offered no objections to her conversion. They were pleased, however, when Cora's children decided to remain in their own church. Only a year ago, Cora and Jacob became the parents of a baby girl. They look forward to giving this child an intensive Hebrew education. Jacob's children by his first wife continue to be observant Jews. They attend the synagogue regularly.

Cora's children continue to attend their church on Sundays. They observe Christmas and Easter at the home of Cora's parents and have never asked that their present home should celebrate these festivals and holy days.

Both Cora and Jacob feel that they have "made" a good marriage. They see no obstacles to their future happiness as a consequence of having two religions in their home.

Arnold Jones

Arnold Jones was born in Milwaukee but was reared in Idaho and Georgia. His parents, nonpracticing Episcopalians, had Arnold attend a Baptist Sunday school for a very brief time. Other than that, Arnold had no religious training. Arnold's parents were divorced when he was about five years old. He has had very little contact with his "real" mother through all those years. Arnold's father remarried, but his second wife died ten years ago. His stepmother had been raised as a Catholic. Following his parents' divorce, Arnold was sent to Idaho to live with his mother's parents. After his father remarried, Arnold joined his father and stepmother in Georgia. He says, "I have been considerably affected by the aftereffects of the divorce." Living with grandparents and later with his father and stepmother, Arnold has often wondered about "what life would be like" if he had had a normal home life. Arnold's own mother remarried too, this time to a Roman Catholic. He believes that his mother has not seen him through these many years because his mother fears what her new husband would say.

Arnold now has a warm, solid relationship with his father even though he believes that, as a child, he was neglected by both his father and stepmother. They were "in conflict" over many years but seem to have resolved their differences.

Arnold attended high school in Georgia. He was always a very good student, enjoying school very much. It was natural for him to go on to Harvard University. Here, too, he received high grades.

His college years were happy ones for him in every way. There were only a few contacts with parents because summers were spent either at school or at some temporary job. All school bills were met by Arnold's father. Determined to go on to graduate school, Arnold worked for several years in order to obtain the necessary funds. His father had found himself unable to assist him further. During those years, Arnold decided to work for a Ph.D. degree in sociology at the University of Minnesota.

Arnold has always liked people. He has enjoyed "dating," paying little attention to the matter of difference in religion.

While at graduate school, Arnold met another graduate student, a Jewish girl in the same department. They began going together and continued seeing each other for a period of almost two years. Arnold and Florence began to be quite certain that they were in love, but Florence hesitated because she knew that her parents' reaction to her proposed marriage to a non-Jew would be unfavorable. Florence's parents are both college graduates. Her father is an attorney. Florence had attended Wellesley College as an undergraduate. She does not regard herself as a religious Jewess, nor do her parents think of themselves as "religious." However, they have objected strongly to an intermarriage. Both parents hinted to Florence that if Arnold would convert to Judaism, they would have no real objection to him, although they still preferred that Florence marry a natural-born Jew. As a consequence, Arnold offered to convert if he would receive the consent of Florence's parents. After further discussion and debate, Florence's parents agreed. Arnold's father, when informed, simply said: "It's *your* life to do with as you choose."

Arnold spent six months in a study of Judaism under the tutelage of the rabbi with whose congregation Florence's family is affiliated. Judaism or any other religion means little to either Arnold or Florence. They have done exactly what has been requested of them insofar as formal requirements are concerned. Arnold now has his Ph.D. degree and is teaching at a nearby college. Florence is also working for her higher degree. They have one child, a girl. There is nothing either Jewish or Christian in their lives. In fact, both state that they are "not interested" in religion.

Laurel Backman

Laurel is an exciting but highly erratic young lady, converted to Judaism because of her love for Larry, a Jew whose interest in and concern for Judaism is purely secondary. It is Larry's father, who is generally regarded as one of the finest, most learned, and cultured Jews of his community, who has influenced Laurel's actions. She determined not to disgrace the Backman family by failing to convert to Judaism. She says "It was bad enough for my father-in-law to hear that Larry wanted to marry a non-Jewess. If I had not offered to convert, I'm sure he would have died."

Laurel came from upstate New York. Her parents are middle-class people. Her father is an engineer. Following high school, Laurel was the recipient of a scholarship to the University of Connecticut. It was there that she met her future husband. Laurel describes her family as "nothing Protestants." Laurel's family have high intellectual standards, and she has followed in their footsteps. But she is "brilliantly erratic." Laurel never went to Sunday school and never attended church. The family disliked "organized religion." Laurel's family was highly regarded as one of the top families in her home town.

Laurel was more interested in meeting "nice boys" than in a college education. Her first years at college were not especially happy ones. She was, at the outset, a failure in most of her courses, primarily because she refused to study.

Larry was a graduate student at Connecticut. He was the son of one of the most conservative of Jewish families in Connecticut. Larry's father was a fine Hebrew scholar and very active in Jewish community life. He was "a believer in books."

Larry and Laurel began going together almost immediately after their first meeting in the university library. Laurel's failure to keep up with her classwork resulted in her "being thrown out of school."

People who knew Larry's family relayed the news that Larry was going steady with Laurel, a non-Jew. Laurel's parents, also hearing about Larry, objected to her dating primarily because he had no definite ideas about his career. Larry's mother, tearfully, objected to Laurel. She asked: "How can I go around in the Jewish community with this shame upon me?" It was this fact that finally "broke" Laurel. Larry finally told Laurel that he loved her but, in deference to his parents, could not marry a non-Jewish girl. He asked Laurel to convert to Judaism. Laurel asked herself: "Do I want to live as a Jew and do I wish my children to?" It took over six months for her to decide to convert.

Laurel began to read about Judaism. She met Larry's family and, as a consequence, agreed to convert to Judaism. This proved to be a shock to Laurel's parents, as it was to Larry's parents. But the love between these two persisted. Every effort was made by both families to break off the romance, but to no avail.

Laurel went to visit the Reform rabbi in the community to try to understand more fully the obligations she would be expected to assume as a Jewess. It was then that she decided to study Judaism with the rabbi. After a study period of six months, she was formally converted and, later, married by the rabbi.

Larry and Laurel have now been married for seven years. Larry has not had an easy time of it insofar as his career as a businessman is concerned. They have two children, a girl and a boy. The parents have relented insofar as their opposition to the marriage is concerned.

Laurel has tried to maintain a Jewish home, and while the dietary laws are not observed, she kindles the Sabbath candles and tries to observe the Sabbath, in degree. Her children attend Hebrew school. Laurel feels that she is a Jewess and is especially concerned that her father-in-law, whom she respects highly, should think well of her. Laurel feels that she would want her children to marry Jews because "this is what they are." Larry and Laurel are very much in love. They both feel that, despite the obstacles put in their way, they would do it all over again.

Fred Davis

Fred Davis is forty-four years old. He was born and reared in Cleveland, Ohio. His parents regard themselves as Presbyterians. Fred's father is a school official. He has received high honors in his field and, throughout his career, has worked with people of all the three major faiths.

Fred has always been a fine athlete. During his high school days, he used to play in gymnasium in the Jewish community center building. Neither Fred nor his parents have been active religionists, although, sporadically, they attended church services.

At the Jewish center, Fred came to know Jewish boys and always got along well with them. His great interest in athletics resulted in close friendships with Jews. He was invited to parties and socials in the Jewish community.

When he went on to college, where he received an athletic scholarship, he also maintained a warm relationship with Jews. Never did he feel that the matter of religion separated him from his Jewish friends. Nevertheless, during those days, he attended the Presbyterian church whenever possible.

When World War II broke out, Fred enlisted in the Navy for a period of four years. In Fred's opinion, he has always felt "at home" with Jews as well as with Catholics. His parents always stressed the need to learn to live with people of all races and religions.

Fred met Alice, a Jewess, on a blind date, after he returned from the service. Alice's parents were very much upset by this romance and urged Alice to break it off. But she, very much in love, refused to do so despite the fact that she and her family regarded themselves as Orthodox Jews. They dated for a period of seven months before they decided that they "were meant for each other." It was especially difficult for Alice's parents to accept Fred even though they liked him personally. No member of their family had ever before entered into an interfaith marriage.

Alice had never asked Fred to convert to Judaism, but Fred, sensing the attitude of Alice's parents, volunteered to do so. Fred had never accepted Jesus as the Messiah, even though he thought of him as a great teacher. He knew that his parents would certainly not object. It took almost a year for Alice to convince her parents that she was in love with Fred and that Fred was sincere in his desire to convert.

Before the parents arrived at a decision, Alice and Fred eloped and were married by a justice of the peace. As a consequence, Alice's parents agreed to accept Fred if he would formally convert to Judaism. For Fred, this meant not only a period of formal study and immersion but circumcision in accordance with traditional Jewish practice, all of which he agreed to.

Fred and Alice have been married for fifteen years. They have three children, two sons and a daughter. The children all attend Hebrew school. Fred, Alice, and family are regular attendants at Sabbath services. Alice's family, her parents, brothers, and sisters, all accept Fred. Fred feels "very much a part of the family." He is also close to his own parents. Fred believes that he is a "good" Jew. "At any rate, I'm trying hard to be worthy of my in-laws. They're good people and I respect them." The children think of themselves as Jews, but, from time to time, raise questions about "what we really are—Jews or Christians."

Dora Reiner

Dora Reiner was born and reared in London, England. Her parents, Anglicans by religion, were not religious people in a formal sense. They were, however, highly respectable people who, Dora says, "lived by the Ten Commandments." When Dora was six years old, her parents emigrated to the United States and to the state of New

Hampshire. The relationship between Dora and her parents was always excellent. There were many friends, socials, and parties to keep them all happy. Dora loved to sing and, as a consequence, she was in demand to entertain at various church socials. She made friends easily.

Early in her high school days, Dora decided to study for the nursing profession. She worked and studied at the Boston City Hospital. Her friendships were numerous. There were persons of many religions; her roommate was a Catholic. Those years were happy and satisfying ones for her. Following graduation, the passing of State Board examinations, and other formalities, Dora returned home to New Hampshire but remained for only a brief period because she found that she had "nothing in common" with those people. She returned to Boston and went to work as a nurse in the Boston City Hospital.

It was there that Dora met Jack, the man who was to become her husband. Jack's mother had been brought into the hospital as an emergency patient, and Dora was assigned to care for her.

As a consequence of his regular visits to the hospital, Jack became interested in Dora. Jack's mother (his father was deceased) was quite Orthodox. When she heard that Jack and Dora were serious about each other, she stormed, making her objections very clear. Jack decided to marry Dora notwithstanding his mother's objections, so they were married by a justice of the peace. The pressures from mother, uncles, and aunts continued, but neither Dora nor Jack saw anything wrong in what they had done. When Jack's mother once again became very ill, Dora offered to nurse her and the offer was accepted. This time, Jack's mother did not recover.

The marriage, to this point, had not been happy because of the pressures that had been placed upon both Jack and Dora. Gradually, however, these two began to build their own lives, independent of their respective families. But Dora recognized the close tie that had existed between Jack and his mother. She sensed too that Jack wanted, in some way, to atone for having "broken his mother's heart." She felt that she could do this best if she proposed to convert to Judaism. At first Jack disapproved, but, as Dora persisted and weeks went by, Jack agreed. Dora then turned to a Conservative rabbi for counsel and guidance. Dora studied with the rabbi for about three months. She was then formally converted to Judaism in accordance with traditional Jewish practice.

Dora has taken her conversion seriously. Even though Jack seldom attends synagogue services, Dora is a regular weekly worshipper. She has insisted upon giving her two sons a Hebrew education. Both sons have been Bar Mitzvah; one son is married to a Jewish girl, the other has married a Protestant girl. Of these two, neither Dora's son nor his wife has given up their respective religions. Dora is unhappy about the marriage, but she is hopeful that, some day, her daughter-in-law will convert to Judaism. Dora is an active member of the temple sisterhood and regards herself as a good Jewess.

Elaine Dansky

Elaine is a native of Vermont, as were her Catholic parents. She describes her parents as "fallen away" Catholics in that they seldom attended church services except when they visited with or were visited by their respective families, all of whom regarded themselves as good Catholics. Elaine's father was a Naval officer; her mother, a housewife. Despite their own lack of devotion, both parents insisted that Elaine should attend a Catholic parochial school, feeling that "she should have *some* religion." Elaine was baptized and received communion in the Church. Her father was moved from city to city in the performance of his naval duties, but always, church school and church attendance were expected of Elaine. Elaine states that a good relationship always existed between her and her parents.

Elaine was graduated from a public high school and then went to work in a large industrial plant for five years. Thereafter, she became an airline stewardess. It was during this time that she met Harvey.

Harvey was a well-established businessman, residing in the Midwest. He began dating Elaine and they became good friends over a period of several years. At one point, Harvey told Elaine that he loved her and wished to marry her, but he would do so only on condition that she converted to Judaism. Elaine realized that even though Harvey was not a religious person, he felt strongly about being a Jew.

Elaine's mother had come to know Harvey and liked him very much. Her father never met Harvey until they decided to get married. During the several years that Elaine was dating Harvey, she seems to have been less regular in her church attendance. Thoughts about Harvey and the request he had made of her, left her in a state of uncertainty. "It wasn't necessarily giving up Catholicism that was the problem. Rather, it was the matter of accepting another. I felt that it would be difficult replacing one religion with another." Gradually, Elaine came to believe that all religions "were basically the same thing, they were all for the good life and it was just a matter of worship." She came to believe that "Jesus was on the same level as Moses," a human being, albeit a great one.

When, after many months of indecision, Elaine finally decided to convert to Judaism, she spoke to her father about her decision. He tried desperately to get her to see that she was making a serious mistake. But Elaine had made up her mind. She felt that her mother did approve of her decision.

Harvey's mother, upon hearing of his intention to marry Elaine following her conversion, remonstrated, trying to persuade her son to change his mind. (Harvey's father had died some years earlier.) Although Harvey felt close to his mother and was regarded as a dutiful son, he made it clear to her that his mind was set upon marriage to Elaine.

At this point, Elaine and Harvey went to call upon the Reform rabbi, even though Harvey and all the members of his family regarded themselves as Orthodox. For a period of three months the rabbi instructed Elaine on the nature and content of Judaism.

Shortly thereafter, a formal, nontraditional conversion ceremony took place, and a week later, Elaine and Harvey were married by the rabbi.

Harvey's mother, deeply distressed by the marriage of her son, nevertheless invited Elaine and Harvey to join in the Sabbath Eve meal on each Friday night, with all the other members of the family, as had been the family practice through all the years.

Elaine and Harvey have been married for ten years. They remain members of the Reform temple and worship there, primarily on the Jewish High Holy Days. Elaine participates in several Jewish community women's organizations and is well received by other Jewish men and women. They "do a lot of visiting and a lot of entertaining."

Elaine does not believe that her studies for conversion have really made her "any different in any way" from the way she thought and lived prior to that occasion. Harvey and Elaine have no children. They appear to be happy with each other. Conversion to Judaism has not really changed Elaine in her beliefs, values, attitudes. Only insofar as the Sabbath Eve meal is concerned, has Elaine changed in terms of ritual practice.

Karen Goldbaum

Karen Deane married Efraim Goldbaum four years ago, in a civil marriage. One year later they were married by an Orthodox rabbi. But for fifteen years prior to the marriage, Karen and Efraim lived together as husband and wife, and became the parents of three children, two sons and one daughter. Karen and Efraim state that their formal marriage would have taken place years ago had it not been that Efraim feared the wrath and indignation of his aged mother, whose Jewish traditional sentiments would have been opposed to her son's marriage to a non-Jewess. Out of regard for his mother, Efraim states, the official marriage never took place until his mother's death.

Both Karen and Efraim are New Englanders. Both were born

and reared in the state of Vermont. Karen is descended from an old and honored New England family, reared in the Protestant tradition. Efraim's parents came to Vermont from Russia in the 1890's. Efraim's father started as a peddler, graduated to a small retail store, and ultimately, as a consequence of the growth of the business, developed into a department-store type of business operation.

Both Karen and Efraim are college graduates. Each is regarded with respect by the larger community. Efraim has been a civic leader. Although there were many persons who knew about Karen and Efraim, it was generally not discussed. Even Efraim's brother and sister never spoke to him about Karen or the children born to them outside the bonds of matrimony.

Efraim insists that the only reason he and Karen were never officially married is because he feared for the health of his mother, who, he knew, was opposed to intermarriage. Further, he knew that she regarded conversion as a consequence of a desire to marry a person of another faith as a meaningless gesture. Efraim says that his mother would never have accepted it.

Karen, very much in love with Efraim, believes that Efraim "did the right thing." Only now, after eighteen years of living together without benefit of clergy, has Karen been able to convert to Judaism. In tribute to Efraim's mother she asked to be converted to Orthodox Judaism.

Karen has spent a year in study of Judaism under the tutelage of an Orthodox rabbi to whose congregation Efraim's mother, Mrs. Goldbaum, "belonged." Karen maintains a kosher home. She and Efraim send their youngest child to the Orthodox parochial school that is associated with the synagogue. She has joined the synagogue's sisterhood.

Efraim is a member of the synagogue's board of trustees. He continues to be a respected member of the Jewish community. One of his friends says, "We love and respect Karen and Efraim very much. We think that what these two have done to keep Efraim's mother from being distressed was a truly heroic act."

Karen regards herself as a good Jewess. Her children think of

themselves as Jews although only the youngest has had any contact with any part of the Jewish community. What will happen to
the older children, insofar as their religious life and affiliation is
concerned, is conjectural.

Augustine Smith

Augustine has always regarded herself as a "poor little rich girl."
She never knew her father, who died shortly before she was born.
Both parents were American-born. They were a wealthy family, so
wealthy, in fact, that Augustine remembers that, even after the
passing of her parents, she had only to ask for anything to have it
granted to her. Augustine was reared by a succession of governesses,
an aunt who tried to fulfill her mother's role, and a bank official who
was in charge of all fiscal matters. Augustine was an only child. She
had never had formal religious training, thought of herself as a
Protestant, but never attended a church. Nor does she have any
tradition about church affiliation. Throughout her early years, she
attended the church that her advisors of the moment suggested.
She had no special feeling for any of them.

Augustine lived in New York City. Her father, an investment
banker, had left both mother and daughter well provided for.
Augustine never attended a public school. She received all of her
schooling from private tutors. She had no young friends at any
time that she presently can recall.

Augustine thinks of her mother as a very beautiful and brilliant
woman whose knowledge of many languages—English, Italian,
French—always fascinated her. She regarded herself as a "very shy
girl" and also insists that she was not good looking. At about sixteen
years of age, following the death of her mother, Augustine traveled
extensively, always chaperoned but apparently never really in need
of a chaperone. "Dates" were few and far between and, therefore,
especially exciting.

Religion played no role in Augustine's life. Even after her
mother's death, there was no such "turning" to the church as
characterizes some persons under similar pressures. Visits to the

homes of occasional friends always left Augustine with the feeling that the great void in her life was her inability to feel "at home" in any religious group.

On an ocean voyage, following her mother's death, Augustine met a young man who "swept her off her feet." She soon fell madly in love with this Californian and, shortly thereafter, married him. Only after the marriage (by a justice of the peace) did Augustine meet her husband's family. But the marriage was not consummated. Somehow, Augustine's fears were too great. After a brief separation, the warm regard of her husband's family brought her back to her husband. Shortly thereafter she became pregnant and later bore a son. Augustine, apparently not very much enamored, decided to divorce her husband, which she did in due process. She returned to New York, established a home, and, only a few years later, met a fine man who proposed marriage. Again, Augustine accepted and married. Her new husband was a Catholic. But Augustine was not prepared to become a Catholic even though her husband proposed it. She did, however, rear her son as a Catholic. Kevin, the son, attended Catholic schools and ultimately married a Catholic girl. Augustine regards him as a devout Catholic.

Augustine's second marriage, too, proved to be an unhappy one for her. Despite the urgings of her husband, she once again was divorced and has, ever since, been living in New York City.

Augustine, now in her later 50's, is very much moved by the religiosity of her son and his family. Three years ago, out of love of her son, she approached a Paulist priest to inquire concerning the possibility of conversion to Roman Catholicism. After a three-month course of study, Augustine formally converted. She is "deliriously happy." It is "the most wonderful thing that ever happened to me."

Stella and George Di Napoli

George is an Italian-American. His parents came to the United States in the early 1900's. George was born in Pennsylvania. Although his father's first job was in the mining fields, he soon became a barber. One of ten children, George remembers his devout Catholic parents with great affection. Both parents "Americanized" quickly and spoke English very well. They maintained a warm relationship with their neighbors and were well-liked.

All of the Di Napoli children attended the parochial schools. Any other form of education would have been unthinkable. All the children were, of course, baptized and confirmed. Only George went beyond high school, and that was due to the opportunities provided by the G.I. Bill. George had served in the Army during World War II.

Stella's parents were Lithuanians. They, too, were devout Catholics but were hardly as well integrated into American life as were George's folks. Stella, too, attended a parochial school. Following her graduation from high school, she entered a nurses' training course in a Catholic hospital in her Connecticut community.

George and Stella met in Stella's hometown when George visited one of his Army friends. Even though both were Catholic, their traditions and their churches differed from each other inasmuch as the Italian Catholics and Lithuanian Catholics maintained their own ethnic ways and looked askance at each other. Stella's priest delivered his sermons in Lithuanian, while in George's church, the Italian language was used. When George told his folks he had met Stella, of Lithuanian origin, his parents objected. National origins "made a difference." George's folks expected him to marry an Italian girl. Only after George made it clear that he was in love with Stella and intended to marry her, did they "stop making a fuss."

Stella's family was equally disturbed by her choice of an Italian. When Stella's two sisters started to date, one, a Lutheran, and the other, an Episcopalian, her parents became thoroughly angered. But, in all cases, the girls persisted and the parents ultimately accepted their decisions.

Stella felt that "religion had been crammed down my throat," to the point that she became completely unhappy and dissatisfied not only with her parents but with Catholicism as well. She gradually ceased to believe in the divinity of Jesus and other fundamental doctrines of the Church. When she questioned these doctrines in home or at school, she was severely reprimanded. George too had "fallen away" from Catholic belief and practice, but, as he had already taken a well-paying job, his parents could do little to change his views. He was already quite independent of them.

George and Stella, very much in love, went together for six months. Despite the opposition of their parents, they decided to marry. Instead of asking a Catholic priest to officiate they eloped and were married by a justice of the peace. Both stated: "We just never felt comfortable in the Church."

Stella and George, anxious to be independent of their families, moved to another Connecticut town where George accepted a position in a large business firm.

For twenty years, these two and their family, three children (two boys and a girl), lived happily. All seemed to be going well with them. Still they were unhappy because they felt that there should be some religion which would make them happy, and they believed that Catholicism was not the religion for them. Although they gave their children a parochial school religious training, they never attended the Catholic church themselves.

Religion became an important topic of discussion in their home. Both George and Stella read considerably about the world's great religions.

Their oldest son married a Jewish girl and converted to Judaism. Neither parent objected. A second son married an Irish Catholic girl.

George and Stella, deeply concerned about their own religious life, gradually became convinced that Judaism more closely approximated their own religious ideas than any other religion. As a consequence, they decided to speak to the rabbi of a temple close by. After several meetings, they were convinced that they should be converted to Judaism. The rabbi gave them many books to read, as a result of which they, after several months, decided to convert to Judaism. "It was all so rational, so reasonable, that we knew almost at once that we were doing the right thing."

George and Stella were formally converted to Judaism after six months of intensive study with the rabbi. They observe the Sabbath, kindle the Sabbath candles, recite the Kiddush, and attend Sabbath services on Friday evening and Sabbath morning, regularly. They do not observe the dietary laws. (They were prepared for conversion by a Reform rabbi.)

Both Stella and George regard themselves as good Jews. They have become members of the temple, participate in its activities, and identify with the Jewish community through their contributions to Jewish philanthropic organizations. They now have Jewish friends as a consequence of their congregational affiliation and claim to feel "at home" with the Jewish people and the Jewish faith.

Mary Updike

Mary was born and reared in Madison, Wisconsin. Her parents, both Protestants, very much alive and challenged by all the intellectual stimulus of their proximity to a great university, gave Mary and her younger brother the opportunities for lively conversation and intellectual growth within their home as well.

Both of Mary's parents are college graduates. Her grandfather, on her father's side, was a minister. Mary believes that her father's interest in the Jews was stimulated by his knowledge of the Old Testament, taught to him by his father. Mary's mother, formerly a Presbyterian and now a Unitarian, "loves all humans regardless of race, creed, or color." Neither parent is a regular churchgoer today. Theirs is a happy home. There is much interest in books, ideas, and the arts. Her relationship with her parents has always been good.

Mary graduated from high school and then enrolled in another state university "just to get away from home and get new ideas." Her brother, too, is now attending a university in a neighboring state.

Almost from the start of her college career, Mary began to associate with Jewish students. She found them to be "highly stimulating and full of new ideas." She joined the Hillel Society on the campus because "more was going on there than in any other of the sectarian organizations."

Although they had never before discussed the matter, Mary discovered that her brother, too, had become a member of Hillel on his campus.

Mary had never attended a Sunday school during her years at home, but, on campus, she found herself attending Catholic and Protestant as well as Jewish religious services out of sheer curiosity. "I wanted to learn about all religions." The search for "intellectual and religious integrity" always seemed highly important to her. There were also the non- and antireligious students on campus who occupied Mary's attention.

The college years were most rewarding. Mary graduated with honors in philosophy. Her parents, though pleased with her progress, were disturbed because she seemed to be searching for some religious view of life that she had not yet acquired. But, aside from brief conversations on the subject, no serious objection to Mary's quest was raised by either parent.

Following graduation, Mary accepted a position as a social worker even though she had no technical training in this field. During this period, she continued her visits to various churches and synagogues. At that time she rented a room with a Jewish family. Once, she attended a synagogue service with them and found herself so moved by the experience that she decided to attend services there regularly. "Now I had a synagogue I could call my own."

As a consequence of these visits, she became acquainted with the Conservative rabbi and engaged him in lengthy conversations concerning Judaism. Never a believing Protestant, she began to feel that Judaism ought, formally, to be her religion. She never discussed the matter with either parent. The kind of life her Jewish friends lived also had a positive effect upon her. Continued synagogue attendance convinced her that "I had found something of tremendous value. It was both intellectually and emotionally satisfying. I was determined to be converted to Judaism."

At this point, Mary wrote to her parents about her religious experiences and of her wish to be converted to Judaism. Much to her surprise they agreed that whatever Mary would decide to do was satisfactory to them.

A series of visits with the rabbi resulted in agreement that, following a short period of formal instruction, Mary would be converted to Judaism. Emphasis must be placed on the fact that Mary was not dating any Jewish boy at this or any other time. There were no thoughts of marriage to a Jew.

Following a three-month study period, Mary was formally converted in the traditional Jewish manner and "I really found myself happy for the first time."

Mary has gone on to graduate school at another university. She has hopes of teaching on a college level some day. Each Sabbath she has attended the local synagogue and joins in the services. She has had no trouble accepting the Jewish theological concepts primarily because she never believed in Jesus either as the Savior or the Son of God.

For the past six years, Mary has lived the life of an authentic convert to Judaism. But she has, as always, been a lonely person. She has no close friends at school or elsewhere. She corresponds with her parents about once a month, with her brother on a less frequent basis. Aside from her graduate school interests, she has little to keep her busy or happy. Mary has recently suffered a mental breakdown and has voluntarily committed herself to a mental health hospital for treatment. There is every assurance that she will recover. What awaits her, upon her return to the outer world, is problematical.

Arlene Smith Metaxas

Four of Arlene's five brothers and sisters have married persons of a faith different from that of her parents. Two have married Catholics; one has married a Jew. And yet another has married a Methodist. Arlene's parents are Southern Baptists. The parents, "good, plain people" with little education, have worked hard to maintain the family during years of living on the brink of poverty.

Each of the children, following graduation from high school, went to work in order to augment the family income. A warm family relationship has existed throughout the years.

Arlene, following graduation from high school, met Jim, of Greek origin, whose company she enjoyed very much. When she spoke to her mother about him, her mother appeared to be upset and tried, in a matter-of-fact manner, to make it clear that there were major differences in religion to consider as well as the "different" customs of the Greek people. These, she believed would create a barrier that would be insuperable. But, upon Arlene's reporting this conversation to Jim, he insisted on discussing the matter with Arlene's parents. That visit resulted in a much friendlier attitude toward Jim. Still, one of Arlene's sisters, herself converted to Catholicism, was deeply resentful and "did everything possible to get Arlene to break it off."

Jim too had his problems with his parents. They did not take kindly to the idea of Arlene's marriage to Jim and explained, as gently as possible, the reasons therefor.

But the love of Jim and Arlene had grown stronger as the arguments against their marriage proliferated. The Army service into which Jim was called temporarily halted any action on Arlene's part to convert to the Greek Orthodox church. But following his release from the service, Arlene went to see Jim's priest and explained her desire to convert and the basis therefor. The priest discussed the matter with Jim's family, securing their halfhearted consent. Arlene, very much in love, refused to discuss the matter further with any of her family and "went ahead."

Arlene took instruction for six months and was then formally converted to the Greek Orthodox religion.

Both she and Jim are extremely happy. Arlene is especially fond of Jim's parents, who are very kind and considerate. She "loves" the closeness of the Greek family and is genuinely pleased because her conversion has resulted in the kind of family unity she had always wanted.

Arlene and Jim and their two young sons attend church each

Sunday together with all of Jim's family. She has joined various church auxiliaries. The sons go to Sunday school regularly. Arlene's parents, well aware of her happy married life, visit their daughter and her family fairly often and find themselves enjoying Jim's parents as well.

Arlene feels that her marriage has not involved any theological or other major shifts in viewpoint. "After all, I was a Christian before I married Jim, and I am still a good Christian. It's only the form that has changed somewhat."

Helga and Joe Silverman

Helga was, at one time, one of the Metropolitan Opera Company's leading sopranos. Her whole life had been devoted to a musical career. But when she feel in love with Joe, she gave it all up. Further, she, a Methodist, formally converted to Judaism and, as she puts it, "I have lived happily ever after."

Helga was born and reared in Maryland. Her parents, both American-born, lived in the same city as their parents and grandparents before them. She was an only child on whom her parents doted. The parents were churchgoers. Both, in fact, taught Sunday school. The Bible was precious to them. Sunday was a *holy* day, not a holiday. Their devotion to Methodism, however, did not prevent them from loving all of their fellowmen. Their love of the Bible led them to have a special affection for the Jewish people.

Helga was about fifteen when she began her voice training. She had studied piano earlier, but parents and friends soon began to comment about the rich quality of her voice. Her first voice teacher was a noted Jewish cantor, whose kindliness and gentility made him very dear to Helga. Following graduation from high school, she enrolled in the Peabody Institute of Music in Baltimore to undertake training as a vocalist. Helga's parents, while doing everything to further her career, insisted that she must maintain her social life, so Helga dated rather regularly.

Almost immediately upon graduation from the School of Music,

Helga was invited to join the Chicago Opera Company. Her mother went along with her because Helga was so young. For six years, Helga sang with the Chicago company.

During those years, Helga met people of all kinds and from many different religions. She had many friends and included among them were some Jews. Helga's mother was distressed because she was dating some Jewish young men and called the matter to Helga's attention. Helga however was certainly not serious about any of her dates so it did not matter very much. When the Chicago Opera Company was dissolved during the Depression years, Helga and her mother returned to New York, and, after a brief period of further study, she received her Metropolitan Opera Company contract. In addition there were European tours, always in her mother's company.

During the years in New York, Helga was happy in her work. She met and dated Jewish young men, among others. Once when suffering from a bad cold, she was advised to give her voice a needed rest. For this purpose she went to a summer resort in New Jersey. It was there that she met Joe.

Joe was a businessman, a bit older than Helga. He came of Orthodox Jewish parents who were observant of Jewish ritual in the tradition of their fathers. Almost at once Joe and Helga fell madly in love. But Joe's parents were very much hurt by Joe's decision, even though he suggested the possibility that Helga might consider conversion to Judaism. Helga's parents too were upset and urged her to reconsider the idea of marrying Joe. But these two were determined to marry, and Helga almost immediately promised to convert to Judaism. Helga says, "I always had a feeling for Judaism. I had been so closely associated with my first teacher, the Jewish cantor, and I loved Jewish liturgy so much, it seemed so natural for me to turn to Judaism."

With parental consent finally secured, Helga and Joe sought the assistance of a Conservative rabbi, who agreed to instruct Helga and, later, to officiate at the formal conversion. This, in turn, was followed by a traditional marriage service. Helga explains, further, that she had "never felt right about the answers given about Jesus, the Messiah, or about the idea of immaculate conception."

Helga and Joe have been married for over thirty years. They are ecstatically happy. They have three sons, each of whom has received a fine Jewish training. They maintain a traditional religious home life. Helga still sings in the temple choir. Joe is an officer of the temple. They worship in the temple on each Sabbath and are highly respected members of the Jewish community.

Both sets of parents maintain close contact with Helga and Joe and their children. Each accepts the other without reservation.

Helga appears to be an authentic convert to Judaism.

Mary Ann Ryan Saulson

Mary Ann was born a Catholic and was later converted to Judaism. But conversion was nothing new in her family. Her mother and father were Catholic, but her mother divorced her father and married an Episcopalian and, as a consequence, was read out of the Church. Her sister, also reared as a Catholic, married an Episcopalian. Mary Ann became a member of the Episcopalian church when her mother remarried. She has only faint memories of her own father.

Mary Ann was devoted to her mother. When she heard from Catholic friends that her mother was living in sin because she had married out of the Catholic Church, she became very upset with the Church. She was distressed too because her mother's parents had resented her mother's remarriage to an Episcopalian. She was particularly distressed because she knew how unhappy her mother's first marriage had been, and she could not understand why church affiliation should have been placed above her mother's personal happiness.

Mary Ann graduated from high school and went on to a junior college but "flunked out" because she failed to study. She then took a series of ordinary jobs just to keep busy. She recalls that she had the reputation of being "terribly wild." She "ran around a lot" and otherwise comported herself in a manner that distressed both her parents and friends.

When Mary Ann suffered a mental breakdown while in her late teens, she had been living alone. A girl friend notified Mary Ann's mother, but there was little that she could do. Mary Ann was in an institution for almost a year. It was then that she decided that she should return to the Catholic Church. "I had a terrible fear of God. I was really frightened. I felt that God would probably hurt me and everyone I loved because I was so evil. I felt that I had turned my back on God."

Mary Ann received communion in the Catholic Church and felt herself reinstated. But still, she felt uncertain and unhappy.

It was then that she met Harry, "a third generation" Jew. A girl friend had introduced them. Harry was a fine boy in every way. He was kind and understanding and "his understanding seemed to work miracles."

For the first time in her life, Mary Ann felt happy and secure. They dated for about seven months when Harry proposed marriage. Because Mary Ann was a Catholic and Harry was a nominal Jew, these two decided to be married by a justice of the peace.

When Harry's family, whom Mary Ann had never met, heard about the marriage, "the roof fell in." Harry's mother was distraught. She kept asking, "How could you do this to me?" Despite her objections, Harry's mother tried to be nice to Mary Ann, and she, in turn, appreciated her many kindnesses.

Mary Ann felt that Harry's mother had been dealt a heavy blow by the marriage and decided to "make it up to her." About the only way she could think of was converting to Judaism. Even though Harry had never spoken of it, Mary Ann felt that he too would be pleased.

Inasmuch as she had lost her faith in Catholicism—after all, she had not become well or secure by virtue of her return to the Church—she felt that conversion to Judaism would create an even greater sense of unity between herself, Harry, and his family.

Entirely on her own, she went to visit the local Conservative rabbi and discussed her desire for conversion with him. He agreed to the conversion provided that Mary Ann would follow his instructions for a period of three months. Only after she had commenced this period of instruction did she inform Harry of her intentions. He appeared to be highly pleased, so the lessons continued. Following the formal traditional conversion, Harry and Mary Ann were remarried in accordance with traditional Jewish practice by the rabbi.

The two have lived quiet, happy lives. They have two children, a boy and a girl. Both children attend Hebrew school. The boy has been Bar Mitzvah in accordance with the Jewish tradition. Harry and Mary Ann are members of the local synagogue. Both are interested in synagogal and Jewish communal affairs. Mary Ann says, "I feel that I am a good Jew." She feels secure and happy in every way. Although she does not see members of her own family, she is fully accepted by Harry's family.

Arthur and Nancy Stout

Arthur was born and reared in Des Moines, Iowa. Of Lutheran parentage, Arthur was an only son whose mother had died when he was eight years old. His father subsequently married a woman who was a Methodist. Arthur's father then left the Lutheran church and joined his wife's church. Arthur continued to attend the Lutheran church until he was about fourteen years old. He remembers that his father and his "real" mother were regular churchgoers. Out of loyalty to the memory of his mother, he continued to attend the Lutheran church even though his father had remarried.

Both father and stepmother were "good" to Arthur. He thinks of them always with pleasant memories. But he felt "unhappy," the reasons for which he claims he does not know.

Arthur graduated from high school and then enlisted in the Army. The Army years too were "unhappy." "I did my job and when it was over I was glad to get out." Even during those years, he recalls, he began thinking about changing his religion. He seemed to find that the Catholic boys in the service were happier about their religion than he. "I was looking for something I didn't have. All the years I had been taught that I shouldn't smoke or drink, and my parents, as Methodists, had impressed this idea on me; but here, in the Army, I saw Catholic boys who didn't regard these things as a sin. So, I began to feel that maybe my religion was wrong and theirs right."

While in the Army, Arthur attended a social and met a Catholic girl, considerably older than he. He had not socialized much. Almost at once, he decided that he was going to marry this girl.

But Nancy, a Catholic of Italian origin, realized not only that she was older than Arthur but that her faith meant too much to her to have Arthur convert to Catholicism unless he was going to be an authentic Catholic in every way.

Upset by Nancy's negative responses, Arthur visited with the Catholic Army chaplain on many occasions and finally determined to adopt the Catholic religion. He informed Nancy that (1) he wanted to marry her and (2) that whether she accepted him or not, he was going to become a Catholic. Even then Nancy hesitated.

Nancy discussed the matter with her parents and, convinced by them that Arthur might be sincere in all that he said, she agreed to the marriage, provided Arthur would take instruction in the Catholic faith. Even after he had completed his course of study and had been formally converted, Nancy hesitated.

In 1962, Nancy finally agreed to the marriage. This was three years after these two had met. Parents and friends seeing Arthur after he had been released from the Army and recognizing in him a sincere convert, finally convinced Nancy.

These two are very happy together. Arthur is a devout Catholic. He attends church service each day, regularly. He is an active member of the church and is generally regarded as a good Catholic.

Arthur's parents have been unhappy because of his conversion, but they have not disowned him. They see each other only on rare occasions, but their relationships are friendly.

Nancy regards Arthur as "a good man and a really good Catholic." Arthur believes that Catholicism is "the only true religion." "Now," he says, "I am at peace with myself."

Gerry Frankel

Gerry, born in New Hampshire, is a Roman Catholic. She has two sisters and one brother, all older than Gerry. Her mother, reared as a Catholic, divorced her first husband and, as a consequence, no longer received the benefits of the Church. Although she later married a Catholic, she still was regarded as a violator of its laws. Nevertheless, she considered herself to be a Catholic.

Gerry was baptized and, later, confirmed in the Catholic church. During her early years, she attended a parochial school, but, when in the sixth grade, she attended the public schools. She knew only Catholics and Protestants in her hometown—never any Jews. Gerry never went beyond high school. When she was graduated, she became an office secretary.

Gerry dated both Catholic and Protestant boys. Her parents never objected. There was always the feeling that, ultimately, she would surely marry a Catholic.

Gerry moved from New Hampshire to western Massachusetts when a good job opportunity came along. Her employer was Jewish; as a result she met many Jewish men. It was there that she met Allan, whom she later married.

Allan was the son of Orthodox Jewish parents. He had lived all of his years in a devout environment where there was a warm and happy feeling about being Jewish. Allan's parents, his two brothers, and sisters were respected members of the community. Allan's brothers and sisters, all older than he, had married Jews.

It was sheer accident that brought Gerry and Allan together. One day, at the office, Gerry broke the heel of a shoe. It happened just as Allan was standing in front of Gerry's desk. He offered to get it repaired, suggesting that perhaps, too, she would have lunch with him. The dating started from that point.

Gerry had been going with a Catholic boy. It had never occurred to her that she would become serious about a Jewish boy. But, after a few dates with Allan, it happened. Allan saw Gerry every day, and, after six months of courtship, he told her of his love for her. But never did he suggest that she meet his parents. This fact distressed Allan, and Gerry questioned him on this score. She was told that not only would Allan's parents be upset if he should marry her, but that all the Jewish community would be distressed as well. Inasmuch as that community was small and they all felt close to each other, marriage to Gerry might prove disastrous to him and his family.

When Gerry discussed Allan with her parents she was told, "If you want to marry a boy of another religion, we'll not fight you. Just be sure that, whoever it is, he is a good boy." But Gerry knew that they would prefer that she marry a Catholic.

Gerry, after six more months of indecision and inner turmoil, decided that there was only one way to resolve the situation and that was conversion to Judaism. Even then she was uncertain about how Allan and his family would respond. She, completely on her own, discussed the matter with the local Conservative rabbi. It was not only that she wanted to marry Allan but the added uncertainty about what she would have to give up as a Catholic that troubled her.

The rabbi, at the outset, was very discouraging. He was, in effect, saying, "Don't do it." Gerry countered by asking for a reading list of books about Judaism. She read avidly. After a few months, it was obvious to her that her love of Allan was greater than anything else, including the Catholic religion. And she was so anxious to be acceptable to Allan's family.

Gerry then returned to the rabbi and declared her readiness to be converted and promised to observe even the dietary laws of traditional Judaism and the other traditional practices.

Allan, who had been kept informed about Gerry's uncertainties as well as her final decision, was highly pleased. He, at first, met strong opposition from his parents and family, but their views changed when the rabbi discussed the matter with them and suggested that they accept Gerry.

Gerry took instruction from the rabbi and, after a period of six months of study, was formally converted. Allan's family also attended the marriage service, performed by the rabbi. Gerry's parents did not attend.

Gerry and Allan have been married for well over six years. They have two children, a boy and a girl, whom they intend to send to Hebrew school. Allan is presently an officer of the synagogue and Gerry has joined the sisterhood and other Jewish organizations. The Sabbath is observed in their home, as are the dietary laws. The Jewish community has accepted them without reservation.

Gerry says that she really hasn't quite resolved her uncertainties about having given up Roman Catholicism. From time to time, there are moments of regret. "But," says Gerry, "I have a really happy marriage. My husband is so good to me and I am so anxious to have Allan's parents think well of me, that whatever doubts I still have are really minor compared with the greater good, a unified and happy family life. Maybe I'm not the very best kind of a Jewess, but certainly I try to live like a Jew and our marriage is a happy one, so what more can I expect?"

Sherrie Grossman

Sherrie's conversion to Judaism came about because "that was the only way I would prove acceptable to George's mother." Although neither George nor his mother were observant, pious Jews, the very act of conversion made Sherrie acceptable to her.

Sherrie was born in Connecticut, just a short distance from New York City. Her parents were good, middle-class people. They were Episcopalians by church affiliation. Sherrie attended Sunday school regularly, was confirmed in the church, and sang in the church choir for many years. When her father died, Sherrie's mother remarried, this time to a Catholic. During this turbulent period in Sherrie's life, she lived for a time with her mother and later with her grandparents on her father's side. Sherrie loved them dearly.

Following graduation from high school, Sherrie learned to type and then secured an office job. Her ties with her mother and stepfather were tenuous.

Shortly after taking her office job, when only eighteen years old, Sherrie met a nice boy and, without fanfare, married him. It took only a short time for these two to discover that they were simply incompatible, but during that time Sherrie bore a daughter. Despite their differences, Sherrie and her husband remained married for sixteen years. During nearly all of that time, Sherrie continued to work in order to supplement her husband's meager salary.

The daughter, Ruth, was the apple of their eyes. But Sherrie, now that her daughter was quite grown, finally secured a divorce. Ruth was reared in the Episcopalian church but later, when Sherrie moved, she enrolled in a neighborhood Congregational church. During all this time there were few contacts between Sherrie and her mother and, even then, they were always very formal.

Sherrie ceased going to church after her daughter was registered in a boarding school. Working each day, Sherrie found that she "needed the rest" on a Sunday morning. Further, she reports, "as I look back on it, I don't think I ever really believed in the divinity of Jesus. Going to church was something that you *did*. It didn't require any special belief on my part."

Ruth, Sherrie's daughter, had a rather bad time of it at boarding school. She got into one scrape after another and proved to be a source of worry for Sherrie.

While working very hard, Sherrie was given many advancements in her employment, until she finally occupied a position of some importance in a large advertising firm. It was there that she met George.

George was a married man. His wife had long been ill, and, in addition, the two did not get along. They had, in fact, been separated on several occasions. Sherrie and George, both lonesome and unhappy people, were almost immediately attracted to each other.

George, a midwesterner, was a Jew, but only in a nominal sense. His parents' marriage had ended in divorce and, as a consequence, George found himself the man of the family. Actually it was his mother who dominated George's life. She always wanted him to be "mama's boy." Even after George married against his mother's will and later separated from his wife, George's mother moved into his apartment and took charge.

When George's mother heard that he and his wife were going to be divorced there was no murmur of protest. When George and Sherrie began to see each other frequently, George's mother offered no objection. However, when George told her that he planned to marry Sherrie, "hell broke loose." She refused to let George consider marriage, and, when finally pressed for a reason, she insisted that her only real objection was that Sherrie was not Jewish.

Little realizing that Sherrie would gladly convert to Judaism since she was not only in love with George but had few real ties to her own family or religion, George's mother was obliged to consent to the marriage when Sherrie accepted conversion.

Sherrie, independently of George, discussed the matter of conversion with a Reform rabbi, who offered to assist her. After a three-month period of instruction, the formal conversion and a week later the marriage of Sherrie and George took place. George's mother did not attend. She claimed to be ill. Sherrie notified her mother of her impending conversion and marriage, but she did not attend either occasion. Ruth, Sherrie's daughter, was present and appeared to be genuinely happy for her mother. Shortly thereafter, Ruth married an Episcopalian boy whom she had known for several years.

Neither George nor Sherrie appears to be very much in love, and this is not a happy marriage. George is recognized as a "good provider," but his whole life seems to be devoted to his business. Sherrie feels that her conversion to Judaism has served no real purpose other than to appease George's mother. Sherrie is unaware that her conversion has affected any phase of her life in any degree.

Notes

Chapter 1. *Conversion and Converts*

1. Charles Y. Glock and Rodney Stark, *Religion and Society in Tension* (Chicago, Rand McNally & Co., 1965), pp. 6–7.

2. William James, *Varieties of Religious Experience* (New York, Longmans, Green & Co., 1902), p. 189.

3. Joachim Wach, *Sociology of Religion* (London, Kegan Paul, 1947), pp. 13 ff.

4. For examples, see Deut. 30:2, Isa. 55:13, Jer. 18:37 et seq., Joel 2:13. See also, Acts 3:19, Acts 9, Acts 22, Acts 26, Gal. 2:1–14.

5. See Earl H. Furgeson, in *Pastoral Psychology,* September 1965, p. 64.

6. See Albert I. Gordon, *Intermarriage: Interfaith, Interethnic, Interracial* (Boston, Beacon Press, 1964).

7. See *The Official Catholic Directory* (New York, P. J. Kenedy & Sons, published annually).

8. David Max Eichhorn, in a personal letter to the author.

9. Daniel L. Davis, Director, New York Federation of Reform Synagogues, in *Jewish Telegraph Agency Daily News Bulletin,* New York, No. 132 (July 12, 1965), p. 3.

10. This figure is based on my interviews with Catholic priests, Protestant clergymen, and rabbis.

11. E. D. Starbuck, *The Psychology of Religion* (New York, Charles Scribner's Sons, 1899), p. 64.

12. Gordon W. Allport, *The Individual and His Religion* (New York, The Macmillan Company, 1950), p. 18.

13. Richard L. Rubenstein, "Intermarriage and Conversion," in *The Reconstructionist,* Vol. 38, No. 5 (April 20, 1962), pp. 11–21.

Chapter 2. *Requirements for Conversion*

1. Walter G. Muelder, Dean of Boston University School of Theology, as reported to the author in a personal interview.

2. Victor Solomon, *A Handbook on Conversions* (New York, Stravon Educational Press, 1965).

3. *The Catholic Encyclopedia Dictionary* (New York, Gilman Press, 1910), p. 254.

4. Information provided by Fr. James Lloyd, S.J., of Paulist Information Center, New York City.

5. Information provided by Fr. Robert F. Quinn, C.S.P., in a personal letter to the author, dated July 24, 1965.

6. See John 18:28; Matt. 3:11.

7. Babylonian Talmud: Sotah, 47A; see also Jerusalem Talmud: Sanhedrin 107B.

8. Babylonian Talmud: Yebamot 47A.

9. Yoreh Deah, Chapter 268.

10. *A Rabbi's Manual,* Rabbi Jules Harlow, ed. (New York, The Rabbinical Assembly [Conservative], 1965), p. 67.

11. *Ibid.,* p. 68.

12. *Ibid.*

13. *Ibid.,* p. 69.

14. *Rabbi's Manual,* rev. ed. (New York, The Central Conference of American Rabbis, 1961), pp. 116–117.

15. Jakob J. Petuchowski, "Realism About Mixed Marriage," in *C.C.A.R. Journal* (October 1966), pp. 34–38.

16. Ira Eisenstein, *Judaism Under Freedom* (New York, Reconstructionist Press, 1956), pp. 239–240.

17. According to the Rev. Father Stanley Harakas, Peabody, Massachusetts, in a personal interview, June 29, 1965.

Chapter 6. *Success or Failure?*

1. Gordon W. Allport, *The Individual and His Religion* (New York, The Macmillan Company, 1950), p. 14.

2. Neil J. Smelser, *Theory of Collective Behavior* (New York, The Free Press of Glencoe, 1963), p. 25.

3. Bert F. Green, *Handbook of Social Psychology,* Vol. I (Cambridge, Massachusetts, Addison-Wesley Publishing Co., 1954), pp. 335–369.

4. *Ibid.*

5. *Ibid.,* p. 336.

6. Charles Y. Glock and Rodney Stark, *Religion and Society in Tension* (Chicago, Rand McNally & Co., 1965), p. 6.

7. *Ibid.,* p. 44.

Index